DAILY
GUIDEPOSTS

2012

Guideposts
New York, New York

Daily Guideposts 2012

Published by Guideposts
16 East 34th Street
New York, New York 10016
Guideposts.org

Acknowledgments

Every attempt has been made to credit the sources of copyrighted material used in this book. If any such acknowledgment has been inadvertently omitted or miscredited, receipt of such information would be appreciated.

All Scripture quotations, unless otherwise noted, are taken from *The King James Version of the Bible*.

Scripture quotations marked (CEV) are taken from *Holy Bible: Contemporary English Version*. Copyright © 1995 American Bible Society.

Scripture quotations marked (ESV) are taken from the Holy Bible, English Standard Version, copyright © 2001 by Crossway Bibles, a division of Good News Publishers. Used by permission. All rights reserved.

Scripture quotations marked (MSG) are taken from *The Message*. Copyright © 1993, 1994, 1995, 1996, 2000, 2001, 2002 by Eugene H. Peterson.

Scripture quotations marked (NAS) are taken from the *New American Standard Bible*, copyright © 1960, 1962, 1963, 1968, 1971, 1972, 1973, 1975, 1977, 1995 by the Lockman Foundation. Used by permission.

Scripture quotations marked (NCV) are taken from *The Holy Bible, New Century Version*. Copyright © 2005 by Thomas Nelson, Inc. Used by permission. All rights reserved.

Scripture quotations marked (NIV) are taken from *The Holy Bible, New International Version*. Copyright © 1973, 1978, 1984 International Bible Society. Used by permission of Zondervan Bible Publishers.

Scripture quotations marked (TODAY'S NIV) are taken from the Holy Bible, New International Version, NIV. Copyright © 1973, 1978, 1984, 2011 by Biblica, Inc. Used by permission of Zondervan. All rights reserved worldwide. www.zondervan.com

Scripture quotations marked (NKJV) are taken from *The Holy Bible, New King James Version*. Copyright © 1997, 1990, 1985, 1983 by Thomas Nelson, Inc.

Scripture quotations marked (NLT) are taken from the *Holy Bible*, New Living Translation. Copyright © 1996. Used by permission of Tyndale House Publishers, Inc., Wheaton, Illinois 60189. All rights reserved.

Scripture quotations marked (NRSV) are taken from the *New Revised Standard Version Bible*. Copyright © 1989 by the Division of Christian Education of the National Council of the Churches of Christ in the U.S.A. Used by permission. All rights reserved.

Scripture quotations marked (RSV) are taken from the *Revised Standard Version of the Bible*. Copyright © 1946, 1952, 1971 by Division of Christian Education of the National Council of Churches of Christ in the U.S.A. Used by permission.

Scripture quotations marked (TLB) are taken from *The Living Bible*. Copyright © 1971 by Tyndale House Publishers, Wheaton, Illinois 60187. All rights reserved.

"Reader's Room" are reprinted with permission from the authors.

Andrew Attaway's photo by Doug Snyder. Brian Doyle's photo by Jerry Hart. Oscar Greene's photo copyright © 2001 by Olan Mills, Inc. Edward Grinnan's photo by Jane Wexler. Rick Hamlin's photo by Nina Subin. Roberta Messner's photo by Jan D. Witter/Camelot Photography. Elizabeth Sherrill's and John Sherrill's photos by Gerardo Somoza.

Cover design by Müllerhaus
Cover photo by Getty Images
Interior design by Lorie Pagnozzi

Monthly page opener photos by iStockphoto
Indexed by Patricia Woodruff
Typeset by Aptara

Printed and bound in the United States of America

10 9 8 7 6 5 4 3 2 1

Peace I leave with you, my peace I give unto you: not as the world giveth, give I unto you," Jesus tells us in John 14:27. But when we look at the history of the two millennia that have passed since He spoke those words—when we look back to the year just past—we see almost anything but peace. Wars, recessions, natural disasters, the struggle to keep up with the pace of change—the world seems always to be roiled by one of these or another. But Jesus points us elsewhere: "Not as the world giveth," He says. And, indeed, as we turn our hearts to Him, we can feel a peace that, even in the midst of turmoil, can give us the serenity and courage to surmount whatever comes our way.

Our theme for *Daily Guideposts 2012,* our thirty-sixth edition, is "The Things That Make for Peace"—those people, places and things that can help us let Jesus' peace grow in our lives. You'll read about a search for peace in the cradle of Christendom, the gifts of peace in the words of the great old hymns, the peace we find in family and friendship, and the peace we find in prayer and Scripture: "the peace of God, which passeth all understanding" (Philippians 4:7).

This year we have a new member in the *Daily Guideposts* family: Sam Adriance, who recently graduated from St. John's College in Santa Fe,

New Mexico. We hope to follow Sam in the years to come as he makes his way in the world. He joins such *Daily Guideposts* favorites as Rick Hamlin, Marion Bond West, Elizabeth Sherrill and Oscar Greene, who are waiting to share their own lives with you.

May God's peace be in your heart every day of the coming year.

SPECIAL FEATURES

❧ THIS I KNOW *13*

Each of us has a personal list of truths we've tested in our lives. Join Pam Kidd early in each month as she shares the truths she's learned in life—the things she knows for sure.

❧ A GRACE-FILLED JOURNEY *31*

Marilyn Morgan King and her husband Robert recently sailed the Mediterranean on a "Voyage to Antiquity." Sail with her to Athens and Crete, Mykonos and Istanbul as she receives the gift of a stronger faith.

⧗ PRAYING THE HYMNS *61*

This past year, Roberta Messner developed a serious lung infection. Plunged into a maelstrom of pain and uncertainty, she was sustained by her memories of beloved old hymns of faith. She'll share them with you in February.

❧ THE CROSS IN FOCUS *150*

Holy Week is an opportunity to walk with Jesus through the most momentous week in history. Marci Alborghetti shows us how focusing on the events of that week can help us walk closer to Jesus every day of our lives.

❧ REDEEMING THE TIME *280*

For many of us, the decision to retire can be a difficult one. Join Brigitte Weeks for a week in June as she tells us how she's filled her own retirement days with richness for herself and for others.

January

*The Lord will give strength unto his people;
the Lord will bless his people with peace.*

—PSALM 29:11

Sun 1

On the first day you shall have a holy convocation. . . .
—LEVITICUS 23:7 (NAS)

On one January first back in the seventies, it was still dark outside when I awoke. The den was toy-strewn; there were supper dishes in the sink. A pile of laundry waited to be washed, while the dryer was full of the last load. I didn't have the traditional Southern New Year's meal—black-eyed peas, cornbread and hog jowl—planned; I didn't even have milk for breakfast. Wearily I tossed scattered toys into the yellow plastic clothes basket with the broken handle. *New Year's Day. Bah, humbug!*

I felt someone watching me and turned. In the dark room stood Julie, my oldest, in her pink nightgown with the top button missing. Sleepy-eyed, she asked softly, "Why are you up so early, Mama?"

"I'm trying to get a head start. It's New Year's Day. You know what that means?"

Silence. I assumed she'd chosen to ignore my strange early-morning question.

"My teacher said that every day is the first day of the rest of your life. Is that what you mean, Mama?"

I stood up straight and looked at her—really looked at her. A smile found my face. "Yep, Julie Babe, your teacher's a smart lady."

Father, You must have been excited on that very first day of creation. I'm claiming a bit of that excitement myself this first day of 2012.
—Marion Bond West

Mon 2

For behold, I bring you good tidings of great joy, which shall be to all people. —Luke 2:10

Taking down the Christmas tree is my least-favorite holiday chore. It's always so exciting to buy one, bring it home, set it in the stand, string it with lights and hang the ornaments we've collected over the years. I pause as I take them out of the box. "Remember when Will made this in nursery school? . . . Look at the crèche Tim drew. . . . I can't believe you made these out of dyed macaroni."

But taking it down? The tree is dry as a bone, pine needles drop to the ground, the ornaments look weary and I'm sad. I wish the singing, the gathering with friends and family, the joy could go on and on.

Last year I took down the tree in record time, just to get it over with. I boxed up the ornaments and lights, dragged the dried husk outside to the recycle bin, vacuumed the rugs and floor of every pine needle I could find and then sat on the couch, my hands crossed over my chest, and glanced at my watch. "Forty-five minutes," I declared.

"Well," Carol said, "you missed this." She picked a little drummer boy off the rug and dangled it from its gold string.

"I've put away the boxes already," I said.

"I'll leave it on the piano."

There it sat, urging me not to give up on Christmas entirely. Didn't some good cheer remain? Couldn't I still feel the glow without the lights and tinsel? Maybe Christmas wasn't something to be rushed away from but carried with me like the painted boy with his drum. After all, these "tidings of great joy" were meant to last.

I don't remember who put the ornament away, but I could smell the piney scent of Christmas for weeks—and sense its joy—whenever I ran the vacuum cleaner.

> *All the good things in life, Lord, were*
> *meant to be lingered over.*
> —RICK HAMLIN

Tue 3   *Everything should be done in a fitting and orderly way.*
—I CORINTHIANS 14:40 (NIV)

By now, everybody who knows me knows how much FlyLady has changed my life. Her real name is Marla Cilley, and she started a Web site for people like me who have a problem with clutter. A friend used to say, "*God* stands for *Good orderly direction*," and if that's the case, FlyLady has helped me become closer to God.

After I'd complained for the dozenth time about not being able to get a handle on my clutter problem, my friend told me to pray about it. I remember being shocked. "Pray about clutter? It's ridiculous to take such a strange problem to God."

But Edie insisted. "If it's important to you, it's important to God."

I couldn't argue with that one, so I prayed. And I was directed (in a good, orderly way) to FlyLady, where I learned to declutter fifteen minutes at a time, where I learned that "my timer is my best friend," and where I learned to listen for "God breezes" (such as friends like Edie telling me to pray about my problem).

More important, I've found a community of people who all struggle with the same issue that I do. Finally, I don't feel isolated but connected to humanity because I'm doing something about it with others.

Connect us to each other in our weaknesses, God, and
help our hearts to always be connected to You.
And thank You for FlyLady.
—LINDA NEUKRUG

Wed 4

Jesus said to them, "Follow Me, and I will make you become fishers of men." Immediately they left their nets and followed Him.
—MARK 1:17–18 (NAS)

This week I celebrate my sixtieth birthday. Amid the cake and candles, the most important question I can ask is, "How will I live the rest of my life?"

During the past few years, I've become more and more focused on the term *ripple effect*. The most powerful creative forces in the world are caused by the ripple effect. Throw a rock into a pond and watch the impact create expanding ripples across the placid water until they reach the shoreline. Sound waves, light waves and energy waves flow across the known and unknown universe. If the *big bang* was one of the means by which God created, then the whole emerging event of creation was caused by God's using the ripple effect to change and shape our massive universe.

Yesterday I sat in my office talking with a first-year student about the future of her life. She wants to be a physician and to practice medicine within rural locales where doctors are scarce and needed. As we explored her life-dream, I became increasingly aware that nothing was more important in my day—indeed in my life—than to help this young woman understand, clarify and achieve her goal.

Long after I have made my bow on the stage of life, she will be continuing to share love and compassion and healing with others. If I can be a small pebble tossed into the fresh and vibrant waters of her young life, perhaps the ripple effect of our conversation will be helping people and shaping history long after I am gone.

I have decided to focus my future on achieving the ripple effect. I want God to throw me into the waters of young life and create ripples that will challenge, enable and energize my grandchildren's generation.

Father, show me today how I can best cause a positive ripple in one single and precious life.
—SCOTT WALKER

THIS I KNOW

Thu 5   *All of you are children of the most High.* —PSALM 82:6

A BIGGER, BRIGHTER REALITY

It was one of those hectic days when life seems little more than a busy blur. I had dashed into the grocery store to pick up dinner. Now, bags in hand, I rushed for the exit. As the door closed behind me, I stopped dead-still on the sidewalk.

There on the bench right outside the store sat Rita, who had worked beside our son Brock at this store during his high-school years. "Hey, Rita, what are you doing?" I said.

"Just chillin'," she answered.

For me, it was a defining moment. I could make a beeline for the car and continue swimming in molasses through another tedious day, or . . .

"Wow, could I sit down and chill with you?" I asked.

Soon Rita was telling me how she caught the bus for work; how she'd never learned to drive a car; how sometimes on her day off, she paid a friend to drive her out into the country; how she loved to just ride along, looking out the window.

Somehow, in those few minutes my life changed.

Now, years later, I still treasure that time when something called me away from my little world and into a bigger, brighter reality. The memory urges me to embrace life with all its extravagant Ritas sitting on a bench, just chillin'.

Father, beyond me You spread lavish life. Give me the good sense to embrace Your offering.
—Pam Kidd

Editor's Note: *Please take time to jot down "My Pathway to Peace" on the journal pages at the end of each month.*

Fri 6   *Opening their treasures, they offered him gifts, gold and frankincense and myrrh.*
—MATTHEW 2:11 (RSV)

On the first Epiphany wise men brought Jesus gifts of gold, frankincense and myrrh. An antique bookcase in my living room holds treasures of a different sort.

There's Tinsy Winsy, a red-sock monkey that my great-aunt Grace made and tucked into my Christmas stocking the year I was five. In the corner are paper dolls from Mum, who graciously spared them from the rummage sale we had when emigrating from Canada to the United States. On top of the case is an ancient teacup with vibrant purple pansies, a wedding gift to Grandma, now a gift to me. But the best of all is a storybook.

It's a Wonder Book, like the one my father used to read to my sisters and me every year in the days preceding Christmas. He'd read it one last time on Christmas night, help us say our prayers and give each of us a kiss. Linda, Tresa and I, every year, would give a big sigh, flop into our pillows and recite the last page: "Oh! We can hardly wait until *next* Christmas!"

At some point we lost that book. For years, every time I went into an antique shop, I looked for it. A few Christmases ago I got the strangest sensation when Tresa handed me a gift, a flat package in the heft and size of that book. And so the beloved Wonder Book sits on the shelf next to a picture of Dad reading to me.

*Lord, I used to think the wise men's gifts odd
things to give a baby, until I realized
they gave the best they had.*
—BRENDA WILBEE

Sat 7 *"Take courage!..."*—ACTS 23:11 (NIV)

Going sledding seemed an appropriate way to celebrate the first Saturday of the new year. We had just the right amount of snow on the ground, and the blue sky beckoned. I couldn't find anyone to share this adventure with me, so I bundled up, called Kemo, my golden retriever, and pulled our slippery plastic toboggan out of the garage. As I headed toward the hillside near our home, I knew my determination wasn't so much about sledding. It was about wanting to mark my resolution to be courageous instead of fearful as I headed into this new year with all its unknowns. My husband Lynn was still on chemotherapy for his recurrent brain tumor and the doctor recently informed us that he might have to stay on chemo for the rest of his life.

So here I was, perched at the top of the steepest, longest part of the neighborhood sledding hill on a cold, clear afternoon. I could see the great sledding path others had already carved out, down through the yuccas in the field.

"Here goes, Kemo," I said as I positioned the sled and plopped down on it. I took a deep breath and pushed off. Instantly I realized the sled run had turned into a sheet of ice and I was picking up speed, flying down the hill, totally out of control. I tried to use my legs as brakes, which turned me around backward, and by the grace of God I twirled into a clump of yuccas and tumbled off the sled. I picked myself up, grateful that all my body parts still seemed to be working, shook off the snow and started trudging back up the steep hill.

"I don't think we need a second run," I told Kemo, but as I took one last look at the hill before turning toward home, I felt kind of proud that I'd gone sledding.

Lord, I'm thankful for the reminder that courage isn't the absence of fear, but going forward into the new year in spite of it.
—CAROL KUYKENDALL

Sun 8

In every thing give thanks; for this is the will of God in Christ Jesus concerning you.
—I THESSALONIANS 5:18

One Sunday my pastor Scharleen Cross related a scary experience from the night before. Just after dark, she decided to water the flowers in her front yard. Because she would only be out a few moments, she left her little dog inside even though he barked furiously in protest. She was about to turn on the water when she sensed something creep up behind her. She turned around, her heart racing. . . .

It was a skunk, fully grown, fully loaded, his tail up and ready to spray. Pastor Schar didn't move a muscle. She looked at the skunk. It looked at her. After what seemed like an eternity, the skunk lowered its tail and ambled away.

"It was a 'Thank You, Jesus' moment!" she told us. "All I could say was, 'Thank You, Jesus! Thank You that the dog was inside. Thank You for keeping me from screaming or fainting! Most of all, thank You that the skunk left!'"

I thought about Pastor Schar's experience several times that day. I'd been trying to develop a grateful heart—an attitude of gratitude. I always thanked God for big blessings, like a bountiful corn harvest and my friend Susan's return to good health following chemotherapy. But I doubted I would have given thanks for an encounter with a skunk.

Was I missing opportunities to thank God because I didn't recognize them? Did blessings sometimes come disguised as troubles? Or as things I simply took for granted? What would happen if I actually tried *giving thanks in all things*?

Lord, give me eyes that see, a mind that understands, and a heart of praise for the "Thank You, Jesus" moments that happen every day.
—PENNEY SCHWAB

Mon 9   *Our oxen will draw heavy loads....*
—PSALM 144:14 (NIV)

I can imagine the scene. It is a chill afternoon in January 1776. General George Washington is standing on the heights overlooking British-occupied Boston. Anchored in the harbor is the largest fleet of British warships ever seen in America. "They wouldn't be so cocksure," Washington says, "if only we had some cannon up here!"

A twenty-five-year-old Boston bookseller-turned-artilleryman overhears Washington. "There are lots of cannon," he says, "at Fort Ticonderoga." But what good is that? Ticonderoga is three hundred miles and several mountain ranges away, in upstate New York. On the spot, Washington commissions the young bookseller to try. Thus began an extraordinary endeavor.

Young Henry Knox rode his horse to Ticonderoga, where sixty cannon lined the walls of the fort. How would he get them to far-off Boston?

Oxen.

Oxen? Humblest of creatures? But the slow, plodding beasts had one virtue: physical strength. From farms and lumber camps, Knox rounded up teams, hitched them to gun-carrying sledges and, for more than two months, goaded the long train over frozen rivers and mountains, reaching Boston on the night of March 17.

Next morning the astonished British looked up to see the impossible: sixty cannon lining the high ground. Quick negotiations followed. The Americans watched as column after column of redcoats were ferried to the ships. Then the great fleet raised its sails and left the New England coast forever. A modest Boston bookseller and a train of laboring oxen had brought about the first victory in the War of Independence.

Father, how often I see myself as plodding and simple!
Help me to know that in Your hands humble
gifts can do important things.
—JOHN SHERRILL

Tue 10

Your name, O Lord, is everlasting....
—PSALM 135:13 (NAS)

I've made some interesting discoveries by asking people how they came by their names. A post-mistress, Modesty, said she was named in the sixties for a character from a *Gunsmoke* television episode. Gypsy, a nurse, told me her parents met as employees at Yellowstone National Park and had pet names for each other—Gypsy and Ranger. When I asked if she had a brother named Ranger, she answered with a surprised "Yes!"

Another time I met a woman named Garnet. Her childhood initials spelled G.E.M. She was determined to keep it that way, so she did not even consider marrying anyone whose last name did not begin with the letter *M*!

My own daughter's recent baby has a Russian name, Natalia, in memory of a friend Tasha who was adopted from a Russian orphanage.

Names overflow with stories. In Exodus, God speaks to Moses in the wilderness, saying He wants Moses to lead the Israelites out from slavery in Egypt. Moses says the people will want to know who has sent him. God tells Moses, "I AM WHO I AM.... Thus you shall say to the sons of Israel, 'I AM has sent me to you'" (Exodus 3:14, NAS).

Imagine a man pasturing sheep in the desert asking God to name Himself! And how superbly God responds with a name that says He is ever-present. *I AM* is an entire autobiography.

It is the best name story I know.

Thank You, Lord, for Your name—I AM—that assures me You are always with me.
—CAROL KNAPP

Wed 11

Weeping may remain for a night, but rejoicing comes in the morning.
—PSALM 30:5 (NIV)

My sons and I walk up the long, unplowed driveway to the cemetery. The snow is deep and heavy and reaches my son Henry's knees. As we climb the steep hill to my sister Maria's grave, Henry grows tired.

We rest for a minute, sitting in the snow, our legs protected by our snow pants. Henry's older brother Solomon falls backward and makes a snow angel, and Henry and I join him. Looking up at the sky, we wave our arms and legs to create perfect angel imprints. "We're going to see Aunt Ree Ree," Solomon says.

Henry was only one year old when my sister died suddenly in her sleep three years ago. Solomon was older; he remembers his aunt. He had his very first sleepover at her house. They stayed up way past his bedtime, eating popcorn and telling silly stories. Right before they fell asleep, Solomon jumped up and hugged Maria, shouting, "I love you! I really *really* love you!" Maria told me about it with tears in her eyes. Yet here we are on this cold morning, getting up out of the snow and admiring our angels on our way to my sister's grave.

"We were lucky to have Aunt Ree Ree," I say.

"I know," Solomon says, "I remember. We *are* lucky."

Dear Lord, thank You for those precious moments when my grief turns to gratitude and I feel love, not loss.
—SABRA CIANCANELLI

READER'S ROOM

When I look back over my life, I see answers to prayers I never even thought to pray. I see a retrospective map of people, time and circumstances that have saved me, guided me and blessed me in ways that are unimaginable showers of blessings. I just have to wonder, and one day in heaven I'll ask, "Why do You love us so?"
—*Joy Shores, Summerfield, North Carolina*

Thu 12

God... comforts the depressed....
—II Corinthians 7:6 (nas)

Our city is known on the Canadian prairies for the extravagant Christmas lights people put up to decorate their homes and yards during the festive season. Contests are held for residences and businesses to see who can come up with the most attractive displays. Buses are available for those who want to view the winning entries without getting caught in traffic. Nor is all the attention restricted to the locals. Pilots often comment that they know they're over Winnipeg by the extra glow they can see on a clear night.

Once the holidays are over, however, the lights go off one by one, and we enter the dark, forbidding month of January, when the sun sets around 4:30 pm and doesn't rise until nearly 8:00 am.

At our Bible study one January night, we had been discussing the dark spots we encounter in our faith walk. I had run into some myself. After experiencing the lighthearted joy of the Christmas season, I felt as if my soul had suddenly been plunged into heavy darkness. It was as if my spirit was a corridor and someone had walked down it and switched off hope, ambition, initiative and expectations.

Then I saw it. Perhaps someone had simply forgotten to unplug his outdoor Christmas tree, but there it was, shining like a faithful beacon.

Remember, it seemed to say, *that Christ has come. He is with you, guiding you, lighting your pathway.*

> *Thank You, Jesus, that when courage fails,*
> *You provide that one spark that*
> *relights my enthusiasm.*
> —ALMA BARKMAN

Fri 13

"The eye is the lamp of the body; so then if your eye is clear, your whole body will be full of light."
—MATTHEW 6:22 (NAS)

I got hit in the eye with a hockey puck. (This is not the first time I've hurt my eye playing hockey, nor is it the second or third. Oh, I was wearing protective goggles . . . which were hanging loosely around my neck, protecting my Adam's apple.) My wife Sandee took me to the emergency room, where she sprang into action. "Is there any chance we could get a handicapped parking tag?" she joked. I laughed through the writhing pain.

The laughing stopped at phrases like "blowout potential" and "surgery." For a few minutes, I contemplated life without my right eye, which is really one of my better eyes. Would I wear a patch à la *True Grit,* or go with the fake eye? I entertained myself like this as a way of avoiding the real question: *What have I done?*

Fortunately, I play hockey with my friend Bob, a gifted optometrist and one of the saints among us. Bob stitched me up (figuratively) and got me on pain meds (literally) and never charged me a cent, with one condition: "From now on, wear a helmet with a face cage, okay?"

So here's the happy ending, but it's not what you think: I've lost some visual acuity. The pupil in my right eye is dilated. I squint a lot. Colors are different. I use a larger font on my computer screen.

And I couldn't be happier. Every day without an eye patch is a gift. Every moment reading or driving or watching the Pirates play baseball (or whatever it is they're doing) is a present from above, a reminder of what I've been given.

Lord, a second chance is one thing, but a fourth chance doesn't ask for gratitude—it demands it: a small price to pay for services received. So thank You. Oh, and a cage. Yes, it also demands a face cage.
—MARK COLLINS

Sat 14

I am sending him to you for this very purpose, that you may know how we are, and that he may encourage you.
—EPHESIANS 6:22 (NIV)

At 10:30 AM I glanced over at the calendar beside my desk and noticed I'd penciled in "Help clean chapel." I'd been noncommittal when the call came from Pamela, our new prayer coordinator, about meeting to tidy up the chapel in preparation for an upcoming prayer service. I was all for the prayer service, but I felt I didn't have the time. Now I was busy writing a Sunday school lesson on encouragement. Some people in our class were very discouraged because lack of funds had caused the shutting down of a mission we had sponsored. I had spent all morning making up a list of "tools of encouragement" we can use to help each other. Logic told me that my job here at home was more important than the chapel cleaning. After all, Pamela only needed one or two people to get the job done.

I continued working, and at 10:45 when I glanced at the calendar, a voice inside of me seemed to say, *Go.* I threw on a pair of shoes and drove over to the church, sure that I was making a foolish decision.

I was the first one to arrive. Pamela, surprised and delighted, said, "I so much appreciate your support!" As I picked up a couple of old bulletin inserts behind the altar rail, I suddenly remembered that one of the tools of encouragement I'd listed on my computer earlier was *presence.* The inner voice hadn't told me to come because I was bringing critical manpower or skills to the cleanup; I was here to do a different job. Sometimes the best way to encourage someone is to just show up.

*Dear Father, show me where You want me
to go today to encourage someone through
my supportive presence.*
—KAREN BARBER

Sun 15

*A single day in your courts is better
than a thousand anywhere else! I
would rather be a gatekeeper in the
house of my God than live the good
life in the homes of the wicked.*
—PSALM 84:10 (NLT)

Adults called him "Brother Joe," but during my
growing-up years, my parents and the parents
of most of my peers insisted we kids address the
man by the more respectful "Mister Gray," the way
all children should speak to grown-ups—especially
the white-haired ones.

No matter which title Joe Gray answered to, most
members of our church knew him as "that man
who greets people at the door." Certainly his name
never appeared on the Elders or Board of Directors
lists.

Had any of us—adults or kids—been asked "Who
turns on the heat and lights every Sunday morning?"
or "Who's responsible for setting up folding chairs?"
or "Who stacks the bulletins, just so, on the table
outside the sanctuary doors?" we'd probably not
have been able to give "Who" a name. We'd simply

taken it for granted, week after week, that *someone* must be responsible. That *someone* was Joe Gray.

I've had the privilege of talking with many Very Important People. Awed friends often exclaim, "You actually *met* him!" or "You have *her* autograph?" "Yes," to both. Doubtless these VIPs deserve the honors they receive. But I'm sure countless Brother Joes are around, only recognized and praised by the King of Kings!

Father, when I feel unnoticed and unappreciated
for the routine tasks I do, help me to remember
that You see, and Your approval means
far more than anyone else's.
—Isabel Wolseley

Mon 16

Remember the days of old, consider the years of many generations: ask thy father, and he will shew thee; thy elders, and they will tell thee.
—Deuteronomy 32:7

Our homeschooling this morning started with history. I read out loud from a book about what America was like in 1963, when the nation was still wracked by the struggle against racial segregation. My kids have grown up in a city where a subway car may carry people of a dozen nationalities; they thought segregation sounded weird.

Then I pulled up a YouTube video of Martin Luther King Jr.'s "I Have a Dream" speech. The people in the video looked different, with their 1960s hairstyles and glasses and clothing. But the children all thought it was a good speech, a remarkable speech. We talked about its literary qualities: assonance, consonance, metaphor, meter. We discussed the biblical references too.

We talked about nonviolent protest, Gandhi, assassinations. I told the kids how my father had headed south for the Freedom Summer of 1964 and how he brought home a stuffed animal for my brother that was ever after known as the Mississippi Tiger. I shared with them what it was like living in East Orange, New Jersey, a mile or two from Newark during the summer of riots in 1967. I described two years in an urban middle school, and how bizarre life seemed when I moved to the suburbs where the race proportions were reversed.

And then we moved on to math, and I let the past slip back into the past, praying I'd planted a few seeds of perspective and hope for the future.

Father, may times of pain and change grow me into a peaceful person.
—JULIA ATTAWAY

❈ A GRACE-FILLED JOURNEY

Tue 17

And the bow shall be in the cloud; and I will look upon it, that I may remember the everlasting covenant.... —GENESIS 9:16

SOMEWHERE OVER THE RAINBOW

My husband Robert was grinning like a schoolboy as he returned from the post office and handed me a flyer. "How would you like to cruise the Greek Isles to celebrate our special birthdays this year?"

"Oh, it sounds wonderful, honey, but can we afford it? What about my eyes? Where would I find a retina specialist in a strange country? Then there's the unrest in Greece right now. It might not be safe!"

Robert's face clouded over. "Oh, I thought you'd love it!... Well, please give it some thought, anyway."

Sorry to have thrown cold water on Robert's excitement, I did give it more thought, and eventually we found ourselves in an airplane headed across the Atlantic.

But on our flight out, things kept going wrong. I had asked for an aisle seat but was given a window.

I'm on a gluten-free diet, so when Robert made our airline reservations he asked for a gluten-free meal for me; I got a regular meal.

Then, somewhere over the ocean, I opened the shade of my window seat and saw a most amazing sight: There was a rainbow—the sign of God's covenant with His people—below us! In all of my flying years, I'd never seen such a thing. And I wouldn't have seen it now if I'd had the aisle seat!

Heavenly Father, I trust your sign that "all shall be well, and all shall be well, and all manner of things shall be well" (Julian of Norwich).
—MARILYN MORGAN KING

Wed 18   *O God, You have taught me from my youth; And to this day I declare Your wondrous works.*
—PSALM 71:17 (NKJV)

Thomas, the ten-year-old son of my colleague Kathleen, is one of the wisest people I know. The stories his mother tells about him help me keep my thinking grounded in reality.

Last winter Thomas asked his mother if he could have a chinchilla for a pet. Although Kathleen was taken aback at first by the prospect of having a chinchilla in her home, she agreed on two conditions: Thomas needed to buy the chinchilla with his own money, and he had to improve his grades at school. To earn the money, Thomas got to work shoveling snow and doing odd jobs for the neighbors.

One evening after dinner, Kathleen and Thomas were in the kitchen chatting about chinchillas. Hoping her son would change his mind, Kathleen said, "Chinchillas are a bit odd looking."

Thomas looked up at her and said, "We're all creatures of God, and it's not up to us to judge them."

A few days later, Thomas could hardly contain his excitement, because he had been graded "excellent" on his religious-education report card. "Mom, it's time to buy my chinchilla," he said.

"I need to see your school report card," Kathleen reminded him.

"This is the most important report card," Thomas shot back, "because if it wasn't for God, we wouldn't be here anyway!"

Thomas's words got me thinking: If God were to give me a report card, what grades would He give me in caring for His creation? In my relationships with the people around me? In my relationship with Him? I hope my report card is as good as Thomas's.

> *Lord, thank You for the ways children*
> *teach us how to live our faith.*
> —PABLO DIAZ

Thu 19

> *In the morning, O Lord, you hear*
> *my voice; in the morning I lay my*
> *requests before you. . . .*
> —PSALM 5:3 (NIV)

My dear friend Sonya gave me the idea: early-morning prayer. Her four children were older than mine, yet somehow she had already learned how to beat the rush and scoop out a quiet time before the children awoke. At my house, where the children were two, four, five and eight when I became a single mom, stress began at daybreak— spilled cereal, pawing through the laundry basket for matching socks, rushing to school, squabbling— and became worse as the day roared on. After supper, homework, baths and bedtime stories, I felt too frazzled for prayer and often fell asleep with my shoes on.

Sonya, on the other hand, rarely seemed stressed. Her tremendous faith, optimism and energy drew me to ask her about her prayer practice. She eagerly shared her daybreak routine and even gave me a devotional booklet to weave into my frayed prayer life. Though Sonya began her day at 4:00 AM, I lingered in bed until 5:00 AM. Slowly, my quick talks with God evolved into more intimate conversations. I recognized God's calming presence in my daily routine and could relax just a bit more.

That was twenty-five years ago. These days, my mornings are cathedral-quiet, and though I could enjoy prayer time anytime I choose, I continue to cherish my morning prayer. I brew my coffee, sit in Mom's old rocker, thank God for so many blessings and let Him know what my friends and I need. I pray. I listen. I read the Bible. And I watch the sun rise, knowing that no matter what happens during the rest of the day, God and I are together.

Heavenly Father, as the hymn says, "morning by morning new mercies I see." I am grateful.
—GAIL THORELL SCHILLING

Fri 20

I will love thee, O Lord, my strength... in whom I will trust....
—PSALM 18:1–2

He is gifted with superlative musical talent, and he could have had a brilliant career as a concert pianist. But his devotion to Christ and a call to the ministry were the top priorities in his life.

The dilemma hit him in his teens: "Should I become a preaching piano player, or a piano-playing preacher?" he asked himself.

Voices in favor of his music bombarded him. He struggled and went to his knees. His decision was as clear as his faith was firm: God first—he would be a piano-playing preacher. That decision led him to seminary, marriage, children, and then over twenty years on the mission field.

His recent e-mail came as a shock: "The tumor in my leg is malignant. I need an amputation above the knee, and there is a possibility it has metastasized to my lungs. I'm so glad I don't have to worry about the outcome. It's heaven anyway, whether I arrive earlier or later. My life is in the Lord's hands. Please pray."

My daughter hadn't opened the piano for years. For the past weeks she's been shakily pecking out "Greensleeves." "It's the first piece he taught me," she said. "I'm playing it as I pray, remembering him before God." As I hear the notes, I hum the tune and join my heart with hers.

Without his leg, his fingers continue to fly across the keyboard, uplifting hearts with consecrated music. One thing is sure: He will always be praising the Lord, now and through all eternity.

How grateful I am that we don't have to worry about the outcome of our lives; it's heaven, Lord, whether we arrive earlier or later!
—FAY ANGUS

Sat 21

The Lord God hath given me the tongue of the learned, that I should know how to speak a word in season to him that is weary....
—ISAIAH 50:4

We'd been hit with a blizzard up in the Berkshires, thirty inches of snow, and it took me the better part of a day to dig out before finally driving into town for supplies.

The air pressure in the right front tire was a tad low, and I decided to stop at a gas station on Route 7 to add a little air. But when I attached the air hose, I felt a rush of cold air shooting out of the tire nozzle. The tire was flat in a matter of seconds. I called a local shop, Steve's, and they told me it would be at least two hours before someone could get to me.

But then Steve himself came rumbling down Route 7 in his tow truck and pulled over. "Didn't want to leave you stuck out here when I was on my way back in anyway. We'll take her to the shop."

That's how I found myself sitting in a small waiting area, talking to a woman who dispensed all sorts of fascinating facts.

"Do you know this is the second oldest Main Street in America?" she shouted over the racket of the mechanics.

"Really?" I yelled back. "What's first?"

"Don't know! But this snow is good for the ski operators!"

It went on like this for a while, until she asked, "What do you do down in the city?"

I told her.

"Oh, I read *Guideposts*! Mother gave it to me way back—the magazine and the book. Love it! You look different from your picture, younger and better looking but a lot shorter too!"

Our talk was interrupted by Steve announcing that the tire had been changed. In a few seconds I was on my way, but not without saying a nice good-bye to my unnamed friend, who warmed a very cold day.

God, thank You for the people You send
my way in times of need.
—EDWARD GRINNAN

Sun 22

Whosoever shall not receive the kingdom of God as a little child, he shall not enter therein.
—MARK 10:15

In the church we've attended since our move, children go to Sunday school during the first half of the adult service, joining their parents for the second half during the singing of a hymn. That is, others sing; I watch the children.

They enter through a door down at the front so that as they walk up the aisle you see their faces. The smallest ones come first, clutching the morning's coloring project—maybe Noah's ark with a red-and-green giraffe. They move shyly, slowly, eyes wide and anxious as they scan the rows of grown-ups. A little girl smiles and breaks into a run, fears vanished as she spies her parents.

The six- and seven-year-olds follow. These are self-conscious, schooled in the decorum of how-we-behave-in-church. But they, too, are searching, seeking. . . . Eyes light up: The hoped-for figure is spotted. None of them run, but steps quicken.

The big kids stroll in last, the boys especially a portrait of cool. They saunter up the aisle displaying a huge indifference to the presence of anyone in particular. But sudden smiles betray them: They too need parents.

As I watch I'm asking the Father, *How did I come to You this past week? Did I live as though I didn't need You at all, acknowledging You in some moment of grace almost in spite of myself? Did I approach You in conventional, well-mannered ways, hyperconscious of how I appeared to others? Or did I seek You eagerly, openly, aware only of the longing to see Your face?*

Heavenly Father, let me run to You as a little child.
—Elizabeth Sherrill

Mon 23

I would hasten my escape from the windy storm and tempest.
—PSALM 55:8

I'd kind of lost contact with God because of my busy schedule at the University of Missouri, taking classes and working part time to help pay my husband Larry's and my expenses as he worked toward getting his master's degree. Between semesters we'd take quick trips to southern Missouri, where I visited my parents in one small town and Larry visited his mother in another town a few miles away.

My parents had already left for work one morning when the phone rang. I answered and heard Larry say urgently, "A terrible storm just went through here and it's headed your way. The TV says there's a tornado in it. Take cover."

My parents had no basement, but having grown up in "tornado alley," I knew about the crawl space under the house. When I went outside, I saw that the clouds had turned a strange copper color and the leaves and grass were fluorescing a brilliant yellow-green. My skin prickled with foreboding. The air was absolutely still.

I slithered under the house, curled my body in a tight knot beneath the cement steps that led up to the porch, and started muttering a prayer: *God, be with me, be with me, be with me, be with me. . . .*

Then I heard the roar. Almost immediately there was a loud *whump,* and the house shuddered as if a bulldozer had crashed into it.

The tornado moved on and I crawled out into a pounding rain. The house was intact but plastered with leaves, as if it someone had painted it green. Later I learned that no one in town had been injured, although some buildings on Main Street were damaged. Now my prayer became: *God, thank You, thank You....*

Today I will share with someone I meet that God is indeed our refuge and strength in time of trouble.
—MADGE HARRAH

Tue 24

But time and chance happen to them all. —ECCLESIASTES 9:11 (NIV)

Wolfing down a peanut butter sandwich as I drove to a meeting across town was not my idea of the ideal lunch. But that's the way it's been these days. Just when I thought work at the television station couldn't get much busier, it did. We had a couple of big documentaries to produce and the deadlines were looming in the not-so-distant future. Now I was on my way to a meeting to talk about a new video we needed to produce in two weeks. My stress level was mounting just thinking about it.

Impatient at the red light that seemed to be taking an awfully long time to turn green, I reached over and turned on the radio. It was tuned to a station I rarely listened to, because I'd never liked its choice of music. This time, though, it was playing a relaxing tune with an uplifting beat and a hint of jazz. I listened, feeling my body unwinding a bit and my grip on the steering wheel easing. The next song was just as good, and so were the two after that. By the time I arrived at my meeting, I'd heard five of the best songs I'd ever heard on that station. I got out of my car with a smile on my face and a swing in my step.

Some might say that hearing those songs was a coincidence, but I know better. So I'll just say a thank-you to God for being there at the right place and the right time, and tuning me into His peace.

Lord, thank You for all the little coincidences in my life that I know come from you.
—MELODY BONNETTE

Wed 25

For we are God's workmanship, created in Christ Jesus to do good works, which God prepared in advance for us to do.
—EPHESIANS 2:10 (NIV)

It's hard to imagine a worse environment for giving a motivational speech.

I was standing between the tables in the center of a hospital cafeteria. The row in which I was standing happened to be between the entrance to the cafeteria and the food itself, which meant a steady stream of people stepped around me as I spoke. There had been no advance publicity for my speech, so the audience was made up of the usual patrons of the cafeteria. I didn't have a microphone to help my voice compete with the giant flat-screen television, and to top it all off, a baby was screaming about ten feet away from me.

I was standing in the middle of all this, attempting to give a talk about my battle with cancer and the loss of my leg. I paused and took a deep breath and remembered what my mother had told me on the phone before the presentation. "Even if it seems like a tough room to give a speech in, maybe you'll be able to touch just one person," Mom said.

Doubtful, I thought.

After I finished, there was a smattering of applause. I was eager to leave, but as I did, a young man grabbed my shoulder.

"I lost both my legs in the war," he said, gesturing down toward his two prosthetic limbs. "I really appreciate you sharing your story today."

Lord, please give me the patience I need to do my work and leave the outcome to You.
—Joshua Sundquist

Thu 26

If we walk in the light, as he is in the light, we have fellowship with one another, and the blood of Jesus, his Son, purifies us from all sin.
—I JOHN 1:7 (NIV)

When I was a teenager I attended Bible classes taught by Dr. Frank C. Torrey, who was pastor of Calvary Independent Church in Lancaster, Pennsylvania. This distinguished man with silver hair and wire-rimmed glasses was a great teacher, and I learned a lot of Bible from him. But what I remember best is a story he told about himself.

As a young minister fresh out of seminary, he felt he had to live up to certain impossible standards, one of which was to always be right. One day he was visiting an elderly woman from his church, and they had a disagreement over some point of order in the service. Later, to his chagrin, he found out the woman was right. With great difficulty he went back to her house to tell her.

He sat in the same chair he'd sat in when he'd been so relaxed and sure of himself. Now, he was on the edge. His hands clenched, he blurted out the dreaded words, "You were right."

The woman smiled sweetly. "Thank you, Pastor," she said. "But you need to go a little further. Instead of saying 'you were right,' could you swallow that last bit of pride and say 'I was wrong'?"

What Dr. Torrey was saying is a paradox that comes back to me again and again. By admitting to God, ourselves and others the hard, humbling truth, "I was wrong," we diminish the fear of being wrong and the hold it has on us. It's only our pride that cringes at those words, and by bringing it down, we free our true selves.

> *Lord, this day and always, may I live in*
> *the light of Your perfect, accepting love,*
> *which covers me with grace.*
> —SHARI SMYTH

Fri 27

"Therefore I say to you, do not worry about your life, what you will eat or what you will drink; nor about your body, what you will put on. . . . "
—MATTHEW 6:25 (NKJV)

How can you say that, Lord? Don't you know how much things cost these days? Have you priced shoes, or health insurance or gasoline?

"Is not life more than food and the body more than clothing?"

Well, yes, but we can't go around naked and eating crackers all day.

"Look at the birds! They don't plant or harvest or store in barns, but they aren't hungry."

Okay, but birds don't have to drive a car or pay for weddings and college tuition or make quarterly income tax payments.

"Look at the lilies in the fields; they don't work nine-to-five, and yet Solomon himself was not so well-clad."

But flowers only live a few days. I might live seventy, eighty, ninety years; that's a lot of house payments and car payments and prescription drugs.

"But you are more important to me than birds and flowers. I know you need all these things. There is nothing I don't understand."

But my wife has always wanted to go to England, and I would like to retire and enjoy a few years before I die.

"I never promised you that all your dreams would come true in this life, or that you would have everything your neighbors have. But if you will put me first, everything you really need will be taken care of."

I don't like surprises, God. I want to know where my next meal is coming from.

"Life is full of surprises, but just take it one day at a time."

My faith is small, Lord, about the size of a mustard seed. But You said that's enough to move mountains, so I'm trusting You to care for me.
—DANIEL SCHANTZ

Sat 28   *Who can discern their own errors?*
—Psalm 19:12 (TODAY'S NIV)

O ur rabbi was going out of town, and she asked our lay leadership to conduct services and study sessions while she was gone. I'd led Torah study before and expected to do it again, but this time she asked me to lead the Saturday morning service.

I gulped hard. I'd never been particularly stellar on the *bema.* The first time I was asked to light Friday-night candles, when I was thirteen, I dropped the match and set fire to the carpet. It wasn't an auspicious beginning.

I studied the parts of the service I'd be expected to read, rehearsed the melodies I'd have to lead and spoke with the other people who'd be participating. I wanted it to be perfect.

But I never thought to rehearse the actions that are as much a part of the service as the words. I first realized my mistake when I sat down in the rabbi's chair and elbowed the pole with the American flag. I had to grab it quickly to keep the flag from falling.

Hoping that would be the only glitch, I went on with the service. It went well until it was time to take the Torah out of the ark. The ark openers came up to the bema and pulled on the doors, only to discover I'd forgotten to unlock them. Once we got the Torah out, I found I was too short to take off its crowns. Later, the silver breastplate crashed to the floor.

By the end of the service, I was convinced no one would ever want me to try it again. But people in the congregation kept thanking me for making the service inspirational.

I asked a friend who had been there, "How could that have been inspirational?"

"The rabbi is very professional," she said. "You're just like us. And if you can do it, we think we can too!"

I know I'm imperfect, God. Sometimes I need to be reminded that You love me anyway.
—RHODA BLECKER

Sun 29

"You are the light of the world. . . . "
—MATTHEW 5:14 (NIV)

Last Sunday I served as deacon for our church's early worship service. Because the crowd is so small, only two deacons are scheduled. We help the elders take the offering, we "dismiss" the rows for communion, we pass out and collect the attendance rosters. And my favorite part of the job is lighting the candles. The service begins with the two deacons "carrying the light of Christ into the sanctuary." We separate at the front of the church and light the candelabra on each side of the communion table.

My very favorite thing, though, comes at the end of the service. The two deacons go forward to extinguish the candles and relight the wicks at the end of their long brass lighters. The bulletin proclaims: "The light of Christ is carried into the world."

My friend Sue was serving with me, and out of the corner of my eye I saw she was having trouble with her wick. While the pastor offered the final blessing, Sue struggled to push a bit of wick forward. On cue, we extinguished the flames and I relit mine. But as we walked out behind the elders, Sue's lighter was dark.

I joked with her in the narthex: "Looks like you were having trouble letting your light shine!" Sue laughed as she headed off to breakfast.

But all day I thought about what had happened. *I was the only one that morning carrying the light of Christ into the world.* What if that were really the case? How much darkness and pain would be pushed back? How many rays of comfort and joy would spread across my community? Would anyone even notice my flicker of Christian love?

I'm sure the wick problem will be resolved by next Sunday. But I have something to think about for a long time. Because I really am the one responsible for carrying the light of Christ into the world.

And so are you.

> *Let me burn brightly this week, Lord,*
> *that others may see Your light.*
> —MARY LOU CARNEY

Mon 30

A woman giving birth to a child has pain because her time has come; but when her baby is born she forgets the anguish because of her joy that a child is born into the world. —JOHN 16:21 (NIV)

A friend of mine shows me his brand-new son, all of two days old, the size of a loaf of bread, his father looking like he's been sleeping in the woods for a week. I accept the infant gingerly as my friend shuffles off to make coffee. The kid weighs half of nothing, and he is sound asleep and drooling on my best shirt, which makes me unaccountably happy.

Do we ever salute and acknowledge and celebrate miracles enough? I watch the kid breathe; his chest is about the size of a sparrow, but it keeps inhaling and exhaling—miracle. His fingernails are the size of the letters in this sentence—miracle. I remember twice being in the hospital watching tiny people emerge from my wife and sobbing for any number of reasons, one being sheer astonishment at the perfect, moist, glistening beauty of those tiny miracles.

Do we ever acknowledge that every breath we draw and word we speak is a miracle? Hardly. Birds, bread, kindness, rain, the dawn that came again today, the silver river of drool filling the pocket of my best black shirt—miracles. Maybe there are too many miracles to sing properly; maybe we would never do anything but gape in awe and mumble, "Oh, bless me, thank You, thank You," if we were really attentive and respectful to the ocean of miracles. But once in a while we should pause and bow, perhaps with a dish towel over one shoulder in case of miraculous rivers.

Dear Lord: Listen, this whole idea of infinitesimal new people emerging from people we love—very cool invention. Your creativity is astonishing all around, but this tiny-new-being-emerging-from-older-amazing-being thing—that is just deft.
—BRIAN DOYLE

Tue 31 *Nevertheless I am continually with You; You hold me by my right hand.*
—PSALM 73:23 (NKJV)

It is late at night, and I have just finished setting the table for our bed-and-breakfast guests. My husband Bill has already gone to bed and so has our precious daughter Brittany. As I climb the "wooden hill" (my mom used to call the stairs that), I smile, knowing that my day's work is done and that soon I'll be having a good night's sleep.

Outside, the full moon lights up the subzero January night. On the stairs a sudden blast of cold air hits me, and I brace myself for the rest of the climb. When we bought this farmhouse, we weren't dismayed by the fact that it had no heat, plumbing or running water. A centrally located wood stove, now long gone, had warmed the house prior to our arrival. The first fall we installed baseboard heating on the main floor, making a promise that one day we'd install heat upstairs. Now, almost forty years later, the bitter cold of winter still sneaks in through every upstairs cranny and crack in our 220-year-old farm home.

I think about my faith tonight, how one minute I'm in the warm presence of my Lord and yet in a split second I can take a step in the wrong direction. I've been at that place of decision many times in my life, yet because of the warmth of His love, I've never been left out in the cold.

Lord, I pray that every step I take be one that draws me closer to You.
—Patricia Pusey

MY PATHWAY TO PEACE

1 _____

2 _____

3 _____

4 _____

5 _____

6 _____

7 _____

8 _____

9 _____

10 _____

11 _____

12 _____

13 _____

14 _____

15 _____

January

16 _____

17 _____

18 _____

19 _____

20 _____

21 _____

22 _____

23 _____

24 _____

25 _____

26 _____

27 _____

28 _____

29 _____

30 _____

31 _____

February

*Great peace have they which love thy law;
and nothing shall offend them.*
—PSALM 119:165

❦ THIS I KNOW

Wed 1   *Our eyes as yet failed. . . .*
—LAMENTATIONS 4:17

THE COURAGE TO HELP

The first day I stood on the street of downtown Harare, Zimbabwe, watching cold, hungry children crawl out of storm drains and into the early morning light, I was livid with anger. How could God allow this to happen? How could He be so cruel as to send me to such a hopeless place, helpless, without money or resources to make a difference?

I had been called to Zimbabwe, where the AIDS pandemic had claimed almost a third of the population, to write about the street children. Later, back home in Nashville, my husband David and I were distraught but determined to make at least a small difference.

At first we simply gave what we could to help support the efforts of a lone woman who took tea and bread to the street children each day. Soon, David was inspiring church members to make small monthly donations to help. Within two years, with the commitment of a family in another state and a church-related foundation, we had raised enough money to buy a compound of buildings in downtown Harare, where the tea-and-bread lady continues to serve homeless people.

Miracle followed miracle, and we found ourselves bonded with a remarkable Zimbabwe couple who were willing to spend their lives welcoming orphans with AIDS into a large, loving family. Next we were buying a farm, changing the face of a rural community, feeding children at two schools, watching our son-in-law Ben open a dental clinic for children with AIDS, and on and on.

This I know: A lot of people out there want to help, and if we can gather the courage to challenge a hurting world, God will find a way to gather His family together to join our efforts.

God, You have shown me that I don't have
to do everything. I just have to be
willing to do something.
—PAM KIDD

Thu 2   *The unfolding of [God's] words gives*
light.... —PSALM 119:130 (RSV)

When I was in college, I asked my preacher-dad, "Don't you get tired of the same old

Bible stories?" Now that I'm the age he was then, I understand his "No!" What drew me from boredom to anticipation? Asking myself one question: *What does this Scripture passage say to me today?* Here's how it has worked with the account of Jesus' wedding-at-Cana miracle, which my congregation reads at Sunday services every three years.

At age forty I heard a *command:* Jesus' mother telling servants to "do whatever he tells you" (John 2:5, NIV). Listen to direction. Follow and obey. For me, this meant joining a different congregation, welcoming new friends.

In my midforties I identified with Jesus' hesitant *response* to his mother's subtle nudge for Him to do something: "They have no more wine." Jesus' reply? "My time has not yet come" (John 2:3–4, NIV). Feeling I wasn't ready for the next stage of life, I prayed for courage and strength. God granted those graces, especially when my parents died.

Approaching fifty, I heard a *blessing* toward the end of the Cana story. Jesus had turned water into wine, and the steward commended the vintage: "You have saved the best till now" (John 2:10, NIV). I claimed "the best" as a promise, which brings me to a recent reading of John 2.

I now sense a *call* in a phrase I previously disregarded: "Jesus, they have no more wine." I've outgrown my earlier resistance ("My time has not yet come") and want to do something. Some unidentified *they* needs refreshment, which God can provide through me. I finally feel ready to serve. Now on Sunday mornings I offer fellow parishioners the Communion cup. And after church I lead a Scripture discussion.

A tired old Bible story? No!

Lord, I'm listening. Unfold the words of Scripture and shed light on my path today. Amen.
—EVELYN BENCE

Fri 3   *Then all the trees of the forest will sing for joy.* —PSALM 96:12 (NAS)

A few months after moving to Texas, my wife Joy and I were back in Washington, DC, visiting our son and daughter-in-law. It was the week of the famed Blizzard of 2010 in DC. All Thursday night Joy anxiously watched the weather reports and worried about what our dog Flag would do if we were snowed in and couldn't pick him up. So we called the airport and caught the last flight for Dallas–Fort Worth early Friday afternoon. As we sat on the runway awaiting clearance to take off, Joy looked wistfully at the blowing snow and said, "If it wasn't for Flag, I would love to stay here and be snowed in with Jon and Beth." Somehow my Southern California girl had come to love snow.

So we escaped the blizzard (which pinned Jon and Beth in their home for nearly a week), picked up Flag and bedded down Friday to a partly cloudy forty-eight degree Texas night. Imagine my surprise when Joy woke me at 5:00 AM and asked, "What is that singing?" Sure enough, some soprano trilling was going on outside our bedroom window. I flipped on the floodlight and was amazed to see (and hear) snow and wind singing through the oak trees in the backyard.

We bundled up in our quilt, went to the front windows and watched all morning as six, eight, ten and finally twelve inches of snow immobilized Fort Worth for the first time in fifty-one years. My wife just kept whispering to me, "The Lord knew I needed this. It's just like home. He knew I needed this."

And I have to tell you, I believed those trees were "singing for Joy."

Thank You, Lord, for constantly amazing us with how much You love us and for whispering that love through the living tapestry of Your creation.
—ERIC FELLMAN

⧗ PRAYING THE HYMNS

Sat 4

Wait for the Lord; Be strong and let your heart take courage; Yes, wait for the Lord. —PSALM 27:14 (NAS)

DAY 1: SWEET HOUR OF PRAYER

You're as sick as some of our patients," Barbara, the hospital chaplain's secretary said to me as I left the chapel where a memorial service had just been held for one of our co-workers. It was true. This was my second bout of pneumonia in as many months, and it was only November. I coughed and gasped for breath as I trudged back to my office. I'd convinced myself that I could complete a report this morning before my 1:00 PM appointment with my physician. After all, I'd already used up nearly a week of sick leave when I had pneumonia in October.

"Let's pray about what is happening to you," Barbara said, guiding me toward a pair of chairs in the outpatient laboratory waiting area. As she thanked God that we can go to Him anytime, anywhere, with our cares and that as I waited in Him, He would make me stronger, I remembered an old hymn I used to sing growing up at Seventh Avenue Baptist Church:

Sweet hour of prayer, sweet hour of prayer,
That calls me from a world of care,
And bids me at my Father's throne
Make all my wants and wishes known.

It was true. Prayer had been my refuge in all the crises of my life. And my Father would surely strengthen me now as I waited for His touch.

In seasons of distress and grief,
My soul has often found relief
And oft escaped the tempter's snare
By thy return, sweet hour of prayer.
—ROBERTA MESSNER

⏳ PRAYING THE HYMNS

Sun 5 *And therefore He waits on high to have compassion on you....*
—ISAIAH 30:18 (NAS)

DAY 2: TELL ME THE OLD, OLD STORY

"I'm afraid you need to be admitted to the hospital right away," Dr. Brownfield was saying to me. Hadn't he heard me say I was two weeks behind on urgent paperwork in my office?

"I'm concerned that you're coughing up blood; you may have a pulmonary embolus." I knew that a blood clot in my lungs was serious and could even be deadly if not attended to immediately. So I walked across the hall to the office laboratory for blood tests, searching for a chair to steady myself every few steps. Then I drove myself to the hospital, feeling more afraid than I had ever felt in my life.

As I headed west on Route 60, I sensed God's compassion enveloping me. "I need Your loving care, sweet Jesus," I prayed. "Remind me of all those times in the past when You were there for me, provided for me." The memory of thirty-two surgeries for tumor growths crowded my mind, but I was certain of one thing: God's love had always been the remedy for any ailment. And it was always right on time, even if God's healing hand seemed to be slow in moving at the moment.

And there, all by myself in my car, I prayed the words to one of my favorite hymns, pleading with God to touch my weak and weary spirit:

> *Tell me the old, old story*
> *Of unseen things above,*
> *Of Jesus and His glory,*
> *Of Jesus and His love.*

—ROBERTA MESSNER

⧖ PRAYING THE HYMNS

Mon 6

I will wait for the God of my salvation. . . . —MICAH 7:7 (NAS)

DAY 3: IT IS WELL WITH MY SOUL

In my hospital room, I was visited by a doctor wearing a gown and mask. This new lung specialist explained that he didn't think I had a blood clot in my lungs at all. Rather, he wondered if I might have tuberculosis.

When I was a brand-new registered nurse in 1974, I had performed mouth-to-mouth resuscitation on a lady who was later found to have active pulmonary tuberculosis. I'd had a positive TB skin test, and the doctor feared that in my diminished immune state, I had reactivated that old infection. I was now to be in isolation for three days until they could test my sputum for *Mycobacterium tuberculosis.*

The irony of the situation wasn't lost on me. In my work as an infection-control practitioner, I cared for patients with tuberculosis. Now I was on the other side of the bed rail.

I knew that studies showed that patients in isolation see hospital staff less frequently because staff members don't want to wear the protective gear necessary to enter the patient's room. Just at a time when I was hoping for a visit from family and friends, I would likely see hardly anyone. Afraid and alone, I searched my mind for an old hymn that might bring me comfort.

Suddenly, I was back at my dear friend Anna's funeral, singing an old hymn that had been a healing balm for both of us: "It Is Well with My Soul." I sang right out loud to the Only One Who could hear me:

When peace like a river attendeth my way,
When sorrows like sea billows roll;
Whatever my lot, Thou hast taught me to say:
It is well, it is well with my soul.
—ROBERTA MESSNER

PRAYING THE HYMNS

Tue 7   *Cease striving and know that I am God.... —*PSALM 46:10 (NAS)

DAY 4: COME, THOU FOUNT OF EVERY BLESSING

Now that I was in isolation to rule out pulmonary tuberculosis, my door had to be kept closed all of the time. The hospital staff wore gowns and masks when they entered my room, and I learned to study their eyes for clues as to what they might be thinking. If they didn't make eye contact at all, I worried that I had lung cancer.

Mostly, I just thought—and thought and thought. I pondered the state of the world, the state of things back at work, the state of anything and everything that could possibly worry me. "Work is piling up back home and here I am flat on my back," I cried out to the heavens. "And how much is all this health care costing, Lord? Insurance only pays eighty percent!"

Help me to stop trying to solve all my problems and just think of something positive, I asked God one particularly trying afternoon. My thoughts took me back to before the pneumonia, when doctors determined that the long-standing tumor in my head, which had been in remission since 2003, had returned. When I got back to work after traveling to the Cleveland Clinic and learning that my tumor was gone, a speech pathologist at my hospital, Rachel Bartram, looked me up. Rachel had just learned that her own cancer was aggressively active again.

But now Rachel was hugging me and rejoicing. "I just learned some good news about you and came to see if it was really true," she said. In her own dark night, Rachel was happy about me.

Alone in my room in isolation, I prayed the words of another old hymn:

Come, Thou Fount of every blessing,
Tune my heart to sing Thy grace;
Streams of mercy, never ceasing,
Call for songs of loudest praise.

—ROBERTA MESSNER

PRAYING THE HYMNS

 For You, O Lord, have not forsaken those who seek You.
—PSALM 9:10 (NAS)

DAY 5: I NEED THEE EVERY HOUR

Nights drag on and on when you're in respiratory isolation. I felt the darkness all around me in my bed at St. Mary's Medical Center. But Jason, one of the night-shift nurses, made all the difference. One night he came into my room with my meds and a cup of coffee with light cream, just the way I like it.

"I heard you used to work the graveyard shift too," he said. "We nurses have to take care of our own."

All at once I wasn't waiting all alone in my hospital room; I was sitting around my friend Sue's glass-topped kitchen table drinking coffee and talking. They say the best friends are those you can call in the middle of the night, so that's just what I did. Sue hadn't been to see me because her ninety-nine-year-old dad was visiting her from Oklahoma, and she didn't want to take the chance of exposing him to something contagious.

Sue was still up watching *The Tonight Show.* We talked and talked, separated by a few miles but joined by the Love that's with us every hour of every day. As I hung up the phone, I thanked God for nurses like Jason, friends like Sue, and the One Who will never forsake me, praying:

> *"I need Thee, O I need Thee;*
> *Every hour I need Thee!*
> *O bless me now, my Savior,*
> *I come to Thee."*
> —ROBERTA MESSNER

⌛ PRAYING THE HYMNS

Thu 9 It is good that he waits silently. . . .
—LAMENTATIONS 3:26 (NAS)

DAY 6: SAVIOR, LIKE A SHEPHERD LEAD US

When my test results came in, I was ever so thankful to learn that I didn't have pulmonary tuberculosis. It was great to be out of isolation and have a steady flow of hospital staff and visitors. But something was still terribly wrong with me.

"I can't push myself up in bed anymore," I told the physician on call. "And when I try to get out of bed, my arms and legs just don't cooperate. They hurt, too, as if there's something wrong with the bones."

The doctor ordered some medication to take care of my pain and loss of movement. But what would happen when I went home from the hospital the next day?

As I waited silently for the Lord, a verse from "Savior, Like a Shepherd Lead Us" came to mind:

> *Thou hast promised to receive us,*
> *Poor and sinful though we be;*
> *Thou hast mercy to relieve us,*
> *Grace to cleanse and power to free.*

It was a tune I often played on my baby grand at home. But if things continued like they had, I wouldn't be playing my piano.

Pushing back my deepest fears, I tried to take a nap. I fell asleep praying the remaining words to the hymn:

> *Blessed Jesus, blessed Jesus,*
> *Early let us turn to Thee;*
> *Blessed Jesus, blessed Jesus,*
> *Early let us turn to Thee.*

—ROBERTA MESSNER

PRAYING THE HYMNS

Fri 10

*I waited patiently for the Lord; And
He inclined to me and heard my cry.*
—PSALM 40:1 (NAS)

DAY 7: LEANING ON THE EVERLASTING ARMS

I was so relieved when my regular physician was back in town and I could speak with him about my inability to use my arms. He quickly diagnosed my problem as severe tendonitis. It was likely caused by the three courses of a particular antibiotic I had taken for the atypical pneumonia they had at long last diagnosed. "I want you to stop the medication immediately and see me in my office in an hour," he told me.

Snow hung on the tall pines like garlands when my sister Rebekkah drove me to Dr. Brownfield's office. When he tested my arms' range of motion, I cried out and tears streamed down my face. He sent me over to the laboratory for some blood work, wrote a prescription for a different antibiotic and pain medicine, and suggested that when the pain was dulled I begin moving my arms as much as I could so I wouldn't lose function.

The tendonitis would likely eventually ease up as the antibiotic cleared itself out of my body, I learned. I was discouraged to know that my symptoms could reappear later, but I would not give up. God was teaching me that courage isn't always like a lion's roar. Sometimes it whispers at day's end, "I will try again tomorrow."

My present and future were unpredictable and entirely in the Lord's hands. But as I faced the challenges ahead, I would not be passive. Stronger than ever on the inside, I'd return to work in three days and begin rebuilding my life patiently as I prayed:

What a fellowship, what a joy divine,
Leaning on the everlasting arms.
What a blessedness, what a peace is mine,
Leaning on the everlasting arms.

—ROBERTA MESSNER

Sat 11

Ye thought evil against me . . . but God meant it unto good. . . .
—GENESIS 50:20

I would love to hear about your trip to Africa," the e-mail said. "I feel like God speaks audibly to me there."

February

Just weeks before, I had returned home from the adventure of a lifetime. I'd flown to Beira, Mozambique, and then taken a chartered plane deep into the bush near Lake Cahora Bassa. I'd spent almost three weeks in a million square acres of wilderness, accompanied by a professional guide and a few native trackers. After seven days, I realized that my adventure had been a clear call from God.

Now here was an e-mail from one of my sister Keri's friends, describing exactly what I'd felt during my time in Africa. I leaned back in my chair and remembered:

We had been tracking a great old Cape buffalo for almost a week when suddenly the huge animal stood before me. Somehow in that moment the heartbreak of my broken engagement fell away, and I heard what I knew was the voice of God: *I am always here,* He said to me.

I returned to Nashville with a new spirit, filled with joy for the Lord, for my son Harrison, for my family, my friends and my career. I knew that I had everything a man needed to be fulfilled. God had given me true contentment.

Now, I was staring at the e-mail on my computer screen, from someone I had never met, someone who somehow knew what was in my heart.

"I think I need to meet this Corinne Barfield," I said to the silent screen.

*Father, You put me in places where I can hear
Your voice and You send messages that
tell me You are near.*
—BROCK KIDD

Sun 12

*Be careful for nothing; but in every
thing by prayer and supplication
with thanksgiving let your requests
be made known unto God. And the
peace of God, which passeth all
understanding, shall keep your
hearts and minds through Christ
Jesus.* —PHILIPPIANS 4:6–7

My grandmother is the only person I have ever known who never showed any fear. She was human, so she must have felt it at some point in her life. Maybe she was afraid when, as a young wife and mother, she became a refugee, fleeing the Japanese as they invaded China. Or maybe she felt it in the late 1960s, when she immigrated to America, a land where the culture was foreign and the language incomprehensible. But I never saw a moment of it.

"You have to pray." I can still hear the words in her warbly voice—a command, a piece of advice, and a grandmotherly reminder all wrapped up in one. My grandma, who died seventeen years ago today, must have said those same words to me ten thousand times: when I was stressed about school, when I was angry at my father, when I was frustrated with some stupid or trivial thing as well as some more important ones. "You have to pray."

She wasn't a starry-eyed fantasist who thought that by turning to God, she'd get whatever she wanted. Certainly, her life showed that plenty of prayer hadn't smoothed out the bumps: She lived through poverty and war and the death of one of her six children and much, much more.

No, it was because she understood that with prayer, she drew closer to God, and with God, she had nothing to fear. The presence of prayer meant the conquest of fear—because she had on her side the peace that passes all human understanding. And that, she taught me, was all you ever needed.

Lord, in good times and bad, in joy and in sorrow,
remind me that I have to pray.
*—*JEFF CHU

Mon 13   *But among you it will be different. Whoever wants to be a leader among you must be your servant.*
*—*MATTHEW 20:26 (NLT)

I was always different as a child, when I so badly wanted to be like everyone else in my class.

Because I'm dyslexic, I didn't start to read fluently until I was ten years old and in the fifth grade. My third-grade teacher told my mother, "Debbie's a nice little girl, but she's never going to do well in school." And I didn't; I struggled with poor grades all the way through school. College was never an option for me.

When I entered high school, my goal was to make the honor roll just once, for one quarter. I gave it my all. Not once did I make that list. On the last report card I received as a high-school senior, I was one point away.

I was different in other ways too. I wasn't pretty, and I struggled with my weight. I had only a few friends beside my cousins. I hated being so different.

Years later, after I started daily Bible reading, I discovered Matthew 20:26. Jesus is telling his disciples that to live the way He wants them to, they need to be servants. I read the verse another way. It was as if Jesus was telling me personally that He made me different for a reason: He had a purpose for me. Because I was different, I could encourage others to become all God intended.

None of us need allow our differences to hold us back in life. Our differences are reason to celebrate; after all, this is exactly the way God wanted us.

Thank You, Jesus, for making me different.
—DEBBIE MACOMBER

Tue 14   *God is love.* —I JOHN 4:8

On this day that celebrates love, I remember a dream I had. . . .

It was two weeks after I'd undergone a quadruple bypass and valve replacement on my heart. I remembered nothing of the seven-hour surgery, but my wife Tib recalled every anxious second—the surgeon had warned her that at eighty-seven, I might not make it.

After some time in the recovery room I was moved to an intensive care unit where, wonderfully, Tib was allowed to stay with me twenty-four hours a day, sleeping (or at least lying down) on the narrow bench against the wall. I don't know how many times a night she was up, adjusting my blanket, bringing me a glass of water, raising or lowering the head of the bed.

At the end of the second week there, I had a dream. I seemed to be walking in a furiously raging stream with slippery, unstable rocks underfoot. Tib was in the stream, too, going ahead of me, feeling out the way. And in the dream she turned and called over her shoulder, "I love you."

Three little words, but as I woke they echoed in my ear. They echo still. Wasn't this what love was all about: the sleepless hours, the quiet standing by, the walking with, one partner maintaining balance for both in turbulent waters.

Isn't it an image, too, of Jesus' love—walking just ahead of us, guiding our steps, pointing the way.

Help me keep my eyes on You, Lord Jesus,
when the water is deep.
—JOHN SHERRILL

Wed 15   *The Lord God of their fathers sent warnings to them by His messengers. . . .*
—II CHRONICLES 36:15 (NKJV)

Searching for something online recently, I stumbled on a list of "Wacky Warning Labels." Evidently, in this era of frivolous lawsuits, manufacturers have felt it necessary to put some (you would think) unnecessary labels on their products. Some of my favorites are:

1. On a blanket: "Not to be used as protection from a tornado."

2. On a carpenter's electric drill: "Not intended for use as a dental drill."

3. On a bottle of shampoo for dogs: "Caution: The contents of this bottle should not be fed to fish."

4. On a string of Christmas lights: "For indoor or outdoor use only."

5. On a hair dryer: "Do not use in shower."

6. On a Batman costume: "This cape does not give wearer the ability to fly."

7. On a cartridge for a laser printer: "Do not eat toner."

8. On a novelty rock garden: "Eating rocks may lead to broken teeth."

9. On a child's car seat: "Remove child before folding."

10. On a household iron: "Never iron clothes while they are being worn."

I wonder if, when God sent the Ten Commandments down with Moses, some Hebrew grandma didn't think: *These sure are wacky warnings. Who would kill another human being?*

The Ten Commandments are just plain common sense, like "never iron clothes while they're being worn." And just like the Wacky Warning Labels, if you ignore them someone is going to get hurt.

Father, before I do something foolish, stop me and show me who I'm going to hurt.
—LUCILE ALLEN

Thu 16

But speaking the truth in love, we are to grow up in all aspects into Him who is the head, even Christ.
—EPHESIANS 4:15 (NAS)

Our seven-year-old Stephen is a tireless inventor. He fills notebooks with diagrams and transforms cardboard tubes, corrugated boxes, strings, pencils and duct tape into Rube Goldberg-like devices. Sometimes I can follow his explanations of what his creations are supposed to do, and sometimes I just look blankly and nod. I'm not the source of the engineering genes in the family.

Stephen is also a *Calvin and Hobbes* fan, and he's particularly fascinated by the "transmogrifier" Calvin makes out of his own collection of boxes. Calvin can enter the transmogrifier (by crawling under the box—it only works upside down) and emerge as a tiger or a toad or a duplicate of himself.

Of course, Stephen doesn't need a transmogrifier; the years are doing their best to change him. While he's still our "Little Guy," the one we can still carry in our arms, that won't be true much longer. "I can see the boy in his face," my wife Julia said one night; I can too—the lingering pre-schooler softness is shaping into planes and angles that will be a mischievous (I'm sure of that, at least) preteen.

I sit with Stephen in our old blue chair, reading him a bedtime story as he draws schematics for his new inventions in his notebook. He fits between me and the arm of the chair, snuggling comfortably in the crook of my arm. Stephen brings up the rear of the parade that's taken his oldest sister to college and will take him too, with his twinkling eyes and his head full of inventions, through boyhood and adolescence and on into a future of his own. And I'll still be sitting in the old blue chair, remembering what it felt like to have a little one beside me.

Lord, when I'm tempted to linger in the past, help me to remember that every day brings me closer to You.
—ANDREW ATTAWAY

❁ A GRACE-FILLED JOURNEY

Fri 17

He went into a ship with his disciples . . . And they launched forth . . . and he said unto them, Where is your faith? . . .
—LUKE 8:22, 25

SETTING SAIL

I was six years old when my father and I stood on the deck of the freighter on which we were traveling to Alaska, watching the foamy wake churning behind the ship. "How deep is the ocean?" I asked.

"Oh, it's many miles to the bottom!" he replied. I shivered as I imagined myself falling over the deck railing into those inky depths and never coming back. For what seemed like months, I often woke in terror from a dream of drowning.

I no longer have that dream, the terror that went with it or my father to comfort me. Yet standing here on the deck of the *Aegean Odyssey,* I sense that same little shiver running up my spine, and I reach for my husband's comforting hand. At just that moment, I see with my inner eye a man in a white robe stepping out of a boat into a stormy sea. His friends try to call him back, but His face shows peace and a solid confidence as He walks lightly on the water.

My father can no longer keep me safe. But a fearless One takes what is left of my childlike terror and shows me how to stay afloat in even the wildest of storms.

My faith is in the One Who calms life's storms
and shows me how to stay safe.
—MARILYN MORGAN KING

Sat 18   *Ask, and it shall be given you. . . .*
—LUKE 11:9

I've lived longer than four score and ten years, yet I'm still embarrassed to ask for help. I have no reluctance to seek assistance from our plumber, electrician or lawyer, but I feel I'm imposing if I ask loved ones, family or friends. On the other hand, when they call on me, I'm instantly available.

Recently I underwent cataract surgery. All was well until one Friday evening when the eye began to ache while I was reading. I went to bed, but the eye throbbed all night. Early the next morning I called my ophthalmologist and my eye surgeon. Both were away on vacation. I left messages on their voice mails.

At 8:30 on Saturday evening, the ophthalmologist called. "I want you to get into the Massachusetts Eye and Ear Infirmary right away. You might have an injury or an infection. Both can be serious."

I gasped. Me drive into Boston at night? Driving into the infirmary and parking during the day was a challenge. I talked with Ruby, and she said, "You're not driving into Boston on your own. Call Betty and Peter."

Peter, a retired physician, and his wife Betty are good friends. But it was Saturday evening and they lived out of town. I overcame my reluctance and called them. Betty and Peter drove me into Boston. Peter took me into the emergency room while Betty parked the car and then walked through the dark parking lot alone. It was 11:00 PM before I was examined and 1:30 Sunday morning before we reached home. I felt so guilty about inconveniencing them.

I had asked for help, and Betty and Peter responded. Why then was I still so ill at ease? I love helping others; why can't I understand that others feel the same way about helping me? Later Peter said, "Oscar, we enjoyed helping." All I had to do was accept.

Mighty Savior, may I understand how to accept the
kindness of others with quiet appreciation.
—OSCAR GREENE

Sun 19   *I will listen to what God the Lord will say. . . .* —PSALM 85:8

I walked into the Sunday school class feeling a bit hesitant. The topic was "Listening Prayer," and I was afraid I'd feel less spiritual than others if I couldn't hear God talking to me. But the speaker diffused my doubts pretty quickly.

"When I first learned about Listening Prayer," she said, "my prayers were always monologues—not dialogues with God. I prayed as if God had an answering machine and I was just leaving messages."

She went on to explain how Scripture tells us that God speaks to us, and that Listening Prayer is a way of learning to listen instead of doing all the talking.

She suggested three "be-attitudes" of preparation for hearing God:

- Be still. Find a spot without distractions and clear your mind of other thoughts.

- Be open to the way you might "hear" His voice. His answers will come to different people in different ways. For some, it may be an image. For others, it could be an immediate thought or a single word or a feeling or a Scripture.

- Be patient. Wait to hear His answers.

Then she gave us the next step: "Simply ask God a question, such as 'How do You want to make Your presence known to me today?' Then write down whatever comes to your mind: a word, a thought, a picture."

As the room grew quiet, I got a picture in my mind of gold-colored leaves swirling to the ground on the whisper of a gentle wind. Not surprising for the month of October. I wrote down that description and then these words: "Spend time outside today."

Ordinary words, but they shaped my afternoon and, now, my desire to listen more and speak less in my conversations with God.

Lord, help me hear Your unique voice in my life.
—CAROL KUYKENDALL

Mon 20

The steps of a good man are ordered by the Lord. . . .
—PSALM 37:23

It was the day before Presidents' Day, but I wasn't thinking about that, or any other holiday for that matter. I had been in labor for more than twenty-four hours and still my baby hadn't been born. "It's just not going to happen," I said to my husband. "This baby is never coming out."

Tony's face was wrinkled with worry and exhaustion as he tightly held my hand. "We'll be okay," he said.

Of course, he was right: Just minutes after midnight, our beautiful baby entered the world.

My sister Maria was our very first visitor. She'd been in the waiting room for hours. "Let me see our little Presidents' Day baby!" she said. "He was holding out for the perfect day!"

I looked down at Solomon, bundled in my arms. *How wonderful for him to arrive on this day*, I thought.

Tony and I took turns holding our new little boy. As we rattled off the names of as many presidents as we could, I put my finger in Solomon's hand and wondered if some day he would join their ranks. Closing my eyes, I drifted to sleep, thinking about the miracle of life and my beautiful newborn son and how all of our presidents began their journey just this way, as a tiny baby in loving arms.

Dear God, thank You for our presidents, past, present and future, and for the mothers and fathers who raised them.
—SABRA CIANCANELLI

Tue 21

Keep on loving each other as brothers. —HEBREWS 13:1 (NIV)

I was at the doctor's office one day waiting to see the doctor. A number of other people were in the waiting room, and we began talking about various things. As we talked, an older African American gentleman said to me, "Ten years ago I heard you speak, and I began to hate you."

Obviously, he got my attention, and I asked him why.

"You were telling people that Christians are supposed to love each other, even white people." He had been involved in the civil rights movement, and he gave us a vivid description of how he had been treated by segregationists. "I thought I had a right to hate white people," he said.

What he said next surprised me. "Thank you for your work. God has changed my heart, and even though it's still not easy for me to accept it, I know your message is right for all of us."

I know how easy it is to hold on to the hurts and pains of the past. But God has something else in mind. He wants us to put the past behind us, fill our hearts with love and, like the man I met at the doctor's office, keep on loving all our brothers and sisters.

> *Lord, help me to be faithful to*
> *Your call to loving service.*
> —DOLPHUS WEARY

READER'S ROOM

I am blessed by and grateful for the wonderful people who helped me this winter, plowing the snow on my driveway hill, shoveling and breaking up ice. We regularly had four- to five-foot snowfalls this winter.
—*White Dove Crow, Mantua, Ohio*

Wed 22

Whosoever will come after me, let him deny himself, and take up his cross, and follow me. —MARK 8:34

I'd long since stopped giving stuff up for Lent, or so I thought, until an acquaintance asked me what I would be denying myself this year.

"Nothing," I said. "I just use these few weeks to stay focused on the message of the New Testament."

My friend, who has a way of gently taking me by the lapels and getting me to explain myself, shook his head, so I continued.

"I got so bored with giving up sugar or a favorite TV show," I tried to explain. "It just didn't seem meaningful."

"Isn't it you who makes the sacrifice meaningful?" he asked. "Not the thing you give up?"

An image flickered in my memory, my father giving up chocolate for Lent, a big deal for Dad because he was a world-class chocoholic. And my mom, who would never tell anyone what she gave up but walked around on Good Friday with a pebble in her shoe to remind herself of her Savior's suffering.

My friend continued, "When I give something up for Lent, no matter how trivial, it reminds me that Christ not only died for my sins, he suffered for them. Terribly. It wasn't as if he died peacefully in his sleep. I can suffer a little bit too, in remembrance of that sacrifice. I can join him in his suffering."

I felt a little flush of shame and remembered how hard it was to give up some of the little things I'd given up in the past, how daily self-denial kept me focused on the meaning of the cross.

"You know something," I told my friend, "maybe you're right." And the first thing I needed to give up was my notion of what Lent was all about. Then I could figure out which one of the small sacrifices I could make this year would have the most meaning.

Father, You sent Your Son to redeem our world
through His suffering. Let me never
lose sight of that sacrifice.
—EDWARD GRINNAN

Thu 23

But thou art holy, O thou that inhabitest the praises of Israel.
—PSALM 22:3

I*'m too old to be doing this,* I thought. I'd driven my son Jeremy to the Social Security office, and my resentment had tagged along with me. Getting Jeremy's life back after more than a decade of addictions and risky living due to bipolar disorder required a tremendous amount of paperwork. His driver's license had been revoked for three years, and I felt like a carpool mom again. Jeremy had seen the light, his restoration was genuine. *Finally.*

About twenty clients waited to be called to a small window where a clerk would help them. We sat mostly in silence, hating the wait and the dreary

February day. An air of anxiety hung in the room; no one smiled.

I looked up startled as the clerk said to a large woman at the window, "Yes, you did receive a check, ma'am." The ecstatic lady jumped up, nearly knocking over a chair, and sang out, "Oh, dear, sweet Jesus, thank You. I praise You, Lord. Bless You." She sort of danced/marched around the waiting room, hands high in the air. "You are so good, God." The startled clerk leaned out the small window for a better view. The woman stopped dancing momentarily in front of the clump of us and said, "People, praise God! Who wants a touch from Him?" Then she sashayed close to each of us, offering to touch our hands momentarily.

All of us in that small room stuck out our hands; Jeremy was the first.

I keep forgetting, Father, that You told us
You inhabit the praises of Your people.
*—*MARION BOND WEST

Fri 24

If any of you lacks wisdom, let him ask of God, who gives to all liberally and without reproach, and it will be given to him. —JAMES 1:5 (NKJV)

Five years ago during Lent, I decided to write down my reflections about my daily devotional reading as a preparation for Easter. I e-mailed my daily reading/writing to my children and to friends who I thought would like them.

At first the project was awkward and almost painful; I was trying too hard to write the perfect thing. Then I began to write whatever came from my heart. As the days turned into weeks, I found that I couldn't wait to get my morning chores done so I could escape to my computer corner. I could feel my faith growing with each passing day and I was surprised to find that my personal reflections actually taught me things about myself.

When Lent was over, I thought my project was finished and I stopped taking my daily time at the computer. Within days I received e-mails from my family and friends asking me what had happened to my daily e-mail.

Now my little Lenten project has grown into a real ministry. I print out my reflections for our morning guests here at the bed-and-breakfast, and many ask to be added to my ever-growing mailing list.

Lord, thank You for using me to touch the lives of others. All that I do is for Your glory, day in and day out.
—Patricia Pusey

Sat 25   *"The father said to his servants, 'Quick! Bring the best robe and put it on him. Put a ring on his finger and sandals on his feet. Bring the fattened calf and kill it. Let's have a feast and celebrate. For this son of mine was dead and is alive again; he was lost and is found. . . . '"*
—LUKE 15:22–24 (NIV)

We all knew it would happen: Angie, my two-year-old niece Sienna's favorite doll, had gone missing.

Favorite isn't really a fair word to describe Sienna's passion for Angie. Angie is loved, celebrated, honored, clutched, stroked and fed any treats Sienna receives. Angie is the first thing packed in the diaper bag and the only thing desired at bedtime. Sienna believes that Angie is her soul mate and general problem-solver. Sienna once gave Angie to a crying cousin to hold and then beamed proudly as she said, "Look! Angie is helping her!"

In the evening of the day we lost Angie, we heard Sienna over the baby monitor talking to her Mom. With tears in her voice, Sienna said, "I miss Angie."

"I know, sweetie," her mom replied.

Then, amid muffled sobs, Sienna said, "I hope she comes back!"

We found Angie the next day. She'd been packed in a purse by a very busy Sienna as she prepared for another imaginary day of playing school and dress-up. When Sienna saw Angie, the joy in her eyes reminded me of the father in Jesus' parable welcoming home his lost son. Granted, Sienna didn't call for the fattened calf, but she did share her marshmallows with us, which I assure you was a sacrifice all the same.

Lord, when I feel lost and afraid, help me remember that I can always come home to You and that my homecoming will be met with rejoicing and gladness—and maybe even a marshmallow or two.
—ASHLEY KAPPEL

Sun 26

The meek shall inherit the earth, and shall delight themselves in the abundance of peace.
—PSALM 37:11 (NKJV)

A footnote in my study Bible defines *the meek* not as timid but as "those who humbly acknowledge their dependence on the goodness and grace of God and betray no arrogance against their fellowman." That reminds me of my friend Jim.

Jim is a church leader. "When I first came to church," he once told me, "I sat in the back and was afraid to speak to anyone. Whatever I've become, I know it isn't my own doing; it's all God's."

Jim is a civil engineer who isn't afraid to get his hands dirty. After being welcomed into the church family, he began to help with building-and-grounds maintenance. He took care of the furnace in the winter, adjusting circulators and responding to frequent breakdowns. If anything needed repair, he was Johnny-on-the-spot. In fact, he even went to the homes of church members to repair door locks or replace plumbing fixtures. No job was beneath his willingness to help.

"I love this church," he said. "I believe God put me here for a purpose, and all I want to do is carry out His will for me."

Jim was elected an elder and became a lay leader and accomplished small-group facilitator. All the while he exhibited a gentle, no-nonsense strength that earned him the respect and trust of the whole congregation.

Oh yes. He's still the go-to guy when anything needs to be fixed.

Meek? You decide. To me, the word carries a lot of strength.

Father, like Jesus, help all of us who
claim to be Your children willingly to accept
the role and label of the meek.
—Harold Hostetler

Mon 27

And it shall be for a sign unto thee upon thine hand, and for a memorial between thine eyes. . . .
—Exodus 13:9

My friend Stephanie, from my old Marland Heights neighborhood in Weirton, West Virginia, was staying with me in Manhattan. She'd just had surgery at Sloan-Kettering for breast cancer and was deciding what course of treatment to pursue. Now she looked at the stuffed piglet with a saucy expression and jaunty stand-up ears sitting on my dining room table. "Who's that?"

"My sister Jeannie gave her to me," I explained. "I was nervous about leading a workshop, and the pig made me feel better. I even took it with me into the workshop. Maybe it sounds strange, but . . . the pig made me laugh and gave me courage. That's why I still always keep it close." I glanced at Stephanie a little nervously. Did she think I was crazy?

Stephanie smiled and spread her neatly manicured hands, each fingernail painted a pretty, warm red. "My painted fingernails do that for me," she said. "They're always with me, and when I see their bright color, I feel centered and optimistic, that I'll be okay. It was great to have them with me in the hospital."

The next day I went with Stephanie to see her oncologist. As the doctor explained her options of chemotherapy, Stephanie calmly took notes. I looked at her smooth hand clasped around a pencil; her colorful fingernails flashed a message of vivacity and hope. My own fingers went to a small cross of turquoise-blue on a chain around my neck that my sister-in-law Jennifer gave to me last Christmas. A prayer resounded in my heart like an echo in a deep well. *Please help me to somehow help Stephanie. Bless and keep her on her journey with breast cancer.*

Jaunty piglets, rosy fingernails, turquoise crosses, unceasing prayer draw us back to our sacred center, so we can face whatever life may bring.

Lord, thank You for all the seemingly small things in life that center us and draw our thoughts to You.
—MARY ANN O'ROARK

Tue 28   *Verily thou art a God that hidest thyself, O God of Israel, the Saviour.*
—ISAIAH 45:15

I've written stories and poems in subways, in traffic, in checkout lines. This one is written in a cold sweat at 3:28 AM. I've awoken with a heart full of doubt. If you've ever experienced such a night, my sympathies. If you haven't, I'm envious.

This isn't the first time. What surprises me is that it doesn't happen more often. Take an unvarnished look around—war, poverty, tyranny, disease. And those are just the headlines before the first commercial. Sometimes it feels as if God works in mysterious ways and sometimes it feels as if God isn't working at all. Sometimes it feels as if God took a few days off or a few decades off, and the little pink "While You Were Out" slips are mounting up on His desk, waiting for His return.

I know I'm waiting for God's return. I don't mean the Second Coming; I mean right now, here in this drafty bedroom full of memories and dust bunnies. Any sign will do: a flickering light; a contented sigh from my ever-patient wife; even the fragile respite of a fitful sleep. Anything, just the smallest hint that I'm not forsaken.

Lord, You have brought me this far and yet You seem so distant. Show Yourself to the lonely sinner who searches but cannot find You in the dark.
—MARK COLLINS

Wed 29

And all were speaking well of Him, and wondering at the gracious words which were falling from His lips. . . . —LUKE 4:22 (NAS)

From my childhood I have loved words. My mother tells me I was forming complete sentences before I was two. It's no surprise my all-time favorite game is Scrabble!

A few years back I discovered among the sons of Jacob, Naphtali—whose descendants comprise one of the twelve tribes of Israel. The patriarchal blessing given him is found in Genesis 49:21 (NAS): "Naphtali is a doe let loose, He gives beautiful words."

I've chosen Naphtali as my "spiritual tribe." I want to live in this promise of giving beautiful words. They might be words of greeting, as at the post office when a customer at the counter said she was new in town, and I called, "Welcome! This is a great place to live," as she went out the door. Or they could be encouraging words: When a grocery store employee was feeling frazzled by holiday shoppers, I gave her a greeting card that said, "Remember that when you're beside yourself, God is by your side."

I also enjoy using words creatively. The other morning I thought the gleaming sun looked like a shiny copper kettle. And one night when a star was just "underneath" the full moon, it looked to me like an egg laid by a fat, white hen.

Beautiful words are wacky and winsome and wise. They transform. What a miracle, this world of words!

Jesus, Word of God—inhabit my words and make them wonderful.
—CAROL KNAPP

MY PATHWAY TO PEACE

1 _____

2 _____

3 _____

4 _____

5 _____

6 _____

7 _____

8 _____

9 _____

10 _____

11 _____

12 _____

13 _____

14 _____

February

15 _____

16 _____

17 _____

18 _____

19 _____

20 _____

21 _____

22 _____

23 _____

24 _____

25 _____

26 _____

27 _____

28 _____

29 _____

March

The meek shall inherit the earth; and shall delight themselves in the abundance of peace.

—PSALM 37:11

Thu 1

Better is a neighbor who is near than a brother far away.
—Proverbs 27:10 (nas)

Moving to Texas last year to take a new job was not easy. After twenty years in the East, Texas was, as the ad says, "a whole other country"— browner, flatter, hotter and farther away from our sons than we had ever lived before. Now it requires a plane flight, not just a long drive, to see our granddaughter Ella Grace in New Hampshire.

My wife Joy had a difficult time adjusting: I had an office with work colleagues and travel to distract me; she needed a map to find groceries. Only Flag, our golden retriever, seemed happier. Our new house has a large backyard with a field beyond and plenty of new critter life to fill his nose with exotic scents.

Meeting neighbors and making friends was a special challenge. No longer did we have kids to enroll in school or church activities where we'd meet other parents. Often Joy was the only one home on our street as couples went off to work. Our nearest neighbors were the age of our kids, one a lawyer and one a government agent. There was no way they would relate to us, or so we thought.

Not long after we moved in, the doorbell rang and there stood neighbor Chris, all six-feet-four, tanned and fit. With a sheepish grin, he asked, "Can Flag come out and play?" It turns out that Chris and his wife Maria have three small dogs who couldn't wait to meet their big new pal. A chorus of barks broke the ice and awkwardness melted as Texas delivered up its first treasure to us: a pair of wonderful new friends.

Lord, thank You for adding friends to my life
at every place in my journey.
—ERIC FELLMAN

Fri 2　　*Even to your old age and gray hairs*
I am he, I am he who will sustain you.
I have made you and I will carry you. . . .
—ISAIAH 46:4 (NIV)

Our grandson Lil' Reggie is six years old, but occasionally he'll still say to me, "Pops, pick me up."

I explain to him that he's getting so big my back won't allow me to pick him up. His response is usually "Pops, you're getting old."

The first few times he said that, I simply shrugged it off, but lately I've had to say to him, "Reggie, you're absolutely right: Pops *is* getting old."

Lil' Reggie enjoys playing tag with me in our backyard. When he tags me and runs away, I run after him and try to catch him and tag him before he gets to home base again. These days, that's not so easy. But it gives Lil' Reggie the pleasure of telling his grandma that I can't catch him even when he slows down.

At this time in my life, some things I once did I can't do so well anymore, but a lot of things—the important things—I can. My back may not let me pick up Lil' Reggie and carry him in my arms, but I can carry him always in my heart.

Lord, help me walk daily knowing that no matter how old I get, You are always carrying me in Your arms.
—DOLPHUS WEARY

READER'S ROOM

I don't know how other *Daily Guideposts* readers use the journal pages, but I use them as my daily prayer list. On these pages are the names I lift up to God in intercessory prayer. As we hold others in prayer, we become one, as Christ and the Father are one. For me, these journal pages are "the tie that binds."
—*Myla Wells, Auburn, Indiana*

Sat 3   *Let them praise his name with dancing and make music to him with tambourine and harp.* —PSALM 149:3 (NIV)

The White Plains High School auditorium was filled with people for a *Dancing with the Stars* fund-raiser to support the local food pantry. The professional dancing instructors and the contestants had practiced for hours in preparation for the event. Our daughter Christine was one of the contestants.

After one of her dancing lessons, she had called home and said, "Mom, I love dancing. It's hard work, but it's me!" My wife Elba and I were excited that Christine was doing something she loved while at the same time helping others.

Choosing a dancing outfit became a big deal. "Mom," Christine said, "I need your help in finding the right outfit to go with my dance number. It's a mambo called 'Cuban Pete.'" When they had chosen an outfit, Elba called her mother, who had worked for many years as a seamstress, and asked her to do the alterations.

Christine's enthusiasm was contagious. The owner of her company bought tickets so Christine's co-workers could attend the fund-raiser. Relatives made long trips to be there and support Christine. The contest became a family affair.

When the emcee introduced Christine and her dancing partner, we couldn't contain ourselves as we cheered her on.

At the end of the night, the judges announced the top dancers, and we applauded all the contestants. Christine didn't get an award, but she was still a winner. Everyone who took part was a star because they'd made a difference in the lives of others.

*Lord, help me use all I have in creative ways
to bless those in need.*
—Pablo Diaz

 THIS I KNOW

Sun 4   *Ye are of more value than many
sparrows.* —Matthew 10:31

SHINY PEOPLE

That nice couple was at church again this morning," I was saying to my husband David. "Shouldn't we—"

"I'd better take care of it," the woman standing next to us interrupted. "I know them well, and we've shared some things . . ."

Every church has what I call "shiny people," and this woman was one of them. She seemed to know everyone and to have all the right answers.

At lunch, my daughter Keri guessed that I was feeling sorry for myself. Soon I was telling her how, near our friend, I always felt that whatever I had to offer was irrelevant.

"Oh, Mama," Keri answered. "If she makes you feel less than you are, it's because you've given her permission. Step back, take a close look at what's happening and refuse to let her make you feel bad about yourself."

In the weeks ahead, I tried to follow my wise daughter's advice. I looked, I listened, and I learned that the problem wasn't mine after all. I saw that our friend seldom listened when anyone else was talking. She almost never made eye contact and habitually finished other people's sentences without regard for what they were trying to say.

"Wow," I said to Keri the next time we had a chance to talk. "You were right about that permission thing. We all need to learn to say no when others make us feel bad about ourselves."

This I know: None of us is perfect, but we're all precious in God's sight. That's a truth that trumps any hard word ever spoken, no matter how shiny the speaker might be!

Father, let me hold on to the best part of who I am.
—PAM KIDD

Mon 5   *Hope deferred makes the heart sick, but a desire fulfilled is a tree of life.*
—PROVERBS 13:12 (ESV)

A series of late-winter snowstorms had pummeled the Northeast, and the damage to the trees was incalculable. All that heavy wet snow and then ice sent boughs breaking and trunks snapping like matchsticks. On my morning jog through the park, I was dismayed to see so many of the fruit trees injured, pruned by nature before they had even bloomed. I picked up a branch of a cherry tree that would have been covered by blossoms in another month. "Take it home with you, anyway," I told myself.

I wasn't sure what I would do with it. Put it in a pitcher of water and hope that it bloomed? Not likely. I couldn't even see any buds on the naked branch, just the dried brown stubs of last year's fruit. Still, out of some instinct to salvage something from the debris or at least to clear the path, I carried it with me. I'm sure I looked pretty silly, running with half a tree in my arms.

The branch still had ice on it when I brought it inside. I filled our biggest pitcher with warm water, trimmed the limbs, and put it in. "I don't think anything will happen to it," I told Carol. "It's too soon to force a blossom out of an old stick." But four days later, a series of delicate pink-white flowers appeared on the branch and new buds on the tips.

Hope doesn't need much to flourish: a bit of water, a willingness to look foolish and the desire to trust. Spring is never too far away.

There is always hope in my soul,
Lord, waiting to bloom.
—RICK HAMLIN

EDITOR'S NOTE: *We invite you to join us on April 6, as we pray for all the needs of our Guideposts family at the annual Guideposts Good Friday Day of Prayer. Send your prayer requests to Day of Prayer, PO Box 5813, Harlan, Iowa 51593–1313; fax them to (845) 855-1178; call them into (845) 704-6080 (Monday through Friday, 7:00 AM to 10:00 PM EDT); or visit us on the Web at OurPrayer.org.*

Tue 6

Let the light of your face shine upon us, O Lord. —PSALM 4:6 (NIV)

I was trying on a pair of slacks in the cramped dressing room of a discount clothing store and feeling pretty low about how terrible I looked. The glaring mirror showed every defect. The teenager in the next booth was having the same problem.

"Mom, I look so awful I can't stand it," she wailed. "My skin looks like paste, and I hate this outfit! Just look at it!" The metal rings of the curtain zinged back so Mom could see.

"Honey, that's a darling outfit on you. It's this awful harsh lighting. Nobody looks good in it."

Amen, I thought. *This glare puts us all in the worst possible light.* I remembered stores where the lighting was designed to make me look my best. I'd come away with a lift and more often than not a purchase.

As I changed back into my own clothes, my eyes avoiding the mirror, I thought about another kind of light that can glare with a vengeance: snap judgments. When I make them I'm prone to put people in the worst possible light. For instance, the driver who cuts me off is "a rude jerk." The clerk who doesn't smile is "unfriendly." My husband who misplaces things while cleaning the kitchen is "sloppy."

But if I shined the light of compassion, I'd see that maybe the driver had a bad day and needs a pass. Perhaps the clerk has a burden that would take the smile off my face too and needs a kind word. And my dear husband? In the glow of love, I'd see the misplaced items for what they are—minor—and offer my gratitude for his cleaning the kitchen.

Good light can make all the difference. And when we cast it on others, it glows back on us as well.

Oh, Jesus, shine on others through me so that
I see them in Your light, not mine.
—SHARI SMYTH

Wed 7

*Into thine hand I commit my spirit.... —*PSALM 31:5

L ast winter when Beth and I moved from Texas to Georgia, we loaded our four golden retrievers into the back of my Suburban. Beau, his mate Muffy and their two-year-old pups Bear and Buddy snuggled into blankets in the back of the truck for a seventeen-hour-long drive.

Our retrievers quickly adjusted to their new home. They loved the large backyard with plenty of room to chase a ball. Soon after we arrived, however, Beau began to have spasms of sneezing. I was sure it was allergies. But our new veterinarian told us that Beau had inoperable nasal cancer and had about three months to live.

Beau was thirteen years old, a ripe old age for a golden retriever. He didn't seem to be in pain; he enjoyed his food and romped with the younger dogs. However, slowly he grew more tired. Finally, as the cancer advanced and his breathing grew labored, I knew that the most loving thing to do was to release Beau from suffering.

As we entered the veterinarian's office, Beau was calm, almost regal. His nose was bleeding badly but he seemed not to care. Walking into the examining room, he suddenly leaned against the wall and slowly slumped to the floor. Beth nudged me and whispered, "Look at him. He's relieved. He's ready to go."

Beth and I held Beau in our arms as the shot was administered and he slipped into a deep and peaceful slumber. We cried a lot, more than I have wept in years. But amid our pain was peace, completion and profound thanksgiving.

Beau taught me a lot about living. And in his final moments he taught me a lot about dying too. Somehow my best friend let me know that all will be well and there is nothing to fear.

*Father, thank You for the wisdom of animals
and what they can teach us. Thank You
that You create and love us all.*
—Scott Walker

Thu 8

Now faith is the assurance of things hoped for, the conviction of things not seen. —Hebrews 11:1 (RSV)

Last night I was ready to give up. I'd spent two days trying to write a devotional, but it wasn't coming together. Here's where I'd started:

One morning my computer antivirus program had told me I needed to update my security software. With hopeful anxiety, I clicked the appropriate links and boxes. Loading fourteen updates, the site said, would require several hours on my dial-up connection.

While waiting, I busied myself with other tasks. Even so, I stayed close to the monitor screen. As long as I focused on a narrow horizontal graph—at first blank and then gradually filling in, left to right, with green bars—it was easy to believe the screen's statement: "The updates are being downloaded and installed." Eleven times, the "full" graph emptied out ("Done!"). The visual movement assured me that progress was being made, streaming in unseen.

Then toward the end of the process, the configuration changed. The screen said "Downloading #12," but the graph remained empty for fifteen minutes. I fidgeted. I left the room for a while to resist the urge to push Cancel. Eventually I saw what I had hoped for: A green graph zipped rapidly across the screen. Soon I read "Installing," promising a final "Done!"

I wrote and rewrote those paragraphs. The sentences themselves assured me that I was gaining ground. But then I stalled. *What's next?* I couldn't see any signs of progress. I felt anxious; by dinnertime I was ready to push Delete. *No,* the Spirit said. *Wait. Sleep on it.*

And now, this morning, I find a fresh lesson in faith, newly assured that the Holy Spirit is working in my mind, in my heart, in my sleep, silently—even invisibly—updating: "Done!"

> *Lord, when I don't see evidence of Your work,*
> *increase my faith.*
> —EVELYN BENCE

Fri 9

We were delighted to share with you not only the gospel of God but our lives as well, because you had become so dear to us. —I THESSALONIANS 2:8 (NIV)

My husband Gordon was being honored at work for forty years of service, and his co-workers were planning a surprise slide show to present during the informal lunch. When one of them called to ask me to e-mail some pictures of Gordon, I asked, "Do you want some funny ones too?"

"Oh, that would be great!" his co-worker replied. Apparently even at work Gordon is known for his sense of humor.

I opened the picture files on my computer and started hunting. Finding funny pictures of Gordon wasn't hard. One snapshot showed him in a Santa suit stretched out on a recliner in our den, pretending to be asleep. In another, he was in a two-person orange kayak in a small swimming pool. There was the shot Gordon insisted I take of him in a drained pool that was undergoing renovation. He had set up a lawn chair on the bottom of the pool and was sitting with a fishing pole, pretending to fish in a small puddle left behind when the pool was drained. And here Gordon was in a classy sculpture garden, hamming it up by posing exactly like the statue behind him! Oh, and here Gordon was lifting a huge fake barbell over his head with a strained look on his face. He was the only adult waiting in line with the kids at a carnival for that photo opportunity!

Of course I picked out a few normal shots of Gordon as well: at our son John's Eagle Scout ceremony and fireside with our boys on a ski vacation.

The slide show was a huge hit, and we all had a chance to smile and laugh. And I had a chance to renew my appreciation for my fun-loving husband.

Dear Father, refresh my memory of the endearing qualities of those around me.
—KAREN BARBER

Sat 10

Be still before the Lord. . . .
—ZECHARIAH 2:13 (NIV)

Sometimes my car serves as my sanctuary—a place for solitude and quiet thinking in the midst of a busy day. That's where I sat one recent afternoon, in a parking lot outside our neighborhood coffee shop, contemplating the conversation I'd just had with two friends. One is a teacher, the other a grandmother, and both described their discouragement with the way children are growing up these days.

Soon the parking lot around me started buzzing with minivans rushing in and stopping, their side doors sliding open and kids jumping out, dressed in white with colorful sashes and disappearing into a door marked "Martial Arts."

One particular van caught my eye. A boy, probably about eight, jumped out the side door. He ran around and opened the back of the van, pulled out a stroller, wheeled it around to the passenger-side door, expertly engaged the brake with his foot, and climbed back into the van. Soon he reappeared, carrying a toddler. He climbed down, put her in the stroller, clicked the straps around her and then jumped back into the van and retrieved a sippy cup, which he placed in the toddler's outstretched hands.

Next he went to the rear of the van and this time pulled out a wheelchair, unfolded it and then wheeled it to the driver's-side door, which had just opened. A woman awkwardly inched her way out from behind the wheel and—with strong arms but lifeless legs—turned and lowered herself into the wheelchair. She said something to the boy, who jumped into the driver's seat and came back out with a water bottle, which he handed to her. He then closed all the doors and began to wheel the baby stroller up onto the sidewalk and into the door of the martial arts studio behind his mother in the wheelchair.

I turned the key in the ignition, and drove out of the parking lot, smiling.

> *Father, I just witnessed a holy moment in*
> *an ordinary parking lot. Thank You.*
> —CAROL KUYKENDALL

Sun 11

Praise him with stringed instruments and organs. . . . Let everything that hath breath praise the Lord. . . . —PSALM 150:4, 6

Most Sundays Sandy and Calvin Koehn and I get to church early to prepare music for worship. Sandy plays piano, I'm at the organ, and Calvin leads the singing. He has a lovely baritone voice but doesn't read music, so the first thing we do is go over the choruses and hymns to make sure all three of us know the tunes.

Then Sandy and I work on selections for the prelude, offertory and postlude. *Work on* is the operative phrase. We're both amateurs, and it usually takes several tries to get a piece service-ready. Once we practiced the first page of "Jesu, Joy of Man's Desiring" in different keys and wondered why it sounded odd. Another time Sandy played "God Is So Good" while I played "He Is Lord." Both are great songs, but not meant to be a duet! When a musical score finally comes together, though, it's as if God is right there, transforming our meager talents into joyous songs of praise.

During the worship service I'm often preoccupied with making sure I play the correct number of verses or whether the offertory is long enough or if I'm getting the pedal notes right. But that little time before, when Sandy and Calvin and I are doing our best to be our best for Jesus and the congregation, that time is my worship. It's my sacrifice of praise, my offering to God.

Thank You, Jesus, for the precious moments when You bless my worship with Your Holy Spirit.
—PENNEY SCHWAB

Mon 12

I have come that they may have life, and have it to the full.
—JOHN 10:10 (NIV)

It's tough going, this road I'm traveling on to get my PhD. I'd just spent the weekend working on my dissertation. So when my daughter Kristen called and asked if I could drive over to her house and watch the kids for a few minutes while she ran some errands, I jumped at the chance.

The minute I arrived, Sophia and Thomas, my two grandchildren, ran up to me. "Will you take us outside so we can ride our bikes? Please? Please?" they asked in unison.

"Sounds like fun," I said. "Let's go!"

I headed outside, bikes and kids in tow. I stood in the middle of the driveway while the children rode in big circles around me. Thomas raced around the driveway on his three-wheeler, skidding and sliding around the corners. Sophia, on her pink-and-white bike, looped around, ringing the bell on her handlebars every time she passed in front of me. She then circled around some more, waving at me each time and giggling all the way. Thomas and I laughed right along with her.

After the umpteenth time around, Sophia came to a quick stop in front of me, laughing and breathless, her cheeks flushed with excitement. She looked up at me with a big smile and said, "This is the best time I've ever had!" Then she rang her bell. *Brrrng! Brrrng!*

Now I'm pretty sure Sophia has had better times in her young life. She's eaten breakfast with a princess at Disney World, and just last summer she went panning for gold in Tennessee. But to her, these moments, on this particular day, became the best time she'd ever had. And, you know, they did for me too.

God, thank You for the moments that wake me up
to this perfectly beautiful world.
—MELODY BONNETTE

Tue 13

I am filled with comfort. . . .
—II CORINTHIANS 7:4

G reta is a *Guideposts* reader in Germany with whom I occasionally correspond. Her English is almost flawless, with just now and then a mix-up caused by the bizarre spelling of our language, like the recent letter that closed with "Blessings to your hole family."

Your hole family . . . The phrase gripped me. There was a hole indeed in our family! My husband John and I had just returned to Massachusetts from Arlington, Virginia, where we'd gone for the double funeral of his sister and her husband.

John's only sibling, Mary had died just a short while before Hugh, a former Navy captain. Their funeral was accompanied with full military honors—an honor guard of white-clad sailors, a caisson pulled by six horses, a Navy band, taps, a twenty-one-gun salute.

But all that was over, we were home, and what was left was the gaping empty place in our lives. *Could God really bless the hole in a family?* I wondered, looking at Greta's letter. Then I thought of Hugh and Mary's children and grandchildren who'd gathered in Virginia from Michigan, Kentucky, California, Florida, North Carolina, Utah, Dominica, Qatar... I remembered the hugs, the tears—the laughter, too, as stories were told of growing up in this widely traveled Navy family. I thought of the things we'd said about our love for Hugh and Mary and for each other, things that might never have been said if we hadn't gathered to acknowledge the hole in our lives.

> *Lord, help me to know that every hole in my life*
> *is simply a space waiting to be filled*
> *with Your blessings.*
> —ELIZABETH SHERRILL

Wed 14

> *Our daughters will be like pillars carved to adorn a palace.*
> —PSALM 144:12 (NIV)

It's my daughter's very last high-school basketball game. I was changing her diapers two minutes ago, and now she's starting at forward on senior night.

She starts out cold, but to her eternal credit, she's rebounding with alacrity and playing terrific defense. Every time she touches the ball, it's immediately gone, which is not the case with her lanky teammates. In another two minutes she'll leave for college, and she'll never be a kid again. Finally she hits a jumper, and then another, and another. Time out. I want to bottle tonight somehow, or make it last forever, and it won't, and I want to weep.

Now that she's scoring, defenders are flying at her, but she stays cool, which also makes me want to weep. She loves this. I love her. I want to weep. She gets the ball in the corner and gives a little shoulder fake, and two defenders sail past like wild birds. My baby girl cruises in for an easy layup, which she misses.

Soon the game is over; her team won. The girls mill around, laughing with their boyfriends and mothers. All the dads stay up in the bleachers wanting to weep. Time is cruel and time is glorious. To have had any moments with that kid was to be the richest man who ever lived. To mourn the loss is to miss the gift, maybe; all the way home in the car, I try to remember that. Because in about two minutes, I'll remember that little shoulder fake and it will make me weep. The defenders flew past like wild birds and my baby girl drove forward into her life as a woman and never was there a richer man than me forever and ever, amen.

Dear Lord: There is more to thank You for than I have words for. Isn't that stunning? So thank You, especially for daughters—and shoulder fakes.
—BRIAN DOYLE

❁ A GRACE-FILLED JOURNEY

Thu 15   *Blessed are the peacemakers: for they shall be called the children of God.* —MATTHEW 5:9

THAT THE WORLD MAY REMEMBER PEACE

The night before we left home, the *News Hour* had stories on the wars in Iraq and Afghanistan, the Iranian buildup of nuclear materials, street protests in Greece, gridlock in Congress and in-fighting within our political parties themselves. *What is happening to our world?* I wondered. *Why can't there be peace on earth?*

These thoughts are running through my mind this morning as our bus driver in Athens stops at the Stadium of Peace and Friendship, built in 1896 to revive the ancient tradition of the Olympic Games, first held in 776 BC. In addition to the athletic events at those ancient games, poets and writers presented their works and leaders of city-states discussed any personal differences they were having with each other. Even during times of war, enmities were put aside so the Olympics could be held.

From this ideal, the Olympic Truce was formed, calling for an end to all hostile activities before, during and after the games "so the world may remember peace" and so the participants and spectators might travel to Olympia and back in safety. And for the most part, this sacred truce was respected and obeyed. Since 1992, the International Olympic Committee has urged all nations to observe a similar truce during the modern games.

Lord, when I'm feeling angry, please remind me of that Olympic Truce. It won't assure peace in the world, but it just might help bring peace to my soul.
—MARILYN MORGAN KING

Fri 16

And Jesus answering said unto them, Render to Caesar the things that are Caesar's, and to God the things that are God's. . . . —MARK 12:17

Every year about this time, with a month to go before tax day, I'm staring at a mass of receipts, canceled checks and other financial detritus that Julee and I have to organize to file our return. And every year I berate myself: *Why didn't I start earlier? Why didn't I do a better job of organizing this mess during the year instead of just shoving it all into a bag until now? Lord, where do I begin?*

I dig in, trying to put things into neat little piles and growing more depressed by the minute. Almost surreptitiously, a familiar Bible verse slips through my mind: *Render to Caesar the things that are Caesar's...*

And to God the things that are God's, I remind myself.

All of a sudden I wonder, *If I were to take stock of my yearly spiritual receipts, would the accounting look this haphazard? This disorganized?* It very well might: prayers said on the run, promises to God that I have not totally kept, commitments I let lapse, bad habits that are still unbroken. *Face it,* I admonish myself, *your spiritual life is a mess, worse than your financial record keeping. You deserve a faith audit!*

Julee pokes her head into the room on the way out the door to walk Millie. "Wow," she says, "you're making progress!"

Another phrase pops into my head: *Progress, not perfection.*

There's no doubt my spiritual life could be better organized; spiritually I spread myself too thin. Yet unlike the IRS, God is understanding and forgiving. I must believe He knows I try and He sees me struggle. I believe He blesses my struggles. He accepts my imperfect efforts to love Him. And in this divine acceptance, I find a deeper faith.

Julee's right; I am making progress.

Lord, I am far from perfect in my worship of You. Yet what I render unto You, I render with all my heart.
—EDWARD GRINNAN

March

Sat 17

The grace of the Lord Jesus Christ, and the love of God, and the communion of the Holy Ghost, be with you all. . . .
—II CORINTHIANS 13:14

Top o' the mornin'! This is the day for the wearin' o' the green and the celebration of the shamrock.

Our yard abounds with shamrocks. One particular clump frequently gives us a four-leaf clover. Through the year, I pick and press these between wax paper and then affix them to greeting cards. St. Patrick used the shamrock to explain the mystery of the Holy Trinity: the Father, the Son and the Holy Ghost; three persons Who are one God. The leaves also symbolize three great virtues of I Corinthians 13:13, faith, hope and love, and when there's a fourth leaf, the blessing of luck!

Many of us will have corned beef and cabbage for dinner. Not in Ireland, though: Their tradition is Irish stew (made with lamb), soda bread and colcannon (from the Gaelic cal ceannann, the name for white-headed cabbage). Colcannon is a delicious mix of mashed potatoes laced with onions and cooked cabbage and then drenched with butter.

In Irish villages, when guests leave the festivities, it's customary for the host to take a burned stick and mark a charcoal cross on the sleeve of each person to remind them of their commitment to the faith and their love of Ireland's patron saint.

> *"May love and laughter light your days*
> *and warm your heart and home.*
> *May good and faithful friends be yours,*
> *wherever you may roam. . . . "*
> (CELTIC BLESSING)

Give us smiles to cheer us, and loved ones near us as we celebrate all that is Irish and wear St. Patrick's shamrock . . . in the name of the Great Three-in-One, the Father, Son and Holy Spirit. Amen.
—FAY ANGUS

Sun 18

Work willingly at whatever you do, as though you were working for the Lord rather than for people.
—COLOSSIANS 3:23 (NLT)

I've never had a lot of exposure to classical music, and I tend to listen to it without much appreciation. But I read a true story about a composer the other day that made me sit up and take notice.

Johann Sebastian Bach wrote each note as though God Himself was scrutinizing every musical bar and phrase. One of his most acclaimed works is *The Passion According to St. Matthew*, which has been called one of the greatest choral works ever written. Now here's what really got my attention: *The Passion* was performed only once while Bach was alive and wasn't all that well received. Just one performance. One.

Then a hundred years later, in 1829, Felix Mendelssohn obtained a copy from his teacher, who allegedly bought the original score from a merchant who was using it to wrap cheese. Mendelssohn's performance of the score was met with an appreciation and love that has never ebbed. This story certainly has God's fingerprints all over it.

What struck me particularly in the article, though, was this: At the beginning of almost all of his compositions, Bach wrote the abbreviation *JJ* for the Latin phrase *Jesu juva*, which means "Jesus help," and ended with *SDG* (*Soli Deo Gloria*), which is Latin for "To God Alone the Glory." This is just the reminder I need as I forge ahead in my life. All I do, every word I write, every action I take, everything belongs to God. To Him be the glory, always and forever.

Father, to You be the glory in all that I say and do.
—Debbie Macomber

Mon 19

Do you have eyes but fail to see, and ears but fail to hear? And don't you remember?
—MARK 8:18 (NIV)

On Mondays after art class, Maggie's friend Tamar comes over to visit. The girls play; Stephen stomps around feeling left out, and then I take him to soccer. As we leave, the girls head over to a fitness class for tweens that's two buildings away. They do circus arts, yoga, ride the stationary bike and make up new (and ridiculous) lyrics to the loud music that keeps them moving. The extremely patient instructor keeps the class happy and active for seventy-five minutes.

Most of the girls in the fitness class didn't really know each other beforehand. Maggie had one good friend there and was pleased to discover a whole new crop of likable girls. She comes back each week full of stories and smiles.

But this week my nine-year-old arrived home to announce that she wasn't sweaty or tired. "Jaya sprained her ankle," Maggie explained seriously. "It was all purple and swollen, so we sat and comforted her instead of doing other things."

"Did the teacher stop the class?" I asked, wondering at the extent of the injury.

"Well, she got ice for her, but mostly we just wanted to help take care of her," Maggie replied.

I looked at my daughter, wanting to say something but not knowing what. I held the image in my mind—a room full of girls clustered on the floor in sympathy around a new friend—and thought, *Some days there's something right with the world. Some days it all works well, even if it's working around a bruised ankle. That's a beautiful thing.*

> *Lord, sharpen my eyes to see and treasure each beautiful thing You give me today.*
> *—JULIA ATTAWAY*

Tue 20

And thou shalt not only while yet I live shew me the kindness of the Lord, that I die not.
—I SAMUEL 20:14

The plants that line our long driveway in Bellingham, Washington, are wild. There are evergreens, blackberry vines, hollyhocks, masses of reeds and tall grasses, opportunistic deciduous trees, snowberries and one huge-crowned sour apple tree. Every spring, the apple tree would burst into pink-and-white blossoms that gave way to small, hard fruit. We left those apples for the birds and deer.

Then last winter, during one of those windstorms that sweep down from Canada, the heavy branches pulled the apple tree apart. It split right down the center of the trunk, both sides dropping onto the ground.

"I guess that's it for the apple tree," I said to Keith. The tall grass shot up as soon as winter was over and hid the double bulk of the fallen tree from view.

I didn't look over that way much when I drove past; looking at the tree in its death throes seemed disrespectful. However, in the middle of April, as I was walking down to the street to pick up the mail, I glanced in that direction. There in the bright green of the tall spring grass were pink-and-white blossoms. I stopped and looked more closely; perhaps half the tree had managed to survive.

I stepped off the drive and parted the grass. Yes, this side of the tree was blooming, just as it had when it was still upright. When I looked over at the other half of the tree, I was astonished to see that it, too, was full of blossoms. The tree might have been knocked down, but it was far from defeated.

I picked up the mail, walked back up the driveway, and told Keith not to count the apple tree out quite yet.

Life and death are in Your hands, Lord, and
You are far kinder than we are. Every year,
You give us Your springtime.
—RHODA BLECKER

March

Wed 21

And be ye kind one to another, tenderhearted, forgiving. . . .
—EPHESIANS 4:32

Recently I received a hurried phone call asking for help that would be both costly and time-consuming. I responded, and I felt good about what I had been able to do. But weeks passed without any acknowledgment from the person I'd helped, so I called.

"If I hadn't heard from you, I would have called," was the annoyed response. "Oscar, you must realize I appreciate what was done without me having to shout about it."

I was stunned. What an attitude! All day I felt resentment. Then, in a devotional book I read, "Have you thanked all the people who have helped you?" The names of the people I'd never thanked came fast and thick.

One was Mother, sharing her meager income to keep me in school. At college, Miss Clark, the dining room director, provided work so I could stay in school and graduate. After I graduated, Aunt Lillian loaned me the train fare to my first job, fifteen hundred miles from home. Later, petite Cousin Florence cared for and supported Ruby and Oscar Jr. while I served in the army. None of them had I thanked or repaid, yet they never questioned me.

They should have taught me to be generous without expecting thanks. None of them are still living, but I can repay them by being kind, understanding and forgiving to others. And I can continue to remember those who touched my life, who gave freely and expected little.

Heavenly Father, the opportunities to help are abundant. Help me to see them and to understand the joy of giving.
—OSCAR GREENE

Thu 22

And I was astonished. . . .
—DANIEL 8:27

For years my friend Helen had insisted, "Marion, the group I work with can help Jeremy with his addictions."

I was certain she didn't understand. My son's problems were magnified by untreated bipolar disorder.

"Doesn't matter," Helen said. "Just read this brochure. God's at work there."

I took the brochure to be polite.

"I'm still praying," Helen called out.

When Jeremy's genuine restoration was apparent, a friend at church suggested to him, "I believe God wants you to attend Celebrate Recovery. Read about it on our Web site."

March

That Thursday evening Jeremy asked my husband Gene, "Would you or Mom drive me to a meeting—for people like me?"

"Sure, Jeremy," Gene said. Jeremy dressed carefully for the meeting at Cleveland Post Road Baptist Church in Athens, Georgia. I suppose only a mother could look at a well-groomed grown man and see a first-grader struggling for courage.

I rode along with them. As we pulled up to the door, two friendly-looking guys came to our car. "Welcome," they said in unison. Jeremy smiled at us quickly over his shoulder.

Gene and I were back at the appointed time. I rolled the car window down to better hear the singing and praising—and laughter. Jeremy came out with the others. He had smiling eyes, which I hadn't seen in decades. "Guess what, Mom? Your old friend Helen Gunter said to tell you hello. Man, I love this group. I fit right in. You can tell them anything, and there's no condemnation. I'm coming back here!"

Shocked into momentary silence, I confessed:

Oh, Father, how often do I miss Your voice when You speak to me through others?
—MARION BOND WEST

Fri 23 *Be quick to listen, slow to speak, slow to anger.* —JAMES 1:19 (NRSV)

Our family has owned (or been owned by) three sets of dogs. With our first two dogs, I was quick to speak and quick to anger. I spoke to the second set a little more calmly and could often control my anger. We now have two dogs, Shadow and Coco, who are puppies in behavior but adult in size—a dangerous combination.

On the first nice day last spring, I rode my bike to our mailbox, about a mile down a gravel road from our house. On the way, Shadow ran into my front tire, turning it ninety degrees and sending me sailing over the handlebars. He sped home, barking frantically, and then stood by the door and continued to bark. Since none of our dogs had ever acted like Lassie, my wife ignored him. When I hobbled home an hour later, Shadow slinked away and hid from us.

I returned from the hospital with a broken collarbone, a torn pectoral muscle, seven stitches in my elbow and abrasions on my left leg from ankle to hip. Shadow slowly approached me, his head down and his tail between his hind legs, whimpering as he knelt beside me. I petted him with one hand and marveled at the new spirit God has created in me these past twenty years. It's a spirit that is sometimes—not yet always, but sometimes—quick to listen, slow to speak and slow to anger.

Dear God, I thank You—and my pets thank You— for tempering my temper.
—Tim Williams

Sat 24

He brings the wind out of His treasuries. —Psalm 135:7 (nkjv)

From a distance they look like angels doing their morning calisthenics. As we get closer to the wind farm in central Illinois, I pull off to the side of the road so we can admire these towering pinwheels on the prairie.

"They're so majestic," my wife says in a reverent whisper.

I nod. "Somewhere I read that they're taller than the Statue of Liberty, and their blades are bigger than the wings of a jumbo jet."

We watch them a long time before reluctantly driving on, and soon the turbines are just little white daisies in my rearview mirror.

The force of the wind has been present since creation, but only lately have we learned to lasso these invisible horses and put them to work. It was just a matter of putting something up there to catch the power.

The rest of the way home I think about all the forces that exist in my life, just waiting to be tapped. I think of all my friends who stand ready to help me when I humble myself and ask for assistance. I think about the energy of positive attitudes: optimism, hope, courage, decisiveness. Arthur Gordon's famous line comes to mind: "Be bold, and mighty forces will come to your aid." I think about the magnetic power of prayer to attract God's help. I think about my library, my Bible, my computer, my family—all treasuries of information and inspiration, when I access them.

"Who has seen the wind," wrote Christina Rossetti. "Neither you nor I: But when the trees bow down their heads, the wind is passing through."

Lord, I bow my head, asking You to fill me with Your Holy Wind, that I might be a source of power to those around me.
—DANIEL SCHANTZ

Sun 25   *Come near to God and he will come near to you....* —JAMES 4:8 (NIV)

My grandson Drake is learning to read. This is a huge thrill for a bookworm and bibliophile like me. I can't wait for the day when he is reading to me. And what amazing worlds will open up to him through the pages of books!

A few weeks ago, Drake was in church with me. When the deacon handed me the service bulletin, he gave Drake a packet for children. In it were a few crayons and some pages to color. There was also a word search.

"Look, Nina," Drake said, placing his thumb over the last letter of a word. "This is the only word I know so far. *Go*." He moved his finger, and I glanced down to see the word was actually *God*.

"If you put a *d* on 'go' you get the word 'God,'" I whispered.

Drake busied himself with the crayons and papers, but I couldn't stop thinking about that discovery. Go *is the first word in the word* God.

Go to Him with all your problems. *Go* to Him in joyful gratitude. *Go* to Him when times are tough—and when they're not. *Go* to Him when you're angry with Him. Go, go, go! Comfort in every sorrow, help in every circumstance, direction in every decision begins with that simple act.

Each week in Sunday school, Drake is learning about God. Soon he will be able to read the Bible for himself. But already he has latched on to a truth it took me half a century to learn: God is all about *go*.

Forgive me, Lord, when I race toward worry instead
of coming to You in faith and prayer.
—MARY LOU CARNEY

Mon 26

And the Word was made flesh,
and dwelt among us. . . .
—JOHN 1:14

I took a class last year on the concept of infinity. We started by reading selections from Greek writers such as Archimedes and Aristotle. These ancients held strongly to the belief that an actual infinite was not possible, meaning that while we could imagine something getting bigger and bigger indefinitely, we were not allowed to imagine something infinitely large. That all changed, however, when we started reading more modern thinkers such as Nicole Oresme. Oresme believed it was perfectly possible to cut up a finite object into infinite pieces. This conceptual leap made calculus possible, and along with it Newton's discovery of gravity.

At first I couldn't understand why Aristotle was so limited in his thinking and Oresme wasn't. It certainly wasn't that Aristotle, one of the greatest thinkers who ever lived, wasn't smart enough. I only began to make sense of it when my professor told me that most of the mathematicians who helped uncover infinity were also members of the clergy.

Even Newton, writer of possibly the world's most significant scientific treatise, considered his biblical commentaries to be his best work. Oresme himself was a bishop.

Suddenly it was clear. These men believed that Christ had been incarnated, that God had been made flesh, and so had no problem imagining that the infinite could exist within the finite. The difference between Aristotle and Oresme was that Oresme saw God in math. His conceptual leap, a critical move in the history of both math and physics, was really a leap of faith.

Thank You, Lord, for revealing the infinite in everything through Your coming among us.
—SAM ADRIANCE

Tue 27 Uphold me that I may be safe. . . .
—PSALM 119:117 (NAS)

Only in Canada, *eh?*

Well, maybe not, but I doubt if too many bridges are paid for with taxpayers' dollars but built for the exclusive use of elk. Yes, elk, those big deerlike, bugling animals that frequent our Rocky Mountains. But if you happen to be driving out of Banff, Alberta, you cross under a bridge designed for elk to cross the highway.

No doubt there were as many scoffers when the bridge was being built as there were skeptics when Noah built the ark. I can just imagine the comments:

"What a total waste of money!"

"So, you think those elk are going to be able to find their way across that bridge?"

"I suppose you think if you build it, they will come. Fat chance!"

But come they did. A photo circulating on the Internet showed at least sixteen elk lining the bridge, looking down at all the potentially dangerous cars passing beneath them. For all we know, maybe two of their ancestors looked out of the ark in a similar way and bugled at Noah's detractors.

Safety is a major concern for both animals and people. Even though we lock our doors and obey traffic laws and line up for vaccinations against the latest pandemic threat, none of us can be certain of what lies in store. For that reason we can only do as the psalmist did in Psalm 4:8 (RSV): "In peace I will both lie down and sleep; for thou alone, O Lord, makest me dwell in safety."

Lord, remind me often to put my faith in
Your never-failing care.
—ALMA BARKMAN

Wed 28

As the deer pants for streams of water, so my soul pants for you, O God. —PSALM 42:1 (NIV)

My prayer life seemed to be going nowhere. I felt numb; distractions overwhelmed me, leaving me directionless. To make matters worse, I couldn't make up my mind where to begin with the projects I'd been putting off at home. Scrape and paint the front and back thresholds? Clean out the basement? Declutter and reorganize my office? Revise our budget?

Everything came to a head when I made up my mind to switch cable and Internet providers and unhook the old service's equipment from my wireless network. The new system worked great—until I tried to hook up a new wireless router to tie my laptop and desktop computers and my printer into the incoming cable modem. I know something about the technology, but apparently not enough. Everything worked but the wireless. Days passed. Calls to tech support didn't solve the problem. Neither did a second router.

"Father, I give up," I finally prayed. "This seems beyond me."

Then on the Internet I found a suggestion: I could use the old router from my former Internet provider with the new service. By chance, that very day a technician from the new provider stopped by to install a ground wire. I asked his advice.

"Let's try rebooting the cable modem," he said, and proceeded to unplug the power cord from the modem. After a few seconds he plugged it back in, and we hooked it up to the old router. In minutes the wireless network was up and running!

Had something similar been the problem with my prayer life? Did my brain need to be rebooted too? I decided it was time to disengage from all the distractions and focus my mind on God and His Word. Then afterward, I'd begin those painting jobs.

Lord, help me clear my mind and focus my thoughts,
so I can stay connected with You.
—HAROLD HOSTETLER

Thu 29

Be strong and of a good courage. . . .
—DEUTERONOMY 31:6

I stand in the doorway of the third-grade classroom feeling apprehensive. This is my very first substitute teaching assignment, and even though I know what to expect in terms of child development (three of my four children have been in third grade), I have never been in charge of twenty pupils for an entire day. I smile and greet the children with as much self-assurance as I can muster.

Then along comes freckle-faced Trevor, trembling with excitement. "Look what I got for Show-and-Tell!" Before I can respond, he jerks the lid off his plastic ice cream bucket. Snakes! He has a bucket of writhing baby snakes! Guess who is afraid of snakes?

While the other pupils take their seats and Trevor "hides" his ice cream bucket in the classroom sink, I think fast. Of course! The high-school volunteer will be here for Show-and-Tell. I'll let him deal with the snakes. But the kids' linebacker-hero blanches at my idea; he's more afraid of snakes than I am. I'm on my own.

Perhaps it's just a coincidence that I instantly remember Mom's teaching experience with snakes, but I feel God graced me this memory: Mom, a city girl, recalled the day in her one-room school when the eighth-grade boys hauled in a six-foot blacksnake. Mom told us how terrified she was, but she knew she couldn't let on. Instead she said, "What a fine snake, boys! But we aren't studying snakes in science right now. You can put it outside, thank you!" So while Trevor basks in the attention of his classmates, I praise his pets and admire them from a discreet distance. Actually, from over here, the wiggly little creatures seem rather cute!

Divine Teacher, may Your grace continue to guide my teaching—and to make my peace with snakes.
—GAIL THORELL SCHILLING

Fri 30   Dear friends, do not be surprised at
the painful trial you are suffering, as
though something strange were
happening to you.
—I PETER 4:12 (NIV)

In the same way that physicians often receive requests for free medical advice from friends and acquaintances, I'm often asked for "inspiration" from those who know I'm a motivational speaker. This happened just a couple weeks ago, in fact, while I was getting a haircut from Steven, my barber.

"Josh, I know you're a motivational speaker," Steven said, glancing up from the back of my head to make eye contact in the mirror. "I've been going through a difficult time recently. I feel like I'm in a dream, and that all I need to do is wake up and then life will get back to normal. Do you have any advice on how to do that?"

I thought for a moment about his question.

"Steven," I said. "I don't think you're dreaming. If anything, I think waking up means realizing that life is full of adversity. A difficult life is a normal life."

I thought about my words as I paid for my haircut and walked home. I'd been ill for several weeks, and the truth was that I was viewing my situation in the same way Steven was viewing his, as if it was a dream, as if it was somehow unreal or unnatural that something negative should be happening to me.

I had to pause and remind myself that the Bible never promises that life will be easy. In fact, it promises the opposite: Everyone, whether you're a barber or a motivational speaker or anything else, will face adversity. Maturity, I think, means accepting this, and finding hope in the knowledge that whatever struggles I'm facing, God is standing beside me.

Dear God, please help me to accept life for what it is now as I hope for what it will be one day when I meet You.
—JOSHUA SUNDQUIST

Sat 31

When Jesus came to Simon Peter, Peter said to him, "Lord, are you going to wash my feet?" Jesus replied, "You don't understand now what I am doing but someday you will.... Unless I wash you, you won't belong to me." —JOHN 13:6–8 (NLT)

It was late at night, and I was in a third-floor hospital room overlooking the parking lot. It had been a rough day, with much pain from pancreatitis and no company. I was feeling very low when a gray-haired nursing assistant came in and asked if I would like to have my back rubbed. I wanted her to leave, but her voice was so kind that instead I agreed.

She left the room and returned a few moments later. I turned my back toward her. "I think this will make you feel better, dear," she whispered. I was expecting an icy cold touch and was surprised to find it warm and soothing. "I always heat the lotion in the microwave before I use it," she said. "It's so much nicer."

If I close my eyes today, I can still feel her soft hands gently rubbing in the warm lotion as she told me that I would soon be well.

Lord, was one of Your angels working the night shift at the Dartmouth Medical Center? Like her, let me do as You did and "wash the feet" of those in need.
—PATRICIA PUSEY

MY PATHWAY TO PEACE

1 _____
2 _____
3 _____
4 _____
5 _____
6 _____
7 _____
8 _____

March

9 _____

10 _____

11 _____

12 _____

13 _____

14 _____

15 _____

16 _____

17 _____

18 _____

19 _____

20 _____

21 _____

22 _____

23 _____

24 _____

25 _____

26 _____

27 _____

28 _____

29 _____

30 _____

31 _____

April

*But he was wounded for our transgressions,
he was bruised for our iniquities:
the chastisement of our peace was upon him;
and with his stripes we are healed.*

—ISAIAH 53:5

⚜ THE CROSS IN FOCUS

Sun 1

I am about to do a new thing; now it springs forth, do you not perceive it? . . .
—ISAIAH 43:19 (NRSV)

PALM SUNDAY: SHOWING UP

Normally I delete those forwarded e-mails with cute or sentimental stories without even reading them. I receive so many, and when it comes to Internet profundity, I just don't have the time. But for some reason I read the one I received on Palm Sunday. It told the story of a little boy who had to stay home from church because he had a cold. After the service, his older sister came home, waving her palm frond in the air. "What's that?" asked the little boy.

She answered smugly, "We wave these in the air and then put them on the ground to welcome Jesus."

The boy started wailing and fled the room. When his mother held him and asked what was wrong, he said through his tears, "The one Sunday I don't go to church, Jesus showed up!"

Today's the day Jesus shows up—in our churches, in our hearts, in our minds. We've been waiting for Him all our lives. Are you ready? Will you be there? Don't let an ailment—physical, emotional or spiritual—keep you from the warmth of Jesus' dramatic entrance into our lives. Today is the first day of the most exciting, harrowing, tragic, grief-stricken and ultimately joyous week of our year. Don't miss it. Don't hit Delete. Show up, take the Lord's hand and begin the journey.

> *Jesus, don't let anything keep me from*
> *You this day, this week, this life!*
> —MARCI ALBORGHETTI

THE CROSS IN FOCUS

Mon 2   *Then Simeon blessed them and said to his mother, Mary, "... and a sword will pierce your own soul too."*
—LUKE 2:34–35 (NRSV)

MONDAY OF HOLY WEEK:
FROM MANGER TO CROSS

One of my Holy Week lessons this year didn't come during that time. It didn't even come during Lent. It came right after Christmas. Our neighbor in New London, Connecticut, assembles a glorious outdoor crèche with carved figures standing and kneeling on straw in a wooden stable. A strategically placed spotlight reveals the figures' expressions and positions. They are poor folk, from the weary parents to the ragged, adoring shepherds.

A few days after Christmas, we were hit by a nor'easter. The spotlight illuminated the crèche while the snow flew and the wind howled. When I looked outside, drifting snow had covered the figure of Baby Jesus. Goose bumps rose on my arms. There was something about the scene that disturbed me; I was seeing a preview of what was to come. The rejoicing of this birthday would lead to the glory and grief of Holy Week.

Then I noticed that the figures around the manger appeared different, now that the baby was covered with snow. Their faces, especially Mary's and Joseph's, looked stunned and sorrowful. The angel no longer seemed radiantly singing praises but grimly keeping vigil. The shepherds' awe wasn't joyous astonishment but amazement that such a sacrifice would be made for them. Even the animals seemed to cower in grief.

Later that Christmas week, the sun came out and melted the snow on the manger. And at the end of this painful Holy Week, the Son Himself will rise and melt the ice around our grieving hearts.

Father, my heart cries out in joy at Your wondrous gift and in sorrow at Your wrenching sacrifice.
—Marci Alborghetti

THE CROSS IN FOCUS

Tue 3

For sin will have no dominion over you, since you are not under law but under grace. —ROMANS 6:14 (NRSV)

TUESDAY OF HOLY WEEK: LETTING GO

I've been told that swans mate for life. I don't know if that's true, but I do know they are very loyal parents. My husband Charlie and I have been watching two swans and their baby for a while, long enough to see the baby grow from a tiny creature carried on its parents' backs to a figure as impressive as its parents in everything but its gray plumage. Whenever we spot one swan, the other two aren't far away. The mother sticks very close to the youngster. If it veers off in a wayward direction, she's right behind. If it tries to befriend a group of ducks, she heads off any intermingling. The father is more nonchalant, gliding off in a show of majestic disdain but never too far. Lately, though, both parents are giving the baby more freedom. They stare after the young adventurer with what seems like longing and fear for its welfare, but they let it go anyway.

I understand that need to hold on. During Holy Week, I usually go to a reconciliation service, where I confess my sins and ask God's forgiveness. The problem is I find it hard to accept that forgiveness and to let go of my guilt. This year, my pastor looked me in the eye and said, "You do know, don't you, that this only works if you believe God has forgiven you and, therefore, you forgive yourself?"

I do *know* it; I don't always *feel* it. So now I'll try to imitate the swans and let go of what's no longer mine—what Jesus lived through this week to take from me.

Lord, give me the strength to lay the burden of my sins at the foot of Your Cross and to leave it there.
—MARCI ALBORGHETTI

THE CROSS IN FOCUS

Wed 4

"*When you are praying, do not heap up empty phrases as the Gentiles do; for they think that they will be heard because of their many words.*"
—MATTHEW 6:7 (NRSV)

WEDNESDAY OF HOLY WEEK: SILENCE

Years ago, when I lived alone, I decided not to speak from Wednesday night in Holy Week to Easter Sunday morning. It wouldn't be too difficult now with e-mail and texting, but then it took a little planning. Early in the week I did my grocery shopping, made phone calls and took care of any tasks that required speech. I took Maundy Thursday off from work; Good Friday was a holiday.

I wanted to be silent because sometimes my mouth works faster than my brain, and it's only when I've finished saying something that I realize I ought to have kept it to myself. That week I wanted to take preventive measures. By keeping my mouth shut, I could be assured of not hurting or offending anyone during those holy days. It worked.

But, of course, God had a lot more to teach me. What I'd considered a sacrifice became a form of worship, and into my silence God poured a torrent of grace. I understood more deeply than ever before the meaning of Holy Week. I felt the flutter of the linen cloth when the disciple fled naked, abandoning Jesus in the Garden of Gethsemane. I saw the shadows of members of the Sanhedrin rushing through the night to their secret meeting. I felt the agony of Peter, bent over in shame at his betrayal, while the cock crowed for the third time. I shivered in the chill of the sudden darkness at the foot of the Cross. I heard the wailing of the women and Mary's soft sobs as she bent over her Son's body. Into my silence flowed the power of Jesus' sacrifice, and I wondered if I'd ever speak again.

Lord Jesus, fill me with compassion as
I become Your silent witness.
—MARCI ALBORGHETTI

THE CROSS IN FOCUS

Thu 5   *"I have said these things to you so that my joy may be in you, and that your joy may be complete."*—JOHN 15:11 (NRSV)

MAUNDY THURSDAY: JOY BEFORE SORROW

When we are in California, Charlie and I attend an African American church in an inner-city Oakland neighborhood. I've never had so much fun. Some churches get a bit schizophrenic about Maundy Thursday. Should they emphasize the institution of the Lord's Supper or commemorate the washing of the feet? At Saint Columba's, they celebrate both, and I do mean celebrate. There's no picking of twelve representatives from the congregation to play the apostles. Everyone's feet are washed, from the smallest infant's to the oldest widow's. The Communion service that follows is equally joyful.

Last year I watched a family with three teenagers. At first, the two boys and their sister did their best to look bored. As the service progressed and the music swelled, the girl moved closer and closer to her mother until they were arm in arm. The boys tried to stay indifferent, but when it came time for the foot washing, they swiftly joined the line, and after having their own feet washed, gently washed the feet of those behind them. By the time we went forward to receive Communion, all three children were singing and clapping with the rest of us.

Too often I allow the grief of Good Friday to overshadow the joy of Maundy Thursday, when Jesus gave us two of the most important elements of our faith: our participation in His very life and our summons to loving service. St. Columba's has taught me that these joyous gifts give me the strength I need to stand with Jesus in what is to come.

Lord, for these few hours, I dance with joy
on feet cleansed by Your love and with a body
nourished by the Bread of Life.
—MARCI ALBORGHETTI

THE CROSS IN FOCUS

Fri 6 *Here is my servant, whom I uphold, my chosen, in whom my soul delights. . . .*
—ISAIAH 42:1 (NRSV)

GOOD FRIDAY: THE TREE

There is a long walk I take when I'm in northern California. It starts in Sausalito, meanders into Mill Valley and ends near Tiburon. The route veers from the road onto a path through wetlands. A number of small wooden bridges cross streams connected to the massive bay. I was walking over one of these bridges on Good Friday, where I sometimes can spot a graceful crane. Floating down the river right toward me came a brown, dried-up Christmas tree.

Had someone finally taken down their tree this week? Or had this sad reject been in someone's backyard and just now been thrown in the stream?

The tree was a real, if strange, reminder that Christmas was over. All the joy over the special birth was gone, dried up like this useless Christmas tree. Today, the baby who'd been the source of all that rejoicing was the man nailed to a different kind of tree. The carols had become dirges, the incense was replaced by myrrh to anoint His body, the candles extinguished in the dark of a day without light. And yet it was this event for which the baby had been born.

Jesus, give me the courage to journey with You from Your joyful birth to this grief-drenched day.
—MARCI ALBORGHETTI

EDITOR'S NOTE: *We invite you to join us today as we observe our annual Good Friday Day of Prayer. Guideposts Prayer Ministry prays daily for each of the prayer requests we receive by name and need. Join us at*

OurPrayer.org and learn how you can request prayer, volunteer to pray for others or contribute to support our ministry.

THE CROSS IN FOCUS

Sat 7

The women who had come with him from Galilee followed, and they saw the tomb and how his body was laid.
—LUKE 23:55 (NRSV)

HOLY SATURDAY: THE TOMB

Oh, how I fear the tomb! I'm willing to follow Jesus into the Garden of Gethsemane and I'm certain I won't abandon Him like the disciples when Judas shows up with the soldiers. I'll stay with Jesus through the Sanhedrin's trial, Pilot's questioning, Herod's mockery, the soldiers' tormenting. I'll stand at the foot of the Cross and, later, weep while Mary holds the body of her Son as Nicodemus and Joseph wait. But, oh, that tomb. I do not want to go there with Him.

As a child, I used to welcome the trip to the tomb at the end of Good Friday. It was a relief for me that, finally, Jesus' suffering was over. Finally, He would have rest. I couldn't wait for the end of Good Friday services, because it meant the end of His pain and the beginning of anticipation.

But the older I get, the more troubled I am by the tomb. And so today I'm trying to recapture the feeling I had as a child when I saw a stained-glass window depicting Jesus' body being placed on a shelf hewn into the rock wall of the cavelike tomb. I went to bed last night and imagined myself lying on the ground below that shelf, keeping vigil with my Lord.

Really, what is there to fear about the tomb if Jesus is there waiting?

Lord, help me to rest confidently in Your Presence, certain of Your power.
—MARCI ALBORGHETTI

 THE CROSS IN FOCUS

Sun 8   *Jesus said to her, "Woman, why are you weeping? Whom are you looking for?"...* —JOHN 20:15 (NRSV)

EASTER: SUNRISE

I think of Mary Magdalene journeying to the tomb at dawn. She has lost everything. The One Who had healed her has been agonizingly crucified, dying by inches over long hours. She knows because she watched. The One Who'd been her first real friend is gone. Her hope—for herself, for her people, for all people—has been crushed. The prospect of an Israel delivered from the Romans is now a cruel joke. The people who had accepted and welcomed her are dispersed, cowering in their hiding places like terrified children.

After dutifully keeping the Sabbath, she has spent the night preparing spices and oils for Jesus' body. And now, when it seems things could not possibly be worse, His body is not in the tomb. It's been stolen!

Mary turns, and in the dim, morning mist, she sees a stranger. Is this the thief? But, no! He murmurs her name, and now she knows: "Rabbi!"

I pray that my life, my prospects, never become as dark, as despairing, as Mary's were that morning. But sooner or later, they will to some degree. And that is when I must remember Mary. That is when I must recall a glimmer, just a pale reflection, of Mary's glorious dawn. That day, as much as today, will be my Easter.

Lord, my rejoicing today knows no bounds. Remind me of this Easter joy when I have most need of it.
—Marci Alborghetti

April

Mon 9

"No eye has seen, no ear has heard, no mind has conceived what God has prepared for those who love him."
—I CORINTHIANS 2:9 (NIV)

A splashy field of bluebells at my grandparents' farm is woven through the Easters of my childhood. This half-acre carpet of stunning color waved at us as we rounded the bend of a dirt lane on the farm. No matter how much we picked—my cousins, siblings and I—we made hardly a dent in their abundance. Back at the house, Grandmother's Easter dinner table was filled with spring flowers newly gathered.

Then one year they were gone: plowed under for potatoes, we were told. It was the way of the farm, but I was devastated. The years have passed and every spring my memory still floods with the sight of that waving field. In the scheme of things a small loss, but holding a huge hope.

In that field I see all the losses of this life, from loved ones to beloved pets to even a spread of blue-bells, and I hear God whisper that someday, when I round the bend of eternity, I will find them restored. All that is good and beautiful and true will come back to us a hundredfold in that wondrous place where "God shall wipe away all tears from their eyes" (Revelation 21:4).

Lord Jesus, in rising from the dead You turned death into life and loss into gain for us and for all creation. How can we thank You?
—SHARI SMYTH

THIS I KNOW

Tue 10

I wait for the Lord. . . .
—PSALM 130:5

THE WAITING GAME

When our daughter Keri was about three years old, she crawled under the table one morning and refused to come out. I called, I sang, I danced, I begged. I offered cookies. She stayed under the table.

After a while I saw her stubbornness as a game and decided to play. I wedged myself into the pantry and closed the door, determined to outlast my daughter. Seconds turned into minutes. The kitchen was very quiet. Surely she would be coming out soon, if only to investigate.

Silence.

Finally my legs were cramping and I could bear the darkness no longer. I crawled out of the pantry and peeped under the table. There was Keri, all curled up in a ball, her head resting on her Lovey Bear, fast asleep.

Not long ago the memory of that day came back in a rush. For weeks I had been in a similar contest with God. I'd prayed and prayed for some sort of heavenly solution to my very earthly complaints.

Wait and see, God had seemed to say to my nagging prayers.

But I was begging, calling, singing, even trying to bribe Him with my special I'll-do-this-if-You-do-that cookies. Finally I just hid myself away.

Still no answer—until the day I finally bothered to stop and take inventory. Hadn't God always shown up at just the right time—His time, not mine?

That's when a new anticipation overcame my anxious heart, and I realized that waiting out God isn't a contest; it's an adventure.

> *I wait, Father, with butterflies in my heart.*
> —Pam Kidd

Wed 11

For you do not know which will succeed, whether this or that, or whether both will do equally well.
—Ecclesiastes 11:6 (niv)

In my new job in Texas I was thrown into dozens of new situations, and well-meaning folks suggested a dozen more new ideas. How was I going to pick the best path or most important activity on which to focus?

Often during our first spring I would find Joy sitting out in back of our home early in the morning, motionless and silent, observing the hummingbirds. Soon I joined her and became fascinated with them.

While I was watching those little birds one morning, I grew exasperated trying to follow the path of just one. They zipped up, down, sideways, backward, forward, making a dozen moves a minute. "Why do they move around so much?" I asked Joy.

"They just try every flower, seeing which one has the most nectar and insects for them to feast on; then they settle on that one for a bit longer."

"How do they do so much so quickly?" I continued.

"That's the amazing thing," she said. "They are the only birds who can fly in all directions, because their wings are so flexible, moving in complete circles and rotating like flaps on an airplane. They actually move their wings in a figure eight when they hover."

Watching a while longer, I had my answer: Stay flexible. Try many things. Keep watching to see what works. Don't get settled in one direction unless you find more nectar and bugs there. Well, maybe not nectar and bugs exactly, but you get the idea.

Are you stuck somewhere today? Move sideways, look up, take a step back, try shuffling left, or maybe right. Or just hover for a while and be ready to head in another direction altogether.

Heavenly Father, thank You for all Your amazing creatures and the wonderful lessons You have written in their lives.
—ERIC FELLMAN

Thu 12

Each of you should look not only to your own interests, but also to the interests of others.
—PHILIPPIANS 2:4 (NIV)

Last night we had a long, gentle rain, the kind that gardeners pray for. When I looked out this morning, my first thought was, *God watered my flowers for me.* My second thought was, *Wow, that was a pretty self-centered thing to think!* It got me to wondering how many of my thoughts today would be centered on me. And was it that way every day?

I once heard a speaker say that we are all listening to the same radio station, WIIFM—What's in it for me? And I think that's true. One of the reasons Christ admonished us to love others as we love ourselves is that, well, we *do* love ourselves! But as believers, we're called to move beyond that self-centered existence, to think about others and what they need.

I'm going to try harder to do just that. In fact, I'll start this very day. After all, I'm going to have a little extra time. Someone already watered the flowers for me.

Today, Father, help me to show kindness to someone in need. I'm ready with a listening ear, a prayer and a fresh bouquet from my garden.
—MARY LOU CARNEY

Fri 13

It doth not yet appear what we shall be: but we know that, when he shall appear, we shall be like him; for we shall see him as he is.
—I JOHN 3:2

For a while, I wondered if our daughter Maggie would ever grow hair. When she was two, her big, almost-bald head caused casual visitors to the playground to wonder if they'd just seen the world's biggest baby. But grow it did, and now at nine Maggie has a healthy mop of honey-blonde hair that, when she doesn't brush it (which is most days), surrounds her face like a golden cloud.

Maggie has always been a natural comedian, and last year she appeared in *Jack and the Beanstalk* at our neighborhood children's theater, giving a bravura performance as the giant's wife in the second act. But it was her small walk-on part in the first act that astonished me.

At first I didn't recognize the girl standing next to our seven-year-old Stephen. I blinked and realized it was Maggie. I'd never seen her with her hair pulled back, the lines of her cheeks and chin setting off her luminous brown eyes. I could feel the tears starting as I turned to my wife Julia and whispered, "She's beautiful!"

Much of the time, somewhat complacently, I think I know Jesus. He lives in a make-believe Judea I've put together from *Ben-Hur* and *The Greatest Story Ever Told*. He's a bearded figure whose face I've constructed from countless paintings and a dozen actors. He talks like a character in an Elizabethan play, His words so formal and familiar that they slide straight through my mind.

For now, one way I can rub off some of the patina that's obscured His features is to read the Gospels carefully and slowly, preferably in a modern translation without the cinematic trappings, praying to know Him better. And someday, John promises, I'll see Him as He is, and know His true beauty for the first time.

Risen Lord, grant me to truly know You and
to live a new life in Your likeness.
—ANDREW ATTAWAY

Sat 14

None of the disciples ventured to question Him, "Who are You?" knowing that it was the Lord.
—JOHN 21:12 (NAS)

The day was memorable. I was visiting my daughter Tamara near Homer, Alaska. My morning Bible reading had been the story of Jesus after His resurrection, preparing breakfast on the beach while His disciples fished. When they came ashore they saw "a charcoal fire already laid and fish placed on it, and bread" (John 21:9, NAS).

That afternoon Tamara's church was hosting a picnic along Cook Inlet. We drove in all-wheel-drive vehicles down a narrow strip of deep sand at high tide, where picnickers gathered in the lee of a grassy bank. There were kids and dogs and driftwood benches and tables brimming with good food.

Sea waves splashed. Mountains ringed us. Bald eagles landed just feet away. The sunlit placid water was dotted here and there with fishing boats. Children waded barefoot in the surf. I sniffed the salt air and sighed contentedly, "Ah—a church picnic, Alaska–style."

One family was roasting halibut in a rack over coals. That's when serendipity struck. I had a beach . . . fishermen in boats . . . fish cooking over the fire. My earlier Bible reading had sprung to life before my eyes!

Above all, I had Jesus, in the people of faith gathered... in the songs of praise we sang... in the beauty of the Alaskan scenery. And in the words He asked His disciple Peter on that other beach: "Do you love Me?"

Yes, Lord, I do.

Jesus, it dazzles me to think of You on the beach cooking breakfast for Your friends. Thank You for opening such moments for me in the life I live now.
—CAROL KNAPP

Sun 15

Having made peace through the blood of his cross....
—COLOSSIANS 1:20

As my son Jeremy continued to make progress in his restored life, I continued to wrestle with "What if?" thoughts—until Easter.

Jeremy chose to attend our church. It's small and loving—they'd been praying for Jeremy for years. At first he sat with us near the front. When he was asked to assist in taking the offering and handing out bulletins, he began sitting at the back of the church in a chair right by the door. His chosen spot was very close to a life-size cross some of the men had constructed. Each Easter, it's covered with fresh spring flowers from our yards so that none of the harsh wood is visible.

On Easter morning I glanced back at Jeremy, just to marvel at seeing him in church after all these years. However, he wasn't in his usual chair by the door.

Then I saw him. Jeremy, slightly over six feet tall, about two hundred pounds, stood beneath the cross with one hand resting on the crossbar. He appeared to be clinging to it, apparently totally unaware of himself.

These days he often stands under the cross at church, holding on to it when we sing. But it's that very first Easter morning glimpse of him that lives in my heart.

Father, as the old hymn says, "Beneath the cross of Jesus I fain would take my stand."
(Elizabeth Clephane, 1868)
—MARION BOND WEST

❀ A GRACE-FILLED JOURNEY

Mon 16   *I will sing with the spirit....*
—I CORINTHIANS 14:15

CELESTIAL MUSIC

Today we wake to find ourselves at the port of Nauplia. We've been sailing during the night on the "wine-dark sea" that Homer wrote about in *The Odyssey*. We're here to explore the Mycenaean culture that flourished from 1600 to 1100 BC.

The high point for me occurs in the tomb of Agamemnon, a cylindrical, domed structure with the only light coming in through the open entrance. As our group stands around talking, a surprising thing happens. A strong, clear baritone voice rises out of the darkness, singing "Non nobis Domine" (Not unto us, Lord, but unto thy name give glory.) Suddenly the voice seems to become a full choir! Our chatter gives way to an awe-filled silence. I look around and see our group leader, Nile Norton, standing in the center of the tomb, his voice circling the walls, resounding, surrounding us. I feel like falling on my knees!

Yesterday, I prayed that I might practice the Olympic Truce in my life, and I said, "It won't assure peace in the world." Now here I am in the tomb of a legendary Greek warrior, listening to a song of praise to the One God. In this unifying moment, I truly believe that peace in the world is possible.

O Holy One, make me an instrument of Thy peace.
—Marilyn Morgan King

Tue 17

"Stop judging by mere appearances, and make a right judgment."
—John 7:24 (NIV)

My daughter Hope had her college sights set on Allegheny, a small, well-respected liberal-arts school in northwestern Pennsylvania. My wife Sandee and I thought it would be a wonderful choice, but . . .

"Mom doesn't think I'm smart enough to get into Allegheny," Hope announced during a college visit.

"*Hmm* . . ." I said. Hope is not like the rest of us, so I've learned how to translate her native tongue. "I've got to say, that doesn't sound like your mother. Is that a direct quote?"

"Well . . . ," Hope said.

"Let me guess," I said. "She told you that you're very, very bright, and you would do well at

Allegheny, but you'll have to study harder and get better grades. Would that be more accurate?"

"It's closer," Hope said, "I guess."

And here's what I wanted to say: *Honey, when you were young your mother and I thought you were a visitor from another planet. You've always been different; you'll always be different. We want so badly for other people to see in you what we see in you, but the world is full of quick judgments and rigid categories; only those who will take the time to know you will understand what a heavenly gift you really are. There's a reason we called you Hope.*

I said none of that. College is a time of self-reflection—my only hope for Hope is that she discovers who she truly is.

And yes, she got into Allegheny College. The Lord and the SATs work in mysterious ways.

Thanks for the help, Lord. And keep
an eye on Hope, will You?
—MARK COLLINS

Wed 18

"Pray for those who mistreat you."
—LUKE 6:28 (NIV)

It was a lovely spring morning and I was on my favorite part of my morning prayer walk—the "thy Kingdom come" section when I pray for blessings and provision for the people I know who do ministries of all sorts. *And, Lord, please bless Monty,* I prayed silently. And then it happened for the hundredth time: My mind jumped the track, and I replayed an unfortunate incident that had taken place months ago on a mission project. Someone else working with us had been extremely critical of Monty's rules and his ways of doing things. The criticism had undermined Monty's authority and dampened the spiritual atmosphere of the whole team.

Every day when I prayed for Monty I found myself becoming upset all over again. I stopped on the sidewalk and thought, *Praying for Monty drags me down because of how disappointed I am with the fellow who undermined him. Maybe I should stop praying for Monty since it always seems to stir up my bad attitude and makes me think about all of the faults and shortcomings of the guy who criticized him.*

A cloud scooted over the sun and I suddenly realized that I never give up my prayer walk, even if it's raining. Why should I give up on praying for someone because it wasn't easy to do? I found myself humbly praying, *Father, I thank you for the difficulty of this prayer.*

Jesus tells us to pray for our enemies. I'm not sure how our enemies benefit, but I can tell you how I do when I attempt praying for them. Praying for those I dislike isn't easy; it involves honestly dredging up feelings of disappointment, hurt, anger and indignation. I continue to pray for Monty daily—only now, I also pray for the fellow who criticized him. It certainly keeps me praying—very hard!

Dear Father, I'd rather not, but You have commanded me to pray for everyone, even _____.
—KAREN BARBER

Thu 19

God . . . bringeth out those which are bound with chains. . . .
—PSALM 68:6

"You can't leave Budapest without seeing the Museum of Terror," a couple I met at breakfast that morning told me. "It's the Hungarian version of the Holocaust Museum," she said. "See it."

Which was how I found myself wandering through the dark, twisting corridors of an old building that had once been the prison and interrogation center every Hungarian feared. Now it was a museum cataloging the oppression visited upon the Hungarian people, first by the Nazis and then by the Soviets.

An exhibit hall was dedicated to propaganda ranging from the 1930s through the 1980s, garbled voices blasting out of old speakers emblazoned with swastikas. In the basement were the cells where prisoners were kept, and an execution chamber that still held a gallows. There was a huge Soviet tank in the museum's vestibule and row after row of headphones to listen to survivors' accounts of unspeakable cruelty. And on nearly every wall were old black-and-white images of men staring blankly at the camera, most in suits and ties, a few in clerical garb, some in military uniforms, and a number of women as well. These were the victims who died here, at least some of them, their faces serving as a kind of grim wallpaper.

I saw a very old woman go up to a wall, touching the images lightly with one trembling hand while wiping away tears with the other.

I walked back to my hotel slowly, watching the people of Budapest bustling through the streets on this splendid day. I couldn't help thinking, and even envying, how sweet freedom must taste to them.

Father, we seem as capable of cruelty as we are goodness. But with our eyes on You, our paths will always lead to freedom.
—EDWARD GRINNAN

Fri 20

And so it was, whenever the spirit from God was upon Saul, that David would take a harp and play it with his hand. Then Saul would become refreshed and well, and the distressing spirit would depart from him.
—I SAMUEL 16:23 (NKJV)

There isn't much I envy about movie stars. Fame is fickle; good looks are fragile; money has wings. But I do envy the soundtrack that accompanies their acting. If it's a sad scene, the theater hums with the sound of melancholy strings. A happy scene is set to dance music. Danger is indicated by low notes from a bassoon.

Music therapists point out that the right music can reduce blood pressure, diminish pain and relax tense muscles. Music, they say, can improve job performance and bring back happy memories for Alzheimer's patients.

Because my life has no soundtrack, I have created one. I'm a whistler. Everywhere I go, I chirp. Although the people around me hear only the soft, piccolo sounds from my lips, in my brain I'm actually accompanied by a one-hundred-piece orchestra, and I have the solo part. "I can always find you in the store," my wife Sharon says. "I just listen for your whistle."

Not everyone can whistle, but there are ways to add music to life. Here are some suggestions:

1. Buy an old-fashioned record player, and dust off those Sinatra LPs in the attic. Bring back some big-band memories.

2. Learn to play a simple instrument: a harmonica, a xylophone, a ukulele.

3. Sing one of David's psalms to a popular tune on your stereo.

4. Drive to the country, shut off the engine and roll down the window. Listen to the sweetest sound of all, the sound of silence.

If You are listening, God, this song is for You:
You are the sunshine of my life, that's why
I'll always be around You.
—DANIEL SCHANTZ

Sat 21

In all thy ways acknowledge him,
and he shall direct thy paths.
—PROVERBS 3:6

One Saturday morning my husband Matt came home from the post office with big news: Our friends Adam and Jocelyne would be moving to France for a year. Would we be willing to care for their dog Reuben while they were away? Matt had volunteered an enthusiastic "yes."

I wasn't so sure. We already had one rather large dog, our eleven-year-old black Lab Nellie. How would she adjust to having another pet vying for our affections? Yet Reuben was hard to resist. Big, fluffy, looking like an old man with a bushy mustache, he loved people and was polite, easy and fun . . . and, he *was* genuinely in need of a home. But he hated to be left alone, and Matt and I now spent many hours each day at work.

I didn't know what to do. I had grown to love Reuben, and I sincerely wanted to help our friends set off with a light heart, knowing their pet was well cared for. But I didn't really want the responsibilities that went along with having another animal, and I worried that Nellie's year would be a fretful one. *Oh, God,* I thought, *please help me know what is best for all of us here.*

Finally I determined that the only answer was to trust the truth I felt in my heart: I told Jocelyne I didn't want another dog. As much as I loved Reuben and wanted to help my friends, I needed to focus my energies on other things.

Our friends left for France and the weeks passed. Then one beautiful afternoon, Matt, Nellie and I took a walk down a side street in town. At a quaint house up ahead, a woman raked leaves while two dogs frolicked in the yard. Matt took a second look and exclaimed, "Isn't that Reuben?" Reuben *had* found a wonderful, happy home for the year.

> *Help me always, God, to hear Your voice*
> *deep in my heart, guiding me.*
> —ANNE ADRIANCE

Sun 22

"You didn't choose me! I chose you!"
—JOHN 15:16 (TLB)

When church members were asked to make prayer shawls for the opening worship at our annual conference, the response was overwhelming. There were nearly five hundred shawls—loose-knit pastels, frothy wisps of net, fringed paisley silks and even shawls featuring cowboy scenes. I quickly saw the one I wanted: a black lace mantilla that would look great with my black dress.

Only I didn't get to choose. After I took Holy Communion, a youth delegate selected a colorful patchwork of orange, green, brown and lilac diamonds, cable-stitched and fringed in black. As she draped it around my shoulders, the word that came to mind was "sturdy."

At home, I draped the shawl over a chair in my bedroom, thinking I might give it away. Instead, I've found myself reaching for it each time I have a special worry or concern. I prayed for my grandson

Ryan when he celebrated his eighteenth birthday by going skydiving, I wiped tears with the shawl when a tragic accident took the life of a friend, I appreciated its warmth when an attack of bursitis made moving painful.

The shawl, I realized, was the best possible choice for me! It was strong, sturdy and comforting—a colorful reminder of God's everlasting mercy and overflowing grace.

> *Thank You, Jesus, for the times someone else chooses exactly what I need.*
> —PENNEY SCHWAB

Mon 23   *And God heard them, for their prayer reached heaven, his holy dwelling place.*
—II CHRONICLES 30:27 (NIV)

My friend Elisa and I were in Washington, DC, attending a conference together. Equipped with cell-phone cameras, we were ready to explore the national monuments.

We took a couple of pictures at one end of the National Mall before heading off toward the Washington Monument. When we neared the base, Elisa got down on the ground to take a picture of me and the monument. Then off we went to the World War II Memorial and along the

Reflecting Pool. All around us were people enjoying the day.

Before we reached the Lincoln Memorial, we took a detour to the Korean War Memorial. The life-size sculptures of soldiers presented another photo op, and Elisa reached into her pocket for her phone. Suddenly, she froze.

"I've lost my phone!" she cried. I understood the panic in her voice. Earlier that morning she'd used her phone to record an important interview with someone at the conference.

"What will I do if I've lost my phone?" Elisa kept asking, while I kept praying, *God, please help us find the phone.*

We called her number on my phone. No answer. We kept our heads down, searching along the sidewalks and in the grass. Back around the World War II Memorial, I began to sense where the phone could be and jogged back to where Elisa had lain on the ground taking pictures of me. There, in the grass, was her phone!

We celebrated. We thanked God. And I took a picture of the phone lying there on the ground. Though we took lots more pictures that day, the one of her phone in the grass is probably my favorite.

Father, amid the awesomeness of those great
monuments is the awesome memory
of Your answer to prayer.
—CAROL KUYKENDALL

April

Tue 24

Look at the birds of the air; they neither sow nor reap nor gather into barns, and yet your heavenly Father feeds them. Are you not of more value than they? And can any of you by worrying add a single hour to your span of life?
—MATTHEW 6:26–27 (NRSV)

St. Francis of Assisi is known most of all for preaching to the birds, but he also inspired Christians to live differently. The other day, I followed a key Franciscan principle, straight from the Gospel: Live less for security and more in joy and anticipation of what God can do in your life.

I live in Vermont, and for twelve years I've driven sturdy, reliable cars for the sake of their longevity and their ability to plow through snowdrifts. I'd driven my latest car as far as it would go—nearly two hundred thousand miles—and it was dying fast.

To replace it, I bought a used Mini Cooper. This zippier, tinier, fuel-efficient car required me to let go of some of my old worries: *Will I get as much use out of this car? Will I end up snowed-in next winter?* I had to accept the fact that I can't ultimately answer those questions. Instead, I bought my car because it would bring me joy.

I realize this is a very little thing in the big picture of life. But St. Francis always told his friars, when they planted the annual vegetable garden, to be sure to leave a portion of the soil for planting flowers. Flowers had no practical value; they gave the friars no security against the winter months; but Francis called them his "sisters" and he loved to look at their beautiful colors.

When you make decisions that bring joy to yourself and others, you can see that Jesus knew what He was talking about when He told us to be more like the birds of the air.

Teach me anew, Lord, to live a resurrected life.
I'm ready and willing to live in joy.
—JON SWEENEY

Wed 25

Your steadfast love, O Lord, is as great as all the heavens. Your faithfulness reaches beyond the clouds. —PSALM 36:5 (TLB)

From the lochs to the lakes, our tour of Scotland was magnificent. We feasted at dinners complete with haggis, and kilts swirled as dancers did the Gille Callum over crossed swords. We were stirred by the pageantry of the Military Tattoo at Edinburgh Castle, the highlight of which was one lone piper standing on the ramparts playing "Amazing Grace."

But from all the glorious memories we carried home with us, the one I cherish the most was that of a small dog named Greyfriars Bobby. A statue of him stands outside the pub that he and his master frequented.

Bobby was a Skye terrier, named after the Isle of Skye, which is the northernmost of the Inner Hebrides off the west coast of Scotland. He was the devoted companion of John Gray, nicknamed Auld Jock, a night watchman with the Edinburgh police.

In 1858, Auld Jock died of tuberculosis and was buried in the Greyfriars churchyard. For fourteen years Bobby kept vigil, sleeping on his master's grave, leaving only for the midday meal doled out to him from the familiar restaurant. Whenever he was led away and offered a home, at his first chance he returned to stay close to the one he loved. He so touched the heart of the keeper of the churchyard that he built a shelter to protect Bobby from pouring rain and cold weather. News of the little dog's faithfulness spread and people flocked to see him.

When Bobby died in 1872, he was buried in Greyfriars near his master's grave. His granite headstone has this inscription: "Let his loyalty and devotion be a lesson to us all."

*Lord and Master of my life, create in me a faithful
heart to stay forever close to You, and through the
storms of life to take shelter under the promise
of Your presence.*
—FAY ANGUS

Thu 26

*Never be lacking in zeal, but keep
your spiritual fervor, serving the
Lord.* —ROMANS 12:11 (NIV)

A book! I was asked to do a book! I signed the
contract and rejoiced, and then quiet paralysis
took hold. I'd assumed I'd dive right in to the work,
but I did other important things instead, like scrub
the baseboards in the dining room. After a week I
asked myself what was going on. *You've never done
this before*, a voice whispered in my head.

Ah—it was my old buddy, Fear. He shows up
from time to time, usually when I have to do something new. But I've figured something out: He's
only an obstacle in my head. He can't prevent me
from taking tiny, practical, real-world steps.

So instead of panicking about putting together
Daily Guideposts: Your First Year of Motherhood,
I wrote notes to Sabra Ciancanelli and Karen
Valentin to see if they were interested in writing
devotionals about being a new mom. They were.
And that was all I did for the book that day.

The next day Fear was back, so I asked him to wait while I scratched out ideas on what the book should include. Prayers? Yes. Helpful mothering tips? Sure. The overall focus: how to keep God in your life when you don't even have time for a shower. Fear got bored and wandered off.

The following day I faked out my nemesis, surfing the Web as if I were wasting time. Instead I searched for (and found) several excellent young writers to contribute to the book.

And so it went, one day and one small item at a time. Soon I was doing two things a day, and then five. I didn't even notice when Fear packed his bags and left. Perhaps that's because his place was taken by Enthusiasm—who, as you know, is an excellent houseguest.

Lord, You're in every new experience that comes into my life. Help me face down fear by looking for Your face instead.
—JULIA ATTAWAY

Fri 27

While I was in my mother's womb, he named me. —ISAIAH 49:1 (NRSV)

Gail. Gail. Gail. My name has always seemed dull and boring to me—like a footstep, a door slam, a hammer blow—not melodious or musical. When I was growing up, my best friends had multisyllabic names such as *Lynda* and *Barbara*. Their names flowed like waterfalls. My name just clunked. *Gail* sounded hard, inflexible. How I yearned for a feminine name with more than one syllable, perhaps a name ending in *a* like *Laura, Elisa* or *Sophia*.

When I married, I made my maiden name into my middle name so old friends could still find me. In so doing, I abandoned my middle name, *Donna*, which I suppose I could have adopted as my first name. After all, it had the two syllables and final *a* I seemed to crave.

I might have remained dissatisfied forever until a friend who knew some Hebrew pointed out that *Gail* derived from *Abba Gael* (Abigail), "Father's joy," or more exactly, "Daddy's joy." I tucked this translation into my heart for safekeeping. Many years later I would learn that my parents had lost a baby before my birth, so they were thrilled not only by my arrival, but by my timing. You see, Mom brought me home from the hospital and placed me in Daddy's arms on their second anniversary. Little Gail was Daddy's joy, indeed. So I've made peace with my plain name, a solid name, like *faith, hope, love*—and *joy*.

> *Abba, Father, You know my name.*
> *May I always be Your joy too.*
> —Gail Thorell Schilling

April

Sat 28

Every purpose is established by counsel.... —PROVERBS 20:18

Corinne Barfield and my sister Keri had known each other for some time. Over coffee, Keri had told Corinne about my heartbreak in the year just past and my experience in Africa. Then she suggested that Corinne might want to share her own African experiences with me.

After I received that first e-mail from Corinne, I wasted no time in asking her to lunch. The following Saturday we met at a local Mexican restaurant. Within minutes we were talking about our joys, our disappointments and, finally, our faith.

Incredibly, she remembered reading a story I had written about my stay-at-home mom that had been published in *Guideposts* almost twenty years earlier when we were both in high school. We shared story after story, amazed at how they all seemed to mesh together.

As I described the shock of my broken engagement the year before, Corinne responded without hesitation. "We all go through tough times. It's how we deal with them and what we learn from them that defines who we are. The Lord has a purpose for them all."

Before we knew it, four and a half hours had gone by. During my time in Africa, my heart had been set on fire for God, and here was someone who shared my passion. I was thrilled to make this new friend. It was as if God had been working, in ways known only to Him, to bring us together.

I walked Corinne to her car and just before closing her door, I blurted out, "How about a walk in the park after church tomorrow?"

"I'd like that," she said.

Father, Your purpose is our good. Let us be aware of the ways You work in our lives.
—Brock Kidd

Sun 29

Put off your shoes from your feet, for the place where you are standing is holy ground. —Exodus 3:5 (RSV)

The monk's instructions were clear. I was on a retreat at Gethsemane monastery near Louisville, Kentucky, and I'd expected some of the guidelines. "No talking," said Father Damien. "Walk anywhere except in the monks' cloister. You're welcome to join us at prayers in the chapel. And, oh yes, don't forget to take off your shoes when you enter your cells."

That one surprised me. How could not wearing shoes make a place spiritual? I did take mine off at the door to my room, but as I expected, no revelation came. Sitting around in socks, as far as I could see, just meant your feet got cold.

Only as the days passed and the quiet of the place seeped into me did I begin to sense the very real presence of holiness in the little room where so many saints and seekers had stayed before me. It was there, in the daily schedule of readings, that I came to the passage in Exodus where Moses sees the burning bush.

"Take off your shoes," God tells him, "for the place where you are is holy."

It wasn't removing shoes that made the spot holy; the act recognized the holiness already there. And having encountered the holy in the little room with the narrow bed and the single chair, I began to see it in other places: in the narcissus blooming in a corner of our kitchen, in the warm "hello" from a crippled neighbor at the end of the corridor. Here in our apartment at such moments I find myself mentally—and sometimes actually—taking off my shoes.

Lord, if my awareness of You were more acute,
I'm sure I'd go barefoot all the time!
—JOHN SHERRILL

Mon 30

Let us also lay aside every encumbrance and the sin which so easily entangles us. . . . —HEBREWS 12:1

Rather than tote the heavy hamper down the stairs on wash day, I sort the laundry on the main floor and carry each load separately to the basement. Even though it makes for more trips up and down stairs, I feel it's safer. But not always. The other day in my haste I didn't bundle the load tightly in my arms, and a trailing apron string tangled itself around my ankle and nearly led to my downfall. Thankfully, I managed to regain my balance just in time.

Our washer can have balance problems too. It usually does its thing without complaining, but once in a while a loud clunking and thumping during the spin cycle puts me on high alert. I go tearing down the steps, stop it in the midst of the cycle, redistribute the load, turn the dial and everything hums right along again.

My life is a lot like that washer: Whenever things begin to spin out of control, it's usually because of an unbalanced load. If I feel as if I'm about to fly apart, I know I have to stop, rethink my priorities and redistribute my responsibilities. When I do, everything falls into place and life resumes the way God intended it to be . . . quietly and efficiently.

Lord, help me maintain a balanced life for
Your honor and glory.
—ALMA BARKMAN

MY PATHWAY TO PEACE

1 _____

2 _____

3 _____

4 _____

5 _____

6 _____

7 _____

8 _____

9 _____

10 _____

11 _____

12 _____

13 _____

14 _____

15 _____

16 _____

17 _____

18 _____

19 _____

20 _____

21 _____

22 _____

23 _____

24 _____

25 _____

26 _____

27 _____

28 _____

29 _____

30 _____

May

Peace I leave with you, my peace I give unto you: not as the world giveth, give I unto you. Let not your heart be troubled, neither let it be afraid.

—John 14:27

❦ THIS I KNOW

Tue 1

What time I am afraid, I will trust in thee. —PSALM 56:3

THE PERFECT PICTURE

For many years I had dreamed of the day our family would be together in rural Zimbabwe, where half my heart lives with the beautiful people we serve, and that our son Brock would finally find a soul mate who would happily become part of our slightly offbeat family. Finally, here we were, all together: our daughter Keri and her husband Ben with Abby and baby Charles, Brock with his son Harrison—and his fiancée Corinne.

Up ahead was a one-room mud hut where a struggling mother and her two children lived. With the help of our donors we were keeping the children in school, supplying seed for their garden, and had recently made the family rich by giving them their own goat. Today, we were bringing medicine for the mother's sister, who was sick with AIDS.

As I lagged behind, I instinctively brought my camera to my eye. Up ahead, in the golden hour of waning day, my daughter bent lovingly over a blanket where the sick woman lay. *Typical Keri,* I thought. As I often do when I'm taking photos, I prayed, "Give this one to me, God."

That evening I was anxious to download the photos to my computer. What I saw took my breath away.

The girl in the picture wasn't Keri at all. It was Corinne!

All Brock's life, I'd been praying for him to find the right life mate. I should have known God would find a clever way to show me He'd answered my prayer!

> *Father, I get the picture: Our job is*
> *to let go and trust You.*
> —PAM KIDD

EDITOR'S NOTE: *Take a look back at "My Pathway to Peace" journal pages, and let us know how God's love has been working in your life this year. Send your letter to* Daily Guideposts *Reader's Room, Guideposts Books, 16 East 34th Street, New York, New York 10016. We'll share some of what you tell us in a future edition of* Daily Guideposts.

Wed 2

I have no greater joy than to hear that my children are walking in the truth.
—III JOHN 1:4 (NIV)

Tonight as my son Henry was going to sleep, he insisted on clutching a chapter book. Although Henry is four and knows his letters, he's a long way from books without pictures, and the allure of this book had nothing to do with words.

"Mom, that's my book!" Henry's older brother Solomon said as he climbed into his bed. "I'm reading that."

"I know," I said, leaning over to tuck him in. "Is it okay if he gives it back in the morning?" I kissed Solomon good night and whispered, "He loves you so much he wants to be just like you." Solomon rolled his eyes.

Having a little brother isn't always easy. Most of Solomon's toys are Henry's favorites. When Henry wears Solomon's hand-me-downs, he grins from ear to ear and stands in front of the mirror as if he were a superhero.

Henry looked down at the book and petted it like a stuffed animal. Solomon laughed.

"You guys are lucky to have each other," I said turning off the light.

Later I went in to check on them. The nightlight streamed onto their beds. Henry had managed to kick off his blankets, but the chapter book was still in his grasp. Solomon faced Henry, his arm stretched toward him. I hope someday they realize how blessed they are to have each other. I know I do.

Dear God, thank You for my family and the lessons of love they show me every day and night.
—Sabra Ciancanelli

Thu 3

"I called out to my God.... my cry came to his ears."
—II SAMUEL 22:7 (NIV)

To say I'm scared of going to the dentist is an understatement. So as I strode down the sidewalk on my way to have a root canal, I felt panicky, almost hysterical. How could I possibly sit tipped backward in a chair with my mouth open while the dentist poked and drilled and maneuvered?

As the dentist's assistant helped me into the chair and fastened the towel around my neck, I looked up at her. We'd always smiled and said hello, but never anything more. For some reason I touched her arm. "How are you?" I asked.

Her eyes filled with tears. "It is my birthday," she said. "I am missing my mother in Poland. We are very close and have not seen each other for a long time."

She continued to talk until the dentist came in and started his work. But by now my focus had changed from the drama inside my mouth to the woman standing beside me, longing for her mother far away. During the procedure I thought about what this mother and daughter must be going through. I prayed for them both, then for mothers and daughters everywhere who were separated by the sea, by events, by misunderstandings. When the dentist finished, I was surprised that the time had passed so quickly.

When I went back for a follow-up visit, a different assistant fastened the bib around my neck. I asked where the other woman was. "She's home in Poland, visiting her mother," I was told. I settled into the dentist's chair and took a deep breath and looked up at this assistant.

"How are you?" I asked.

Dear God, whenever my cares and fears have me turned toward myself, let me turn to You in prayer.
—MARY ANN O'ROARK

Fri 4

"If you have faith as small as a mustard seed, you can say to this mulberry tree, 'Be uprooted and planted in the sea,' and it will obey you." —LUKE 17:6 (NIV)

Our umbrellas were scant protection against the driving Tennessee rain as we sloshed across the crowded parking lot and into the Kingston Springs Elementary School to register my grandson Frank for kindergarten.

Frank's teacher-to-be, Miss Candi, a petite, bouncy woman radiating enthusiasm, welcomed us into a cozy room filled with colorful blocks, teaching aids, books and an up-to-date computer just for the children.

May

"Your room is awesome," I said to Miss Candi. "I can't wait for Frank to be here!"

"We work hard," she said with a grin.

But that very night Mother Nature trashed all Miss Candi's hard work with a once-in-a-century flood that inundated the school. In the morning, I stood as close as I could get to the rushing, brown water rising above the school windows. I tried not to picture the ruination inside: Miss Candi's room, the thick rug, the brightly painted walls, the computer, the shelves of books, the puzzles, the teaching aids. *She'll be crushed*, I thought.

And there she was: Miss Candi, a drenched figure stranded on the roof. She had been trying to save her classroom. Now a boat was going out to save her. "Don't worry," she called to the gathering crowd. "We'll get it all back, better than ever!"

The crowd cheered, buoyed by her optimism, which spread through prayers in homes and churches and echoed in a sign stuck in the mud across from the school: Hope is springing in Kingston!

In August, my daughter and I brought Frank for his first day of kindergarten in the rebuilt school. Miss Candi was back in her room . . . and it was truly better than ever.

> *Lord, thank You for faith and hope that*
> *no storm can wash away.*
> —Shari Smyth

Sat 5

Freely you have received, freely give.
—MATTHEW 10:8 (NIV)

There wasn't far to go, yet the journey was difficult: down two flights of stairs to our basement, where I gathered three shopping bags; then up three flights of stairs to our attic, where I looked under the eaves and pulled out three boxes of books.

These were my treasure chests: books purchased at church fairs, yard sales, thrift stores and from long-closed bookstores in Boston. Books I loved and cherished and hadn't read for years. Among them was *To Kill a Mockingbird* by Harper Lee, now fifty years old and still in print.

I looked at the books and my heart ached. These were my old friends, but it was time for us to part, to downsize and to ease the clutter. As I eased each book into the shopping bag, I mentally kissed it good-bye.

I drove to the local supermarket and placed the books neatly in the giveaway bookcase out front. It was time others shared the joy of owning and reading these fine books. Nevertheless, the parting was painful. I wanted to keep all of them for the rest of my life.

I went into the store to do some shopping. When I came out, two ladies were at the bookcase. "I wonder who donated these lovely books," one of them said. "I live alone, and I can't afford to buy books."

My regrets and my heartache were gone. I had given out of my abundance and this lady was repaying me with her appreciation. I'd hurry home, look through my bookcases and select some more books to donate. My friends would be well taken care of.

Gracious Lord, parting with beloved books is far from easy. But You help me clear away the clutter from my home and the possessiveness from my heart.
—OSCAR GREENE

❧ A GRACE-FILLED JOURNEY

Sun 6　　*With gladness and rejoicing shall they be brought: they shall enter into the king's palace.* —PSALM 45:15

THE PALACE OF PURIFICATIONS

Before we left home, Robert and I read to each other about Knossos, where King Minos's palace had been partially restored by Sir Arthur Evans, a Victorian archeologist. Now we stand in the throne room of that very palace, admiring the beauty of the wall paintings as well as the throne itself. But one structure we wonder about: a rectangular enclosure opposite the king's throne. Our guide Vicky tells us it was once a pool of water used for purification rituals. Before the king's subjects could have an audience with him, they had to enter into the water to be cleansed.

It made me think of the words of Psalm 51:7, in which the Psalmist prays, "Wash me, and I shall be whiter than snow." Our King is not named Minos, but He, too, offers a purification ritual. It's called the forgiveness of sins. Jesus asks that I confess my sins, not for His sake but for mine. When I bring to Him my unclean thoughts and unkind words, my unholy actions and all the sinfulness in my life, He gives me the most beautiful gift I can receive—a clean heart, worthy to live in His healing presence.

Wash me, Lord, and I shall be whiter than snow.
—MARILYN MORGAN KING

READER'S ROOM

It is the "ordinary-ness" of everyday living that I am grateful for—the day-to-day sweet companionship of my husband and the love of family and friends. In this I feel blessed!

—*Sally Tidmarsh, Varna, Illinois*

May

Mon 7

Thy will be done....
—MATTHEW 6:10

I've never met a cat who loved to be brushed as much as eighteen-pound Prince does...when he's in the mood. He can stand, heavy on my lap, for up to fifteen long minutes while I brush his fur. If I seem to slow down, he gives me a sharp tap with his paw to remind me to pick up the pace.

I find the activity relaxing, so one evening, tense from a day of dropping off job applications with no results, I thought, *Why don't I brush Prince now?* So I picked up the brush and Prince. He purred for all of about thirty seconds and then jumped off my lap and ran away, as if to say, "That's quite enough of that!"

That's a lot like the way I've been with God.

When I'm job hunting, I pray, "God, please find me a job today!" I want Him to listen to me and magically throw one at my doorstep. But when God seems to have something to say to me, such as, *Maybe it's time to update your résumé* or *Perhaps See's Candy Shop*—with its sign in the window saying, "Yes, if you work here, you CAN eat all the candy you want!"—*is not the best place for you to work at this time,* I jump off His lap.

All cat owners know that we have to deal with cats on their terms, not ours. But as a friend of mine said when I told her exactly what kind of job I wanted God to find for me, "Sounds like you're willing to serve God, but only as an adviser! Why don't you *listen* to God more than *instruct* Him?"

That was good advice. I've taken it, combining some prayer time with the time I spend brushing Prince.

God, when You want to speak to me, let me listen.
And when I want to speak to You, let me listen too.
—LINDA NEUKRUG

Tue 8

Give her of the fruit of her hands; and let her own works praise her in the gates. —PROVERBS 31:31

Aunt Kate organized the fun puzzles and games at my bridal shower. One of them inspires me to this very day.

She gave each of us a piece of heavy cardboard. It was long and narrow, about the size and length of the button strip down the front of a man's shirt, and was accompanied by a needle, thread and a paper cup full of small white buttons.

"This is the prize for the winner," she said, holding up a charming wickerwork basket fitted out with scissors, tape measure and other sewing supplies. That was a prize I wanted to win.

"I'll give you three minutes. Whoever sews the most buttons on her strip in that time wins the basket." She looked at her watch. "Go!"

I threaded my needle and speedily attached the buttons, helter-skelter, thread going in and out of only one or two of the four holes in each.

"Time!" said Aunt Kate. "Put your name on your card and hand it in." I was jubilant; it was obvious that my card was the one with the most buttons.

Aunt Kate tested the stitching on each card. She was able to pull off several buttons on most of the cards. When she came to mine, she easily snapped the thread looping large flimsy stitches through each button. Every one of them fell off. "None of these held!" she sniffed with disdain. She then held up Donna's card. It didn't have as many buttons on it as some of the others, but the thread was doubled and the buttons were carefully attached with crossed-over stitching through all four holes. Despite tugging and pulling, they held firm.

"Whatever you do," Aunt Kate said as she awarded Donna the coveted prize, "do with diligence!"

Whether they be major accomplishments or little day-to-day things, I will give the task my best, Lord.
—FAY ANGUS

Wed 9

He answered: "Love the Lord your God with all your heart and with all your soul and with all your strength and with all your mind'; and, 'Love your neighbor as yourself.'"
—LUKE 10:27 (NIV)

For the past twenty years I've swum laps at the local high-school pool. For those of us who gather in the pool lobby, there's nothing like the smell of chlorine in the morning to get our blood pumping. Over the years we've become good friends.

Recently, someone new joined our group. Arriving a bit later than the rest of us, she seemed to have trouble sharing the lane. She wanted her own space and started dishing out instructions. I heard plenty of grumbling about this newcomer. "Someone needs to tell Ms. Ponytail about pool etiquette," I complained to the lifeguard. When I went in for my shower, I got an earful about the newbie who seemed to think the pool was her private property.

Back at home, I told my husband about the unpleasant woman who'd recently started swimming. Wayne asked me if I was going to invite her to our annual Swimmers' Tea.

I snorted softly and shook my head. "Hardly." She was the last person on my list. I couldn't imagine why Wayne would even suggest she be included.

The next morning, as I finished up my devotional time just before I changed into my swimsuit, I ran across a quote from Dorothy Day: "I really only love God as much as I love the person I love the least."

Hmm... It seemed God knew when to send me the message I needed the most. I looked at my invitation list for the Swimmers' Tea, sighed and added one additional name.

Father, thank You for every person you send my way, even the prickly ones.
—DEBBIE MACOMBER

Thu 10

*The Word of the Lord came to me.... —*EZEKIEL 6:1 (NIV)

My wife Rosie and I have been walking for our health for the past year. We've found that it works best if we take our walk at five thirty in the morning.

As we walk to the park, we can count on barking dogs at certain houses, ducks standing at the edge of the lake waiting for someone to give them food, and the chirping of the birds as they wake up. But what gets our attention most are the magnificent stars that grace the sky. Our house faces east, and the first thing that greets us as we walk out is one very bright star that seems to say, "Look at me and all my grandeur." Its sparkle seems to radiate God's special love for us through His creation. Every day the star is there; every day we get to see the sun as it peeps up and greets us with a smile. What glorious reminders of God's constant presence—whatever we're going through, He is always with us.

During these special walks together, as we marvel at His creation, Scriptures will come to mind, and Rosie and I will discover new facets of their message, new ways to step out on His Word.

Lord, You are great and greatly to be praised.
Thank You that we can be assured of
Your constant presence at all times.
—DOLPHUS WEARY

Fri 11

And so, from the day we heard of it, we have not ceased to pray for you. . . .
—COLOSSIANS 1:9 (RSV)

For a brief time during my childhood, my family lived at a Bible camp in northern California. A major sideline of the organization was housing welfare cases—unwanted men of every age, all incapacitated in some way by alcoholism, blindness or mental retardation. Those who had any capabilities at all were overworked and neglected. My two sisters and I grieved the most for Richie.

Richie was twelve. All day long and late into the evenings, he was put to work. During that summer

May

of 1962 one of his many duties was to plant and tend petunias. But California's hot sun and hard soil made the task impossible and, sure enough, Richie was always in unwarranted trouble.

My family lasted eight months at that camp. We moved on, but over the years petunias came to symbolize for me the sorry plight of Richie and all the others we had to leave behind. Out of loyalty, I never planted a petunia. I just couldn't.

A couple of years ago, however, my son was to be married, and his bride wanted their wedding pictures taken in my yard. Her favorite color is purple. What purple flower could I use to fill the back gardens with bright, cheerful color?

For a long time I stared at the array of petunias in Fred Meyer's garden shop. Tears stung my eyes, and I found myself praying, *Dear God, wherever Richie is now, be with him.* Suddenly, out of the blue (or perhaps straight from heaven?), I realized that if I took these brilliant purple-and-lavender petunias home, the planting, watering, weeding and dead-heading would remind me to pray for Richie. And wasn't prayer for my childhood friend a better response than loyal grief?

Dear Lord, wherever he is, be with Richie today. And Joe, too, and dear Jack and Ken and Uncle Earl and Howard. And, oh yes, thank You for petunias!
—BRENDA WILBEE

Sat 12

Now his heart yearned for his brother.... —GENESIS 43:30 (NKJV)

Eleuthera was as exotic a place as I'd ever seen. On this small Bahamian island, my family and I swam in glass-clear seas, bright fish in sight as we swam. We drove miles and miles without encountering another car, and ate dinner in restaurants that were really small homes with a room set aside for customers. But the really exotic experience was seeing my brother Ned.

Ned had been living in Eleuthera for the past several months. He was attending the Island School, a small program for high-schoolers that focused on building community and living environmentally conscious lives. I imagined him spending his four months in the Bahamas lying in the sun and taking classes he could pass just by showing up. When my parents and I visited for parents weekend, however, I quickly saw that this wasn't the case. Ned—notoriously cranky in the morning—told us he had to get up at 6:00 AM each day to run several miles and then attend a day of classes followed by more activity on the water.

My first night on the island, Ned and I talked for hours—about my feelings of loneliness in my freshman year of college, about how scared he was to return to his normal life. And eventually we hugged and both said, "I've missed you so much."

Until that night, I'd never realized just how much I longed to be closer to Ned. We were always friendly, but we were never brothers. We kept a measured distance between us.

Now he looked different. He was happy and engaged. He looked you in the eye and told you the truth. He was having a life-changing experience; he was growing into himself, and I saw him for the first time for who he was.

Thank You, Lord, for even when I've hardened my own heart, You show me how to soften it.
—SAM ADRIANCE

Sun 13

A child is known by his doings, whether his work be pure, and whether it be right.
—PROVERBS 20:11

Mother's Day" said the header on the e-mail. *Did I forget?* I wondered. No, I reassured myself, I had already dropped the card in the mail to Mom. It would surely get there in plenty of time. I could call her too.

"Dad," the e-mail said, "what should we get Mom? —Will"

Oh dear. I hadn't come up with any good ideas for Carol. The weekend before had been our twenty-seventh wedding anniversary; I was congratulating myself for remembering that—and now this.

"Don't know," I e-mailed back. Carol was usually good at dropping heavy hints—catalogs with dog-eared pages, e-mails with links to her favorite fragrance. "She hasn't said anything."

Twenty minutes later there was another message in my inbox. "Dad, how about a gift certificate to this?" with a link to a chocolate site.

"Perfect," I said. "She'll love it." But what was *I* going to get? A blouse? New socks? Flowers? There was a time I used to get things for the boys to give to their mom. At least they were now thinking of these things on their own.

"Okay," came Will's response, copied to his brother Timothy. "Let's split it three ways."

"Wow!" I wrote. "That's great. You're shopping for me. Let me at least cover half of it. You've done all the research."

"I'll cover half of Timothy's share," Will e-mailed back. "He doesn't make much money yet."

"Thanks," Timothy chimed in.

"Very thoughtful." Carol would be very pleased. She might have had a laggard husband this year, but she had a son—two sons—who more than made up for him. What better gift for Mother's Day?

Lord, let me be known by what I give.
—RICK HAMLIN

Mon 14

"Remember, O Lord, how I have walked before you faithfully and with wholehearted devotion and have done what is good in your eyes".... —ISAIAH 38:3 (NIV)

My dream had come true. After several months of unemployment and a move to a new state, I landed the perfect job: I was going to work at a bakery.

Baking has long been a passion of mine. I'd longed to find a bakery in our new hometown that would allow me to work part time, so I could keep up with my freelance work and get to know the people in my community.

Finally I'd found a bakery I loved and landed an interview. Now I had an e-mail in my inbox letting me know that the bakery wanted me and asking when I could start.

But my heart faltered. *Is it enough money?* I wondered. *I've never done work like that. What if I do a terrible job and get fired?*

As I spiraled down the staircase of self-doubt, my husband Brian interjected, "You want to do this, right?"

"Of course!" I replied.

"Then do it," he said. "Run the numbers, evaluate your options and then do it. Have a little faith."

His last comment was made in passing, but it really struck me. Here we were, miles from our old hometown in a new city, a city we'd trusted God to bring us to. Yet He'd already done so much more: He'd provided my husband with an amazing career opportunity and me with not merely a job, but my dream job. And what was I doing? Fretting and doubting.

I took a deep breath, said a prayer and accepted the offer. Sure, I've messed up a few transactions and needed help filling certain orders, but I've learned to do the job. And I've learned that sometimes I just need to stop worrying and trust God.

Lord, thank You for allowing me to live my dream.
—Ashley Kappel

Tue 15

I urge, then, first of all, that requests, prayers, intercession and thanksgiving be made for everyone.
—I Timothy 2:1 (NIV)

Your EKG looks better than mine," whispered the triage nurse. I'd come into the emergency room because I'd had burning chest pain early in the morning. I was pretty sure it wasn't heart trouble, but better safe than sorry.

May

Three hours later I was still waiting to be seen by a doctor. There was plenty for me to see, though. A little woman with a droopy eye stopped by to chatter in Spanish about her suspicion that her stroke symptoms began when she ate canned salmon. A twenty-something man gently helped his father follow directions for neurological tests for balance and strength. The man next to me had kidney stones—huge ones—but lay patiently on a gurney without complaining, except to say quietly, "This hurts a lot." The silent woman on my other side had waited seven hours for a doctor. I encouraged her to speak up and eventually reported her situation to the attending physician myself.

I'd prayed about whether to go to the hospital and got a clear *yes* for an answer. But several hours into my stay, a part of me wondered why all this was necessary. I wasn't in pain, and I wasn't convinced I had a serious problem. Then I remembered that life isn't always about me. Perhaps the point of my presence was simply that all those worried, sick people needed my prayers.

It turned out I had an inflamed ligament in my rib cage—and that spending a day praying for others was a fine use of my time.

Lord, show me more people who
need my prayers today.
—Julia Attaway

Wed 16

The sluggard is wiser in his own eyes than seven men who can give a discreet answer.
—PROVERBS 26:16 (NAS)

Some of my college students are gifted, especially at making excuses.

"Hey, Mr. Schantz, my absences last week were due to global warming." (When he got his grade, he discovered the Ice Age.)

"Mr. Schantz, I worked on this assignment for two months; how come I only got a C-minus?" (I only gave the assignment a month ago.)

Some excuses are actually believable:

"Professor, I missed your classes because I always set my alarm right after I shower, but I haven't showered all week."

"Dear Favorite Teacher, I have that paper written, but I can't get to it because the health department has sealed my room."

"Sir, I skipped your classes to attend a workshop on ethics."

I'm thinking of writing a book called *The Seven Habits of Highly Successful Fibbers*. I should have plenty of material.

It's natural to want to explain our failures, but making excuses focuses on the past, which cannot be altered.

I, too, make excuses. When I don't have their papers graded as promised, I say things like, "I had company drop in this weekend" or "I wasn't feeling well and couldn't concentrate." They aren't interested in the "why"; they just want their papers. It's better if I just say, "I don't have your papers graded, but I will have them in your box today before I leave the campus."

In short, I need to fix the problem, not talk about it.

*God, help me not to be wise in my own
eyes, but to be more honest.*
—DANIEL SCHANTZ

Thu 17

"When He ascended on high, He led captivity captive, and gave gifts to men." —EPHESIANS 4:8 (NKJV)

I love calendars, schedules and lists. If I'm flying, I start packing days ahead of my departure time and keep a running list on the refrigerator of things to take, jotting them down as they come to mind:

> phone charger
> medication
> sunscreen
> shampoo
> lip balm
> umbrella

I write myself a reminder to print the boarding pass twenty-four hours before my flight, as if I might possibly forget that I need one. I'm a bit compulsive about getting to the airport on time, too, always arriving hours early. I'd rather be sitting at the gate alone drumming my fingers than back at home where people's needs might get in my way and I might be slowed down by unforeseen situations or an unexpected phone call. Caring about others takes time.

I've been thinking about Jesus and His ascension, His trip into heaven. After He was raised from the dead on Easter Sunday, He could have high-tailed it on home. His mission here was accomplished; He could check us off His to-do list and head to glory.

But not our Lord, our Savior, our Friend. He remained on earth for forty more days, hanging out with people in his hometown, loving His friends, giving out spiritual gifts, encouraging others, sharing meals, and allowing Thomas time to touch His nail-scarred hands.

Jesus knew what mattered most. He still does.

Father, help me lay aside my self-imposed schedule and spend more time doing what really counts.

—Julie Garmon

May

Fri 18

We will restore them, and will require nothing of them....
—NEHEMIAH 5:12

Every year, the music company I worked for gave holiday gifts to its employees. Sometimes the gift was a sweatshirt with the company logo on it or a book of passes to local movie theaters or a box of food from a gourmet company. I figured that when I moved to Bellingham, Washington, we wouldn't see any more gifts, but they must have left my name on the list because that first December a box arrived from the company.

The gift inside looked like a long basket filled with sphagnum moss, but without any kind of plant or flower. The directions said to add water to it when the bulbs began to sprout. I dug around in the moss and, sure enough, there were three bulbs inside. They looked completely dead.

"They must be dormant," my husband said. "That's how bulbs work."

I was skeptical. The tulip bulbs we had bought and planted were in dirt and fertilizer, and it seemed only reasonable that they would sprout. But the bulbs in the moss in a basket with a plastic liner didn't seem to have anything to feed on or root in.

For months, the basket sat there on our kitchen windowsill. Every so often I would glance at it and resist the urge to tell Keith that nothing was happening.

Then, at the end of April, green appeared. Long, flat leaves pushed out of the moss and shot up more than a foot before they curved downward again. A stalk began to grow amid the leaves, and at its top, about the middle of May, huge pink-orange blossoms opened. From nearly nothing—and as I thought, against great odds—amaryllis appeared.

God, help me to see that Your plan includes times of growth, even when there is no visible sustenance.
—RHODA BLECKER

Sat 19

And they shall beat their swords into plowshares, and their spears into pruninghooks: nation shall not lift up sword against nation, neither shall they learn war any more.
—ISAIAH 2:4

You would think that after thousands of years of wars and fruitless yammering about wars, there is nothing wise to say about ways that wars might finally go out of business, but you would be wrong.

This morning I was watching a tall child receive a medal for "bravery in action against enemy forces with disregard for his own safety," as an older man in uniform says while pinning a medal on the tall child. I seek him out after the ceremony. He's standing under a cedar tree; he looks about twenty years old.

"Really, I'm almost thirty; can't believe I'm so old, man," he says. "The fight was nine hours long; felt like nine minutes. I'm honored by the medal, absolutely, but every guy there earned a medal, and the women too. There were five women in my unit. The name of the valley where we were still spooks me: When someone says that name, I check my weapon.

"I'm a student here now, studying history. I'd like to be a teacher and teach my students never to know what the words *weapon check* mean. Teach them disputes are best settled with chess pieces or basketballs. Teach them Bronze Stars are given out now for bravery in not-wars. There's got to be a better way. I'm not smart enough to see it clear, but I bet my students might be. So I'm going to be a teacher. We done here, sir? Because I have to get to class, sir."

Dear Lord: Please, please, have patience with Your muddled children. A day will come, a day must come, when all the men and women who pointed to the brilliant country beyond violence are proven right, and our vast creativity and imagination discovers how to make war merely a dark memory. Keep giving us tips and hints. Keep sending us gentle agents of Your peace.
—BRIAN DOYLE

Sun 20   *"How awesome is this place! This is none other than the house of God...."* —GENESIS 28:17 (NIV)

The morning worship service had just begun when a young couple and their child slipped into the pew in front of me. The little girl—about five years old—began chatting.

"*Sh,*" her mother whispered, "this is God's house."

The child fell silent, but that didn't keep her head from turning this way and that as she looked over the many other members already seated in the congregation. Then in a whisper loud enough for those several rows away to hear, she asked, "Which one is God?"

"God's not here. He's in heaven," her mother quietly replied.

The girl continued glancing around the sanctuary. Then she announced, "Well, God better get home pretty soon! He's got lots of company waiting for Him."

As the piano prelude continued during the opening services, I chuckled to myself and thought, *God really does have lots of company*. And I began thanking Him for all those innumerable people throughout the ages who were or, like me, still are part of His vast family.

*Thank You, Father, that wherever You are,
it's an awesome place. But the place seems especially
awesome when it's filled with a whole
company of Your children!*
—ISABEL WOLSELEY

Mon 21 — *Fear not: for I am with thee. . . .*
—ISAIAH 43:5

Gracie, the two-pound abandoned kitten I found at our back steps four years ago, is making progress overcoming her fears. She's even begun, on special occasions, to purr.

I'd stopped taking her to the veterinarian because of her terror. Because she's an inside cat, my vet reluctantly agreed. But the problem of trimming her nails remained. Somehow Gracie knew when I was about to do it and hid—often avoiding me all day. Or else we'd struggle together, and maybe I'd get two nails trimmed.

One day, I sat down by her on our favorite chair. Usually she vacates a chair if she can't have it all, but she stayed there and even purred and shut her green eyes. It was a lovely moment.

Why not trim her nails now? The tiny red-handled feline nail scissors lay within my reach. Rather than hold Gracie down, I laid the scissors by her paws. Startled, she sniffed them cautiously. I continued rubbing her gray head and whispered, "I'm going to trim your nails, Grace Face." She reached out and touched the scissors with one apprehensive paw. Finally, she glared at me. "It's okay, Sweetie." I moved my hand down to one foot and massaged it tenderly. Her purring resumed as she shut her trusting eyes. Gently I exposed a couple of very long nails and snipped them quickly. No struggle! *Snip, snip, snip* . . . In less than a minute, both front paws were properly trimmed. Her sandpaper-like pink tongue licked my hand.

> *Lord, enable me to trust suddenly like Gracie*
> *when You must prune me.*
> —MARION BOND WEST

Tue 22

I will remember the deeds of the Lord; yes, I will remember your miracles. . . . —PSALM 77:11 (NIV)

The worst thing about moving to Texas was being twelve hundred miles farther away from our granddaughter Ella Grace in New Hampshire. So you can imagine what a big deal it was when her mom and dad brought her for her first visit last spring.

My wife Joy was especially anxious that we have everything ready, so for weeks we shopped for the perfect high chair, the perfect sippy cup, the perfect books and toys. More important, however, Grandma was worried that Ella wouldn't recognize her and, after two plane changes and twelve hours, Ella's response would be tears and fear. I had a bit more confidence because of the wonder of computer video calls and her parents' faithfulness in keeping us all connected.

Finally the day came. Joy was waiting at baggage claim, while I sat with my cell phone out in the parking lot. The phone rang and I drove up to the arrival curb. I saw Joy standing in front of a stroller that held a tired and confused Ella. Careful not to rush in too quickly, Joy stayed back a bit, knelt down and said, "Hi, Ella. Do you remember Grandma?" Ella scrunched her nose, squinted her eyes and then, wonder of wonders, reached up her arms to Grandma to be hugged and held.

Watching the thrill on Joy's face and knowing the agony of anticipation she had gone through, I wondered if God doesn't feel like that sometimes. At times we seem to be far from Him, and days go by without much communication. Does God wonder if we'll remember him? Does He long for that face-to-face meeting when we reach up to be held and loved? Would it make God's day today if you paused right now and asked Him for a hug? Want to give it a try?

Lord, help me remember to reach out to You with the same trust and faith as a granddaughter reaches to her grandmother.
—Eric Fellman

Wed 23

Have this attitude in yourselves which was also in Christ Jesus: . . . He humbled himself by becoming obedient to the point of death, even death on a cross.
—Philippians 2:5, 8 (NAS)

When my grandson Caleb was seven, he created an eye-catching solar system penciled on a standard sheet of white paper. From a center circle, six spokes extend to corresponding outer circles. On the left in descending order are "sun," "satrn" and "mars." On the right in ascending order are "erth," "juputr" and "moon."

And the central, largest circle? That, of course, is labeled "caleb." Astronomers who prod and poke the heavens need only knock on Caleb's door for an update. He knows full well that *he* is the center of the universe!

While this seems comical to me as a scientifically informed adult, it's also a needed reminder. Every day I wrestle with Philippians 2:3 (NAS), "Do nothing from selfishness or empty conceit, but with humility of mind regard one another as more important than yourselves."

Jesus is my model for resisting the gravitational pull of a me-centered universe. At times He understandably fortified Himself, withdrawing alone or with close friends to pray and renew a spirit of perseverance. But He never lost His vision for doing His Father's will. He genuinely and ceaselessly cared for others. He refused to allow self-interest to mar the good that He could do—even to the personal cost of death on the cross.

Not surprisingly, on the days when it doesn't all spin around me—when I put God and fellow-humans in their rightful places—heavenly gifts of peace and joy pop up on my horizon.

Lord, this vast universe is Yours, yet You came seeking me. Help me to be centered in You.
—CAROL KNAPP

Thu 24

For He Himself knows our frame; He is mindful that we are but dust.
—PSALM 103:14 (NAS)

I teach a class of nineteen freshmen entitled "Composing the Self." For one semester we've studied how life-dreams are formed and actualized over a lifetime. The students have written essays on various aspects of their lives; they've read books and articles about adult developmental psychology and how religious faith is formed and matures. We've had vigorous discussions and debates. And in the quietness of their own dorm rooms, they have kept personal journals of reflections. Now I must pull out the grade book and assign each of them a final grade. I struggle with this process.

If, indeed, at the end of our lives we must answer to our God for our short semester spent on earth, how will we be graded? Jesus addressed this question in many stories. But the parable that lodges in my memory is the separation of the sheep from the goats (Matthew 25:31–46).

It's a simple story with straightforward meaning. For our final exam, God will ask one question: "How well did you love your neighbor when that neighbor was hungry, thirsty, lonely, naked, broke or imprisoned by addiction or lack of education? How much did you share of your means? More important, did you treat your neighbor like you would treat God if He visited you?"

When I consider this parable, I know I've tried hard, but I've flunked the exam. And a lot of graciousness will be needed for me to pass "Living and Loving 101."

Tonight as I enter grades in my grade book, I will need to follow the "letter of the law." But I will also consider that my students are freshmen; they are young and inexperienced, just learning to study.

They think they're "bulletproof." But I know their frame; I am mindful that they are but dust. And part of the grading scale is grace and compassion.

Merciful Father, You know our frame of dust.
Have mercy on us all.
—Scott Walker

Fri 25

Husbands, love your wives, even as Christ also loved the church and gave himself for it.... —Ephesians 5:25

I had two tickets to a hot sporting event and I knew just the person I'd offer the extra one to: Desmond. He'd be totally thrilled.

"Um," he said hesitantly when I called with the exciting news. "I don't think I can make it."

For a second I was speechless. These were the best seats in the house for the biggest game of the year.

"You're kidding me, right?"

"No," he said softly. "I just can't."

Now I was really worried: "Des, is everything okay?" I asked.

After a long pause, he finally said, "Pauline and I are having some problems. Real problems."

I didn't know what to say. Des and Pauline had a great marriage, or so I thought.

"We've started going to counseling," Des continued, "and it's really, really hard. I'm so used to not talking about the way I feel, I don't know if I can."

Pauline, Des said, had been depressed for a long time. "I didn't even realize it! I've got a lot of work to do on myself, and it starts with Pauline and me spending more time together and learning to communicate."

Suddenly I felt like a total jerk for trying to cajole him into going to some pointless sporting event. "I'm really sorry you guys have to go through this, Des. I'm pulling for you."

"Pull with prayer," he said, and—before hanging up—promised we'd get together soon for coffee.

I thought about those two tickets. Julee had been a little down lately. Maybe I could give them both away.

Lord, no couple is perfect. You bring us together
so that in growing closer to each other in love
we grow closer to You.
—EDWARD GRINNAN

Sat 26

The Lord sitteth upon the flood; yea,
the Lord sitteth King for ever.
—PSALM 29:10

The lights flickered and went dark. The last power outage had lasted eight hours, leaving us without water because the well pump is electric. I had about three minutes to drain the lines, so

May

I quickly filled two pitchers with drinking water; then I shut the bathtub drain and opened the tap to collect more water. The electricity was still off half an hour later when my husband Don and I left for a Little League baseball game.

We returned to a brightly lit house and the sound of running water. The tub overflow had failed; the bathroom and parts of the kitchen, hall and bedroom were soaked. Water was two inches deep in the basement and had drenched two of my storage cabinets.

In the midst of the mess, I received three blessings. The first was that Don never once called me careless. He just got the wet-dry vacuum and started sucking up water. The second was that there was no permanent damage to the house.

The third blessing was the greatest. *Someday*, I'd promised myself, *I'll clean the basement.* I planned to sort through five hundred-plus books, check eBay to see if any of our old LP covers were valuable, put newspaper clippings in scrapbooks and throw out the yellow lampshade that didn't fit my lamps.

Someday was here—and it had arrived with a splash.

It took two days to sort through the mess and haul out the trash. I expected to be sad over the losses, but when I finally finished I felt—*free!* I was free of a task that had seemed too big to tackle; I was free of sixteen garbage bags of junk. And best of all, the bare shelves reminded me that my real treasures are in heaven.

Thank You, Jesus, for the blessings of the flood.
But would you please remind me to turn off
the water next time I leave home?
—PENNEY SCHWAB

Sun 27

But the fruit of the Spirit is love, joy, peace, forbearance, kindness, goodness, faithfulness, gentleness and self-control. . . .
—GALATIANS 5:22–23 (NIV)

It was not the kind of announcement you want to hear from your pilot an hour into your flight.

"Uh, folks, our control panel is indicating that one of our engines has failed," he said over the intercom. "It's probably just a problem with the indicator light, but as a precautionary measure we're going to be making an emergency landing at the nearest airstrip."

Within a few minutes, we had descended and an airport was in sight. From my window seat I could see a small army of firetrucks gathered on the runway.

I took a deep breath and asked God to keep us safe. Then I looked around the plane and was surprised to see that no one was panicking. People looked afraid, but not terrified. Then, as we made what turned out to be a smooth and safe landing, many of the passengers joined hands and began singing "Amazing Grace."

As I walked up the jetway into the terminal, I marveled at this reaction. I'd been on flights before where a mere fifteen seconds of wind turbulence caused hysteria among the passengers. It was obvious, I decided, what had made the difference on this flight: I was en route to Central America with fifty-six members of my church. Their serenity during our emergency landing had been a manifestation of the fruits of the Spirit: self-control, gentleness and, most significantly, peace.

After the mechanics fixed the indicator light and gave the go-ahead for us to reboard the plane, I said a prayer of thanks for the Comforter Who was traveling with us.

Lord, thank You for sending Your Spirit
to guide and comfort me.
—JOSHUA SUNDQUIST

Mon 28

Mercy, peace, and love be multiplied to you.
—JUDE 1:2 (NKJV)

Fifteen years ago, early on the Sunday of Memorial Day weekend, I took houseguests into Washington, DC, to see the Vietnam Memorial. We found easy parking on Constitution Avenue. Hardly anyone else was there except a few young soldiers in shorts who had volunteered to wash the monument. I remember a stillness that I associated with early light: the sight of mist, the smell of cleaning, the sound of songbirds.

This morning I drove into DC, intending to recapture the moment. But new realities had changed the scene. Curbside barriers forced me to park farther north. At the monument I saw no evidence of a fresh-faced cleaning crew—and more visitors than I wanted to share the landscape with. Disappointed, I almost left. Maybe because someone was playing a bagpipe, I lingered to watch: Two men searched a tall panel for a specific name. A veteran cried, another sat soberly in a wheelchair. An intergenerational host of people connected to the 199th placed memorial cards below the names of the brigade's fallen. I overheard a leathery motorcyclist credit the Holy Spirit for the inexplicable nudge he'd had in Vietnam not to hop into a Jeep beside his army buddy on one fateful day, one fatal trip.

Coleridge said that the present already walks in the past. I'd set out in search of a duplicate day. God used that unrealistic motive to enrich my life with new memories, including one more: A storybook drama unfolded on Constitution Avenue when a mother mallard stepped boldly off the curb. A street vendor and I rushed out and waved down traffic to make way for twenty-nine ducklings crossing over in single file.

> *Lord, this weekend as I celebrate memory,*
> *expand my view of Your mercies, still multiplying*
> *in the present tense.*
> —EVELYN BENCE

Tue 29

> *"Ask and it will be given to you; seek and you will find; knock and the door will be opened to you."*
> —MATTHEW 7:7 (NIV)

My two-year-old grandson Mace is just beginning to get the gist of stringing words together. Instead of the single-word announcements I've become accustomed to, I'm now treated to "More grapes" or "Hi, Nina!" or (my favorite) "Uv you."

But Mace surprised me last night by coming into the kitchen while I was putting the final touches on dinner and blurting out, "Knock, knock."

I turned from the stove in surprise. Was it possible one of his brothers (Drake is seven and Brock five) had taught him a joke? Truth is, I love knock-knock jokes. So I responded appropriately, "Who's there?"

Mace doubled over in laughter as he howled, *"Chicken!"*

Okay, so much for two-year-old humor.

I thought of Mace's "knock-knock" this morning as I prayed for my family. How I long for their protection, health, success! But sometimes I knock on God's door and then stand there, like an awkward visitor fingering her hat on the front porch. I'm not sure what to say. I want the very best for my loved ones, but I've lived long enough to know that sometimes what's best isn't what's easiest or happiest. I visualize bright, perfect futures for them all, but are these prayers?

More often than not, words fail me. I have only the longings—and love—of my heart to offer. Fortunately, God's hearing is astoundingly acute. And His will, ultimately, is what I desire most—for myself and all those precious souls I love.

God promises that when I knock, the door to heaven's wisdom and provision will be opened. So...

Dear God,
Knock, knock...
—MARY LOU CARNEY

Wed 30

All the believers were one in heart and mind. . . . They shared everything they had.
—Acts 4:32 (NIV)

I confess that I am something of a *Glee*k, a fan of the TV show *Glee,* which does a great job of reminding me of how awful high school was and making me laugh about it.

One of the beauties of the show is its ambition at tackling, in the context of satirical comedy, some of the big questions of life: parent-child relationships, love and identity. In one episode, *Glee* addressed faith. Toward the end of the episode, Mercedes, one of the main characters, takes her friend Kurt, who has said he doesn't believe in God, to church. "You've got to believe in something—something more than you can touch, taste or see," she tells him. "Because life is too hard to go through it alone, without something to hold on to and without something that's sacred."

I thought about what Mercedes had to say, and I'd add something to that: Not only is life too hard to go through alone, though it is, but also we weren't designed to go through it alone. We are, Scripture tells us, creatures of community, meant not only to help support others but also to be backed up by them.

Today, it's easy for us to try to go it alone, but it's hard, if not impossible, to succeed. That, curiously enough, is the message of *Glee*. It's about a bunch of seekers finding their true home, together, amid the tumultuous world of high school—which makes it a pretty good metaphor for believers trying to make sense of this crazy thing called life.

Lord, thank You for all those around me where I live, work and worship, companions on the way.
—JEFF CHU

Thu 31

Thou art near, O Lord. . . .
—PSALM 119:151

One of the things I've missed most since we moved from a house to an apartment is the screened porch that was our summer living-room, dining-room, prayer-room, everything-room. Here in our new home we do have a bench just outside. It seemed like a good place for my morning meditation, but without a screen, wouldn't insects be a problem?

May

The bench has turned out to be a delightful place for those meditations—with insects part of what makes it so right. This morning a dragonfly lit on my forearm. I'd never seen one so close before: dark wings folded above the needlelike body. And then the wings opened, so incredibly fragile and lacelike it seemed impossible they could lift even this tiny creature. The wings closed and then opened again, spread wide like the petals of some unimaginably delicate flower.

Closing, opening, she remained on my arm, balanced on six thread-thin legs, for nearly five minutes. I couldn't take my eyes off her, reveling in my closeness to a being so lovely. "You're beautiful!" I told her. "I wish I could tell you how beautiful you are!"

I couldn't, of course. The dragonfly was unaware that it was a living being on whose arm she rested. The dragonfly couldn't hear the words I spoke. *And am I always aware*, I thought, *of the Being in whose arms I rest? Do I hear the Voice forever telling me—as He tells each of us: "You are beautiful"?*

Lord, You haven't screened Yourself off from my small life. Give me moments throughout this day to rest in the awareness of Your presence.
—ELIZABETH SHERRILL

MY PATHWAY TO PEACE

1 _____

2 _____

3 _____

4 _____

5 _____

6 _____

7 _____

8 _____

9 _____

10 _____

11 _____

12 _____

13 _____

14 _____

15 _____

May

16 _____

17 _____

18 _____

19 _____

20 _____

21 _____

22 _____

23 _____

24 _____

25 _____

26 _____

27 _____

28 _____

29 _____

30 _____

31 _____

June

For thus saith the Lord, Behold, I will extend peace to her like a river . . . .

—Isaiah 66:12

Fri 1

Having then gifts differing according to the grace that is given to us, let us use them.... —ROMANS 12:6 (NKJV)

My friend Jo has something I don't have: a knack for decorating. So I was thrilled when she agreed to help me give my home a makeover. Day after day, we went through closets, cabinets and cubbyholes deciding what to keep, what to toss and what to put where.

On the third or fourth day, I noticed something: After a couple of hours of work each day, Jo was like a SuperBall, gaining unstoppable momentum. She so enjoyed working her magic to transform my domestic blandness that she could barely finish one area of the house before moving to another.

As for me, after a few hours I felt like a wrung-out dishrag. Every decision—*Like it? Don't like it? Keep it? Toss it? Put it here or put it there?*—sucked energy and life out of me. After three days, all I cared about was when this was going to end.

When we did finally finish the house, I thoroughly enjoyed its newness and Jo's occasional splash of color. But even more, I enjoyed the freedom that came from knowing that doing the things you love and are gifted to do is energizing, while doing what you don't love and aren't gifted to do is draining and exhausting. Now I feel better about my house and the gifts God has—and hasn't—given me.

Father, give me grace to do the necessary things I don't love to do, and opportunities to do the things I love.
—LUCILE ALLEN

Sat 2

We proclaim to you what we have seen and heard, so that you also may have fellowship with us. . . .
—I JOHN 1:3 (NIV)

"Why?" our grandson Konner demanded when I told him not to take his iPod into the restaurant where Carol and I were treating him and his brother Brennig to dinner one evening. At eight years of age, Konner loses himself in all sorts of electronic gadgets, such as television and game consoles. The music player was simply his latest craze.

"Because I want you to be with *us* while we're here," I told him. He began to cry, evidently not understanding what I meant. Finally we persuaded him to go in empty-handed.

When the waiter delivered the menus, both Konner and Brennig eagerly grabbed their kids' menus and began coloring and filling in crossword puzzles, animatedly swapping answers and showing us trails they had drawn through the mazes. The scene reminded me of when their mother was about four and our TV set broke. Instead of sitting in front of the tube, she and her sister ran outside to play. We didn't replace the set for years.

Now as our grandsons took part in the meal and table conversation, I spied a group of young people at another table. A number of them were texting on their cell phones, barely interacting with the rest. It was quite a contrast from what was happening at our table—a difference of day and night, as far as I was concerned.

After dinner, we went back to our house. Later, when we took the boys home, Konner forgot his iPod, leaving it in our living room. So much for technology when you're having real fun.

Father, when I get too caught up in technology, free me to be more alive to those around me.
—HAROLD HOSTETLER

THIS I KNOW

Sun 3   *For they love to pray standing in the synagogues and in the corners of the streets, that they may be seen of men. . . .* —MATTHEW 6:5

FATHER TALK

The memory of the moment still gives me shivers. I was sitting by my daddy during an evening church service when the minister asked, "Harrison Dunn, would you please lead us in prayer?"

I couldn't breathe as I watched my six-foot-four father stand hesitantly. Didn't that minister know that Daddy had never prayed in public? He certainly didn't have the fancy language that so many of the "praying people" in our church used. I looked up at my mother and saw that she, too, was holding her breath.

Daddy's booming voice trembled as he said what seemed to me to be a perfect prayer: "God, walk with us. Help us be good. Amen."

I grabbed his hand as he sat back down, pretty sure that this was the last Sunday evening service we'd be attending for a long time to come.

We've all endured public prayers who glory in flowery words and Bible quotes and whatever else it takes to keep their audience captive. Nothing's changed, it seems, since Jesus talked about the os-tentatious worshipers of His day. But apart from the grandstanders, what about the rest of us, those who hesitate because we feel inadequate or are intimi-dated by the soliloquies that some church leaders deliver?

In light of that long ago night when Daddy was called on to pray, I've worked to understand what God might really want from us. So far, this is what I know: God is a breath away. He wants to hear what you have to say. He hopes that you will choose to come as you are. And to God our Father, nobody says it better than you!

> *Father, I can make anything complicated, even talking to You. But You make everything simple.*
> —PAM KIDD

Mon 4   *For the gifts and calling of God are without repentance.*
—ROMANS 11:29

Early this morning I found myself thinking back to June 1941. On May 27 of that year I had graduated from college, and my birthday was May 28, but we had no celebrations. I was concerned about my future and about getting a job. I went to West Medford, Massachusetts, seeking work in the Greater Boston area. I was promised an interview with a company on July 1.

One week after reaching West Medford, I received an application for a teaching position in East St. Louis, Illinois. I began filling out the application until I came to the question, "What salary do you expect?" I wanted to ask for eighty dollars a month. But was I worth that? I had just gotten out of school, with no teaching experience. I tucked the application away in a drawer.

Then on the evening of June 19, the telephone rang. Mother was calling from Williamstown. "Os," she said, "you have a telegram from a Mr. Joseph Taylor in East St. Louis asking if you'll accept a teaching position for one hundred and twenty dollars a month." And I was hesitant to ask for eighty! My answer was a resounding yes.

I hurried the 133 miles home, borrowed money from Mother for the trip and traveled to Illinois, where I found I enjoyed teaching. And in October in East St. Louis, I met my Ruby, who has been my wife for sixty-eight years.

> *Thank You, dear Father, for Your guidance*
> *when my trust was paper thin.*
> —OSCAR GREENE

Tue 5　　*"If you seek Him, He will let you find Him. . . ."*
　　—II CHRONICLES 15:2 (NAS)

As a toddler, I often played hide-and-seek with my mother in the shady front yard of our old farmhouse. When I went looking for her, I could usually spot a bit of her cotton print housedress peeking out from behind the tall elm tree or the 1936 Studebaker parked in the driveway. But I had to look, making the thrill of discovery that much more exciting.

Sometimes my three-year-old patience wore thin, and I would lose interest in the game before I spied her. Usually, however, Mother would reveal just enough of her presence to make me squeal with delight: "Ready or not, here I come!" Then she would race me to home base, and for some strange reason, I could always get there on my short, stubby legs long before she did.

Sometimes life itself seems to be a spiritual game of hide-and-seek, and I feel that God isn't revealing His presence to me in ways that I can see. At those times, I have to seek Him in Scripture, look for Him in nature or discover Him hidden behind the exemplary walk of another believer. Sometimes my patience wears thin and I give up much too soon, convinced that God just doesn't want me to find Him, that He's not even involved in this game called life.

However, nothing could be further from the truth! When I sincerely seek God, He lets me find Him, and what a delight to discover Him hiding in the most unexpected places.

Father God, You aren't far from each one of us,
for in You "we live, and move, and
have our being" (Acts 17:28).
—ALMA BARKMAN

Wed 6

"Where you die I will die, and there I will be buried. May the Lord deal with me, be it ever so severely, if anything but death separates you and me." —RUTH 1:17 (NIV)

Ten days after my wedding, my dad died suddenly and unexpectedly. Mom and I were forced to shift gears from celebration and joy to grief and bewilderment. As we rushed around, welcoming friends and family, arranging the funeral service and pausing for moments of silent tears, we were blessed to be surrounded by children—my six nieces and nephews, ranging in age from nine months to almost four.

Lily, who was almost three at the time, said to her mom as they talked over snacks, "I think Grandpa is up there flying around the world with Jesus."

Surprised, her mom replied, "That's right, Lily. He is."

Thoughtfully, Lily asked, "Do you think that if I'm really good he'll come back to see me?"

I remembered how often I'd believed that I could make things better because I did something good or change God's plan by making a bad choice. I knew that God had something planned for me and, in spite of my grief, I would find out just what it was. For now, I knew my purpose was to help little hearts understand that their grandfather still loves them, just from a little farther away. And with that, I began to understand a little better myself.

> *Lord, remind me every day that You have a*
> *plan for my life and that You are with me always,*
> *even in times of sadness.*
> —ASHLEY KAPPEL

Thu 7

How often I have wanted to gather
your children together, as a hen gathers
her chicks under her wings. . . .
—MATTHEW 23:37 (NAS)

Friends often talk on and on about the cute or smart or clever things their dogs or cats do and then politely ask me, "Do you have any pets?" When I answer, "Yes, I have a pair of chickens," they laugh. To them, *chicken* means merely a table meat or an egg producer—certainly not a creature with a personality and a maternal care for its offspring.

In defense, I add, "Jesus favored chickens, too, or He'd not have likened Himself to one," and remind them of the verse above. Jesus used common, ordinary objects—chickens in this case—to make a point, so I'm sure He must've observed something similar to what one of my hens did during a recent rainstorm.

The downpour happened so quickly that she had no time to find shelter for her vulnerable chicks.

She simply squatted in place, and the yellow fuzz balls scuttled beneath Mom's wings, where they stayed snug and dry while water cascaded down her sides and tail.

Then there was the day she gave a distinctive sharp call—*Danger!*—when a hungry hawk swooped onto an overhead branch. Again the chicks dashed beneath her wings, knowing this was their place of safety.

Most of the time, however, her little ones, their tiny crops (*stomachs* in bird jargon) filled with food, rest in warmth under her, at peace in their secure sanctuary.

> *You alone, Father, are my refuge, my place of safety.*
> *For You will cover me with Your feathers,*
> *you will shelter me with Your wings.*
> *(Psalm 91:2, 4, NLT).*
> —ISABEL WOLSELEY

Fri 8

Fear not, for I am with you; be not dismayed, for I am your God; I will strengthen you, I will help you, I will uphold you with my righteous right hand. —ISAIAH 41:10 (ESV)

For five years, the newspaper delivery person and I had played a daily game. He hid our newspaper, and my husband and I found it.

We tried to remedy the situation; we worked with customer service and tried communicating with the delivery person directly and indirectly. Once, in desperation, my husband posted a big sign in our front lawn with the words PUT PAPER HERE! and bold black arrows pointing to our doorstep. All our attempts backfired; the paper was flung farther from our house. So a few weeks ago, when my husband announced that he was too busy to read the newspaper and that we should cancel it, I gleefully agreed.

The first morning without delivery, I stood at my bedroom window, scanning the yard for the blue wrapper of the newspaper. I looked across the street and down the neighbor's hill, in the field next door, beneath our expansive walnut tree, and on the slope of our front yard before I remembered we'd canceled it.

For the next few mornings, I found myself at the window searching the ground for the newspaper, as if I needed something to be upset about. Had I been doing that with other things in my life? Had I been holding on to frustrations and resentments, even after their causes had vanished?

Dear God, help me conquer the habit of holding
on to things to be upset about, so I can
be a beacon of Your peace.
—SABRA CIANCANELLI

Sat 9

He saved us through the washing of rebirth and renewal by the Holy Spirit.... —TITUS 3:5 (NIV)

Two years ago a hundred-year flood—the kind that is equaled or exceeded only once in a hundred years—inundated our beautiful town park bordering the Harpeth River. It uprooted and toppled trees, washed away trails, and left behind a scarred, barren, muddy wasteland dotted with rocks and fallen trees.

I couldn't believe the devastation. "There's nothing left," I said tearfully to my husband Whitney.

Yet, today, as I walk through the same park, I'm amazed. The wasteland has become a green meadow. The fallen trees are wood sculptures framed by ferns and wildflowers. Nature has restored and blended herself into a whole new landscape. Looking at it, I feel the wonder of God's transformation, not just in the park, but somewhere else I didn't think possible.

My marriage. "There's nothing left," I'd said tearfully to Whitney twelve years ago. And I'd left, convinced my marriage was a hopeless wasteland. Yet out of it grew a willingness for counseling. And out of the counseling grew a new start. Today our marriage, rooted in love, is restored.

A wasteland transformed. It happens in nature. And it can happen in our lives if we but plant ourselves in the faith and hope that lie in every devastation.

Almighty God, nothing is too hard for You!
—SHARI SMYTH

Sun 10 *But as for me. . . .* —JOSHUA 24:15

It was a proud day for me, age twelve, when my father announced that I was old enough to have my first suit—and one made by his own tailor! Dad always had his suits hand made by Mr. Epstein. It wasn't that Dad had lots of money; quite the opposite. He was a teacher and saved money by ordering well-made suits and rotating them so they lasted many years.

We went together to Mr. Epstein's shop on the second floor of a redbrick building near the river in Louisville. I chose a dark gray wool fabric just like Dad's. Fourteen days later we went back to Mr. Epstein's, and there was my suit! I put it on and stood before the full-length mirror, turning this way and that, feeling grown up indeed.

Sunday came, the first occasion to wear my suit in public. Dressed in my glory, I headed to church with the family. I was glad to see four of my friends just ahead. Determined not to strut, I assumed a casual stroll.

To my consternation, the four boys burst into loud guffaws. "Look at the little gentleman! Hey, Lord Fauntleroy!"

After church that Sunday, I hung up my suit and never put it on again.

My parents were baffled. They'd made a considerable investment in that suit, in that Depression year of 1935. Though he said nothing, I knew Dad was hurt. But I'd come up against something stronger than finances and parental sensibilities. I'd encountered the power of peer pressure, the tyranny of *What will people think?*

I've met it many times in the more than seven decades since that Sunday morning. And more often than I like to remember, I've given in to it. But occasionally, remembering that new suit, I summon the courage to say, as Joshua did to the pressures of his day, "But as for me . . ."

Lord, help me listen today for Your voice alone.
—JOHN SHERRILL

Mon 11

I looked, and there in front of me was a white horse . . . he rode out to conquer in many battles. . . .
—REVELATION 6:2 (TLB)

On June 27, 2009, my granddaughter Olivia, eleven, was bike riding with her friend Peyton when she hit loose gravel and went airborne. She landed with a force that fractured her skull and caused a concussion. The diagnosis was traumatic brain injury.

The next months were sad and stressful. Olivia tired easily, yet couldn't sleep at night. She had severe migraines. She'd been an honor student but now struggled to read, remember lessons and follow instructions. She had to quit her favorite sport, gymnastics. "I used to be a gymnast," she said one day. "Now I'm nothing." We besieged the doors of heaven for healing or the return of our shy but smiling and sometimes sassy little girl. Our prayers seemed to go unheard.

Enter Peso, a frisky white gelding with grey freckles on his nose. He and Olivia chose each other the day she began equestrian therapy. For an hour each week, Olivia groomed Peso, rode him around an arena and practiced responding to his moods. She soon progressed to guiding Peso through courses of barrels and poles. Then her counselor asked if she'd like to try vaulting—gymnastics on horseback. With the first vault, Olivia began to improve. Each new vault brought renewed confidence. When she mastered the back walk-over dismount, she was able to stop therapy and just enjoy riding and vaulting.

Problems with memory, schoolwork and occasional migraines continue but no longer drag Olivia down. Time and a new school helped, but it was

Peso who was the unexpected answer to prayer. It was on Peso's broad back that Olivia again became herself.

Thank You, Jesus, for a girl, a white horse and Your promise of strength for the life battles ahead.
—PENNEY SCHWAB

Tue 12

Husbands, love your wives, even as Christ also loved the church. . . .
—EPHESIANS 5:25

My 7:00 AM train from Carmel to New York City was quiet as riders followed the etiquette of the morning commute: no talking on cell phone or to others; catching up on sleep is okay. Grand Central Terminal was bustling with people crisscrossing the station floor on the way to their destinations. I headed south on Madison Avenue, walking eight city blocks to the Guideposts editorial office.

I was just a few steps away from the building when my cell phone rang. "Honey, I was in a car accident," my wife Elba said. The city became silent and came to a standstill. I could feel my heart beating.

I took a deep breath and asked, "Are you okay?"

"I'm fine," Elba said. "I'm just a bit shaken up." I could feel the tension in my muscles relax. She explained that on her way back home after dropping me off at the train station, the driver of a van lost control on the slippery road, crossed into her lane, and slammed into the car. "She's okay too," Elba said.

Earlier in our marriage, when I was young and foolish and in a similar situation, the first words out of my mouth were "How's the car?" This time I knew better.

That evening at home Elba said, "Thank you for asking me how I was doing when I called you. It meant a lot that you thought of me first."

This time around, I got it right.

Lord, make sure that my loved ones are always first in my heart.
—PABLO DIAZ

Wed 13

But when he saw the multitudes, he was moved with compassion. . . .
—MATTHEW 9:36 (NKJV)

My red riding mower roars to life, and I head for the front yard. The grass is fluorescent green, and the red corn poppies at the edge of the lawn are rocking back and forth in the breeze.

I've been mowing only a short time when the swallows arrive out of nowhere. Round and round me they circle, swooping down at the grass, swallowing insects, and then climbing, banking and heading straight for my face. Suddenly it's 1914, and I am the Red Baron in my red Fokker triplane, taking on Sopwiths and Nieuports. The dogfight rages; then, suddenly, the swallows are gone.

Imagination!

It's a wonderful quality, a uniquely human trait, this ability to see things in our minds. From it have come great novels, spectacular movies, lifesaving inventions and cures for disease, all "imagineered" by visionaries.

Best of all is imagination's ability to create compassion. When a friend of ours lost a son, it wasn't hard to imagine how terrible they felt—at least enough to want to help with food, a card, a hug.

No wonder Einstein said, "Imagination is more important than knowledge." Knowledge may provide information, but imagination provides inspiration that leads to action.

Thanks to imagination, I have some idea what it might mean to be single and alone. I can imagine how hard it must be to be a national leader, whose every move is criticized and second-guessed. I can imagine what it might be like to live in a country where there is no freedom, my every action observed by sinister forces.

No, imagination isn't perfect, but it is a kind of sixth sense that enables us to see what our eyes miss. I need to use it more than I do.

Thank You, Father, for this gift of extrasensory perception that enables us to sympathize with those around us who are in pain.
—DANIEL SCHANTZ

Thu 14

And in the name of our God we will set up our banners. . . .
—PSALM 20:5 (NAS)

Our flag atop its tall post often billows and whips in the wind sweeping the edge of the Great Plains. From my window, I often watch the Stars and Stripes move against a sky of blue or gray or, sometimes, pink-streaked in the setting sun. It's then I feel drawn beneath an outspread wing—a wing promising strength, freedom, compassion, welcome.

One stormy spring morning a fierce, straight line-wind struck the flag, snapping its pole and throwing it to the ground, where it lay in the grass, sodden and still. Startled by the strength of my feelings, I ran from the house into the ugly weather to pick up the flag and carry it inside.

It took us a while to replace the flagpole, and until we did, the flag's absence was like a hole in the sky. I was surprised by how much I missed it.

Finally, on a sunny summer day, the flag shimmied up its new pole, eager to fly. Now from my window I can again watch it gracefully lift and sway in the breeze, waving reassuringly over the land and, I discovered, in my heart.

Lord, even as I look to our flag, I'm reminded that
You reign supreme over all.
—CAROL KNAPP

❊ A GRACE-FILLED JOURNEY

Fri 15   *The isles shall wait upon me, and on mine arm shall they trust.*
—ISAIAH 51:5

ISLE OF MY DREAMS

According to last night's lecture, the island of Santorini was—and is still considered to be—an active volcano. The speaker ended his talk by saying, "By the way, Santorini is now due to erupt again." It was definitely not a joke!

It's a scary thought, but I've heard good things about this quaint island and I don't want to miss it. So when I find the above Scripture from Isaiah, I breathe a silent prayer to the One in Whom I have always trusted.

As we disembark onto the island, my rock-solid husband Robert takes my hand and I feel steadied, safe. The little city named Oia is built on the slope of the volcano, its houses nestled into the now-solid volcanic ash. Standing on a high point by the bell tower of an old church, we look out over blue-domed, cylinder-shaped churches and whitewashed, blue-roofed dwellings to marvel at the turquoise-bright waters of the Aegean, a sea colored like none other anywhere on earth!

I sense a distinct awareness of being grounded, held up by two firm hands. One belongs to Robert. The other is invisible.

> *Thank You, Heavenly Father,*
> *for that most firm of all hands.*
> —MARILYN MORGAN KING

READER'S ROOM

One of my great-great-grandfathers planted a row of boxwoods on either side of the dusty, sandy walkway that went to his house in Cluster Springs, Virginia, where I visited my grandparents for many years. I wish my grandchildren could smell those woodsy, small, tight-woven, taller-than-life green bushes the way I can without being there. At Christmastime next year, I think I'll give each of my grandchildren a boxwood plant.

> —*Tiffany Traynham Klappenbach*
> *Mount Gilead, North Carolina*

Sat 16

"I will give you the keys of the kingdom of heaven...."
—MATTHEW 16:19 (NIV)

My husband Gordon and I decided that it would be a huge help not to have to mail keys to our beach house renters. So we went to the home improvement store and bought one of those keyless entry locks that use a numeric code.

At the beach house, I watched Gordon remove the old lock and try putting in the new one. Gordon shook his head, saying, "The hole in the door is too small for the new lock. And I don't have the right kind of saw to make the hole bigger without tearing up the door." There we were, with the old lock dismantled on the foyer rug and a gaping hole on our now unlockable front door!

In a panic I ran to the kitchen and furiously looked up locksmiths in the phone book. One answered the phone and said, "No problem, I'll be over at noon."

The locksmith had a gizmo that looked like a round steel template that he fastened to the door before sawing. He told me he had previously worked a high-pressure job with a telecom company and had been laid off. He'd been out of work for quite some time when someone suggested that he train as a locksmith. "I like it," he said. "I go out to a variety of locations and I feel like I'm really rendering a service. Besides, everyone is always really happy to see me. When you need a locksmith, you've got a problem. Nobody ever says, 'Oh dear, the locksmith is here.'"

Now, I'm not an outgoing person, and I'm often hesitant to say anything about my faith to others. But when I do, no one ever says, "Oh dear, I'm getting another word of blessing and encouragement." On the contrary, people who have problems are looking for a few good keys—love, compassion, mercy and encouragement—to help unlock their worried hearts.

Father, remind me when I see people with problems
that You've given me the keys to Your kingdom.
—KAREN BARBER

Sun 17

And he shall turn the heart of the fathers to the children, and the heart of the children to their fathers. . . .
—MALACHI 4:6

My friend Kathleen recently gave me a book she and a lot of other people were reading. I can't actually tell you the title, but it refers to memorable "stuff" the author's father said.

Justin Halpern's dad was crude, profane, brutally blunt and, there's no denying it, often really, really funny. So when Justin created a Twitter page devoted to his father's outrageous utterances, it quickly drew more than a million followers, landing him a book deal and a TV spin-off.

My father was taciturn, reserved and rarely even mildly profane. In fact, what shocked and disturbed my father most back in 1973 when the first of the infamous Watergate tapes were released was President Nixon's cursing. Dad simply couldn't abide it. My mother's uncle, Father Jim Morrisey, a Jesuit priest, used to say, "I curse worse than your father!"

So why, as I read through Justin Halpern's book, did his dad and mine seem more and more alike?

Because they both, despite their sometimes odd way of showing it, dearly loved their sons and wanted to guide them into manhood. Halpern was terrified of his dad ranting at him when he made a mistake or said something dumb; I dreaded my father's stony, disapproving gaze. Yet each of us revered his father's opinion, sought his approval and thought better of him as we grew older.

Dads aren't perfect, and no one knows that better than dads. Neither are their sons, but they want us to be as good as they can help us to be. Their styles may be different but the motivation is the same: Love.

Heavenly Father, You are the ultimate source of wisdom, grace and love. Guide me each and every day through this journey of life.
—Edward Grinnan

Mon 18

This is the day which the Lord hath made; we will rejoice and be glad in it. —PSALM 118:24

In quaint Littleton, New Hampshire, the Ammonoosuc River meanders past a wooden waterwheel and under a covered bridge. On nearby Main Street stands the brick library, where a bronze statue of an exuberant young girl waves a flat straw hat at passersby. The youngster is Pollyanna, heroine of the book by the same name and creator of the "Glad Game." Littleton native Eleanor Hodgman Porter published her story in 1913. Even now, nearly a hundred years later, the name "Pollyanna" suggests a person of irrepressible optimism, someone who consistently sees the bright side of things.

In its heyday, the book was translated into twelve languages. That didn't stop cynics from criticizing *Pollyanna*—unfairly, I think—as overly sentimental, saccharine and unreal. Yet the author herself never denied the presence of evil and pain in the world; rather, she actively focused on the positive things of this life, however simple or obscure. Pollyanna has the right idea. Like this happy child, I try to focus on the best parts of each day instead of the setbacks, even when my rose-colored glasses seem to need a stronger prescription.

So when it pours rain, I'm glad I don't have to shovel it as snow. When I face a pile of dirty dishes, I'm glad I have so much food. When I grow homesick for my old Wyoming home, I'm glad I have discovered so many new friends in New Hampshire—including Pollyanna.

Father, thank You for the optimists among us, who remind us of Your goodness everywhere.
—GAIL THORELL SCHILLING

Tue 19

Let us not lose heart in doing good, for in due time we will reap if we do not grow weary.
—GALATIANS 6:9 (NAS)

Last year I published a book, *The Edge of Terror,* that tells the story of a group of American missionaries and gold miners who were trapped by the invading Japanese army on the small island of Panay in the Philippines during World War II, hiding in the remote mountains for the duration of the war. I first heard their story as a child when I lived in the Philippines with my missionary parents.

Several months ago I received a travel-worn letter from the island of Panay. It was written by an aging

Filipino pastor who lived in the remote province where my story took place nearly seventy years ago.

The pastor wrote that his daughter, a nurse in Nashville, Tennessee, had seen my book, purchased it and sent it to her father. He was fascinated by the story and thanked me for writing the book. Then his letter took a surprising turn.

More than forty years ago, my father and mother had been his professors at the Philippine Baptist Theological Seminary in the city of Baguio on the northern island of Luzon. He told me several stories about them I had never known. While he was in seminary, his wife developed a severe infection in her hand. My father provided the funds for her successful surgery. A few months later, my young father died from a heart attack caused by a rare blood disease he contracted in the Philippines.

As I read this letter, tears filled my eyes. I was grateful that this friend had taken time to write me. He introduced me to stories about my parents that I now cherish. And he also helped me realize that the good we do during our lives endures long after us. Indeed, we may never be aware of our greatest contributions.

Father, may I trust that You will transform loving actions into ageless good.
—SCOTT WALKER

Wed 20 *And God called the dry land Earth . . . and God saw that it was good.* —GENESIS 1:10

My husband Keith is the plant person at our house. He feeds, waters and trims them, and is very proud when they grow.

When last spring came, it was time to repot the bromeliads that stand on the kitchen windowsill. Keith bought the appropriate-sized clay pots, each with its own matching tray to catch the water. And, as he usually did when we lived in Los Angeles, he put a layer of pebbles in the tray to protect the bottoms of the pots from the water when it drained through.

I've always thought of pebbles as a sterile medium—just decoration, and not very pretty decoration at that. The market, the craft store and the discount stores sold bags of attractive glass beads in many colors. Why couldn't Keith use them instead of the mottled black-and-gray pebbles?

Then summer arrived, and the sun shone brightly on the bromeliads.

"Come look at this," Keith said, waving me toward the kitchen window.

"Are the bromeliads blooming again?" I asked him.

"No," he said. "The pebbles are."

Emerging from the pebble layer under both bromeliad pots were the uncurling fronds of ferns. "Wow," I said. "There must have been spores in with the pebbles."

I think I would have taken the glass beads for granted in a short time. But for the next few weeks, as the fronds continued to unroll and share their space in the window with the bromeliads, the pebbles I'd thought ugly gave me an unexpected gift of loveliness.

I apologize, Lord, for considering any part of Your creation worthless. Thank You for the surprises You bring with summer's warmth.
—Rhoda Blecker

Thu 21

Give to every one who begs from you.... —Luke 6:30 (RSV)

I was sitting outside on a bench near the office, having a sandwich, when a scruffy fellow with a backpack came up to me, asking for change. "I'm sorry," I said. "I can't give you anything." The usual reasons flashed through my head: *I don't know what he's going to do with the money, probably spend it on drugs. I don't want to encourage that. How can I trust him?*

But then I thought of all the biblical exhortations to give no matter who asks. What did I know of this guy's situation? Why couldn't I help? I started to get a little more worried about me. Why couldn't I be more generous in my thoughts? Why go through life so suspicious? *Next time*, I promised, *I'll do better.*

Be careful of such promises. No sooner had I got up from my bench than I saw the guy again, now standing outside a deli, staring at the food inside. "Can I buy you something to eat?" I offered.

"Sure," he said. He picked up a bag of chips and a Coke.

Suddenly I felt like his mom. "You should also have something more nutritious than that," I said. I put a banana in his hands. He took the items to the counter and I paid for them.

"Do you know anybody who's hiring around here?" he asked.

"No," I said.

"Do you know a place where I could stay?"

"A church a couple of blocks away has a shelter. They also offer counseling. You might talk to them." I gave him the address and we parted ways.

I haven't seen him since, but there are others like him all over town. When I do something for any of them, I do something for me.

God, give me a generous heart.
—RICK HAMLIN

June

Fri 22

Behold, how good and how pleasant it is for brethren to dwell together in unity! —PSALM 133:1

Mom's seventy-fifth birthday was approaching. How could we possibly give her a gift that would honor all that she is to us? The question hung in the back of my mind for close to a year.

Petite, gentle, a wiz with a needle, a steadfast friend, a quiet source of brainpower and energy, and a passionate lover of her family, Mom focuses on others and on making their lives better. She's the center around which our family circle revolves.

Finally I found the answer to my question: We'd make Mom a quilt! We'd each contribute fabrics of our own choosing to make the quilt a tangible reflection of the people she loves so dearly.

My sister Priscilla brought her great design sense to the undertaking. Katrina, my other sister, helped us find a color scheme. Then we sent each family member off to find two fabrics through which to reflect him or her in the quilt.

And that's where the real challenge began! As I opened the packages of fabric from my nieces, nephews, children and father, my heart sank—*Oh, Lord, how would all these swatches ever come together into something of beauty?* All I could see were clashing designs of tawny chickens, multicolor peace signs, Dad's fabric stamped with a symbol of the high school where he'd met Mom, the subtle batik we'd chosen to represent her.

That any pattern could bring so many different elements together was hard to imagine. And yet, as the quilt was stitched, a miraculous beauty began to appear from the multiplicity of designs, styles and colors. And there before my eyes appeared Mom's gift to all of us: These disparate swatches, representing the people she loved, came together piece by piece into a beautiful interconnected pattern.

Dear Lord, help me to always discern the pattern of my connectedness to others.
—ANNE ADRIANCE

Sat 23   *You will keep in perfect peace him whose mind is steadfast, because he trusts in you.* —ISAIAH 26:3 (NIV)

We lost our son Reggie on June 23, 2004, and we always face the anniversary of that day with heavy hearts. As June 23 approached a couple of years ago, my wife Rosie told me about an experience she'd had.

"Dolphus, I was driving the other day, in pain and feeling discouraged, when I saw the most beautiful rainbow. I remembered how, after the flood, God made the rainbow a sign of his promises.

"On that same day, I was reading a card we'd received from a group formed to connect those who had lost children. It had pictures of a rainbow and a butterfly on it, and the word *hope*. God surely used the rainbow and the card to remind me that He is our hope."

Rosie's story was a welcome reminder that our God and Father watches over us and sends us messages of His calming presence when we need Him most.

Lord, when my heart is heavy, open my eyes every day to the signs of Your presence around me.
—DOLPHUS WEARY

Sun 24

Many waters cannot quench love; rivers cannot wash it away.
—SONG OF SOLOMON 8:7 (NIV)

Louis Molinneli was born in Italy more than one hundred years ago. When he became a young man, he fell in love with Angela Lazerato. Louis lived a long day's hike from Angela. He visited her for a few precious hours in the evening and, after staying overnight at an inn, hiked home the next day. One day when he hiked to see her, she was gone. Her parents had sent her to America to work as a servant for five years.

Louis didn't know where in America Angela was. He hoped America was smaller than Italy and that she would be less than a day's hike from New York City, his ship's destination.

When he wasn't working, Louis searched for Angela. But no matter where he went, no one knew anyone named Angela Lazerato. Louis decided to try to find her all the way across his new nation in California. During his journey by train, he stopped to see a friend in Chicago. The day before he was supposed to continue his trip, he went to church in North Chicago.

On that same day, a lonely young woman who still had four years to go in her five-year contract as a servant working for a family in North Chicago also decided to go to church. She missed the man she loved, who lived an ocean away.

Louis never did use his train ticket to California. There in church, against all odds, he found Angela.

Louis and Angela's grandson Bob, one of many people I have grown to love at our church, shared this story with me. I hope every church—in Chicago, in a small town in Colorado or anywhere in the world—is always a place where people find love.

Dear Father, thank You for allowing us to find people to love, and Your own great love, in Your house.
—TIM WILLIAMS

⁂ REDEEMING THE TIME

Mon 25 *I sought the Lord; and he answered me; he delivered me from all my fears.* —PSALM 34:4 (NIV)

DAY 1: THE DECISION

Y ou should retire," they kept saying. I found that I resented these well-wishing friends. Were they implying that I was no longer good at my job? Certainly I was tired more often, frustrated by day-to-day management changes. But retirement? That seemed to be an end-of-life marker or a trip to a sparkly new community with safety bars at every step.

I pray through choices like this. I have prolonged conversations with the Lord, always trying to listen for a hint or a direction. And the hints came. My doctor suggested that retirement would give me a healthier lifestyle, with no more long days and exhausting travel. I listened. My husband thought it was time. My best friend announced her own retirement. But still I hesitated. I worked in the world of books: How would our readers manage without me? And I would painfully miss my colleagues of twenty-plus years.

More prayer. More hesitation. Then quite suddenly, the way became clear. I wrote a short note announcing my formal retirement and was looking at five more weeks in the world as I had always known it. I told people about my decision, knowing that would make it harder to change my mind.

But I did it. I got the party and a lovely necklace, lots of hugs and good wishes. And then I sneaked out of the office alone, unable to deal with any more good-byes.

Hello, new life.

> *Dear Lord, thank You for always listening to*
> *my conflicts and confusions. And thank You*
> *for Your constant presence.*
> —BRIGITTE WEEKS

 REDEEMING THE TIME

Tue 26

"Blessed are you who are poor, for yours is the kingdom of God. Blessed are you who hunger now, for you will be satisfied...."
—LUKE 6:20–21 (NIV)

DAY 2: MAKING A DIFFERENCE

One of the hardest things about trying to reinvent your life as a retired person is the helpful suggestions others offer to fill up all the free time they're sure will materialize. And then there are those who tell you how wonderful it will be to have nothing to do. The former made me feel like a failure ("I don't have any hobbies," I'd point out in subdued tones), and the second just terrified me.

From looking around, thinking hard and praying some more, I knew learning a new language or building ship models were not for me. I wanted to do something with people, something that would feel worthwhile even though I was convinced that nothing could ever replace my lifelong love affair with books.

Eventually, two ideas came quietly into my muddled head and I knew somehow that I should listen and explore them both. "Seek, and ye shall find" (Matthew 7:7), and I did. I'm now a trained and certified volunteer in end-of-life hospice care, and I've qualified as a tutor to help adults learn to read. That was another horrifying idea—a lifetime without reading, no travel, no medical visits, no way to help with children's homework. My students want to get driver's licenses, know which subway stop they're at and be able to order lunch from a menu. In hospice training, I learned that hundreds of seniors in the busy city of New York are living alone and struggling to stay in their homes. I knew I had lots still to learn, but I saw that I could be *useful* and that was what really mattered.

> *Thank You, Lord, for listening and helping me to begin to find my way.*
> —BRIGITTE WEEKS

 REDEEMING THE TIME

Wed 27 *The blessing of the Lord makes one rich....* —PROVERBS 10:22 (NKJV)

DAY 3: COUNT YOUR BLESSINGS

I had made some steps toward a new life, but no one promised me a rose garden. One day I woke up with no classes on the calendar, no meetings with friends. *So this is what busy people envy: having nothing to do.* It's hard to admit, but I began to panic. This didn't look like leisure; it looked like a black hole. *What's the matter with me?*

As someone who has struggled with depression from time to time, the whole scenario unrolled before me as I sat over my morning coffee: *I'll just grow old in a flash and be useless. My children will find me a burden. Whatever made me think I should retire?* "It's too late to change your mind," I told myself and heard my late mother's stern voice: *"Now, Brigitte, count your blessings!"*

So I took a deep breath and counted my blessings. There was my loyal and patient husband of more than forty years; the five small grandchildren, exhausting but full of life; and then the books—learning to read purely for pleasure wasn't easy either, but I could read just for me rather than on behalf of hundreds of unseen readers. Simple ideas helped: Put at least one item on the calendar for each day. Reach out to busy friends. Wage war on the scattered piles of paper. And, not to be forgotten, count your blessings!

Dear Lord: Only with Your help can I build a new life and dedicate it to Your service and Your people.
—BRIGITTE WEEKS

REDEEMING THE TIME

 *Thu 28*   *Precious in the sight of the Lord is the death of his saints.*
—PSALM 116:15 (NIV)

DAY 4: TAKING CARE

My first hospice patient was very sick indeed, but that's what I had been trained for: to help her or her caretakers, to take a small part of the burden. During most of my visits she was either asleep or had nothing to say. I understood that, and wondered if a quiet activity would be helpful or disturbing. There's a lot to learn about hospice care; each patient is entirely different. But on my third visit I brought my knitting, a simple blanket. She raised her hand to touch it, and so I began to knit while her full-time caretaker dashed out to do the grocery shopping. We were alone together. She seemed soothed by watching me.

I knitted; she dozed. Then suddenly she said quite clearly, pointing to the work on my lap, "What's that?"

"It's a blanket for my grandson," I answered. She nodded and closed her eyes.

Parkinson's disease won the battle a few weeks later. I wasn't there, but her daughter was and told me she had slipped away very peacefully. *Another life to turn over to God,* I thought, and prayed that she continue in peace. I felt glad to have done the small amount that I could. *Maybe I can be useful after all,* I thought, and silently thanked my late patient.

> *Dear God, bless all those at the end of life and hold them safe in Your love.*
> —BRIGITTE WEEKS

REDEEMING THE TIME

Fri 29

*A heart at peace gives life to the body.... —*PROVERBS 14:30 (NIV)

DAY 5: SERENITY

Serenity is a beautiful word. I've always loved the way it sounds, but during those first few weeks and months of retirement it seemed as elusive as a butterfly.

Then came three-year old Andrew, a middle child, to visit Grandma all by himself for a few days. Grandma, who now had time to entertain him as the king of the roost. "Get Play-Doh" followed by "Puppets?" were at the top of my to-do list instead of "Negotiate contract, Write report, Schedule meeting about meetings."

Then there was my bicycle, covered with dust and in need of a tune-up. New York had sprouted miles of bike paths while I wasn't paying attention. And reading a book just for fun felt wonderfully daring.

It turns out that serenity isn't staring into the peaceful distance; it's cycling across town and picking pieces of Play-Doh off the floor and passing on the amazing gift of reading to others, to mention just a few ingredients. Serenity will come and go;

I know that. But now that I have it by the tail, it won't escape me for too long.

Thank You, Lord, for sending me the gifts of joy and peace of mind. Help me to keep them alive and share them with others.
—BRIGITTE WEEKS

Sat 30

I do set my bow in the cloud . . . a token of a covenant. . . .
—GENESIS 9:13

It started as a sweet friendship between two people who had gone through their own dark seasons and had found themselves in a better place because of it. Soon Corinne and I discovered that we shared much more. Both of us are native Nashvillians and have a passion to serve our city. We both grew up in close loving families, and we both believed that commitment to church provides a solid foundation for life's challenges.

Although Corinne had never been married, she doted on her nephews and nieces and was great with children. So when it was time for her to meet my son Harrison, they were a natural fit.

One night, sitting in a Nashville restaurant known for its view of the city, we began talking about our grandmothers. Corinne's maternal grandmother had been known for her kindness to the "least of these," something else we had in common, since my grandmother Bebe's good works are many.

I began telling Corinne about Bebe's importance in my life. When I was a little boy, we were staying at our family cabin when a fantastic rainbow spread across the lake. As we stood there in awe, Bebe began telling me that God sends rainbows to remind us of His love. "And don't forget, Brock, God also expects something back for all that love He sends."

Suddenly we were interrupted by our waitress: "You might want to turn around and enjoy the view," she said. "It's something I don't think we've ever seen here before." There, spread across the city sky, was the most vibrant and perfectly formed rainbow we had ever seen.

Less than three months later, I asked Corinne to be my wife.

> *Father, let us live our lives giving back,*
> *as You have given to us.*
> —BROCK KIDD

MY PATHWAY TO PEACE

1 _____

2 _____

3 _____

4 _____

5 _____

6 _____

7 _____

8 _____

9 _____

10 _____

11 _____

12 _____

13 _____

14 _____

15 _____

June

16 _____

17 _____

18 _____

19 _____

20 _____

21 _____

22 _____

23 _____

24 _____

25 _____

26 _____

27 _____

28 _____

29 _____

30 _____

July

Now the God of hope fill you with all joy and peace in believing, that ye may abound in hope, through the power of the Holy Ghost.

—ROMANS 15:13

Sun 1

*And God saw every thing that he had made, and, behold, it was very good.... —*GENESIS 1:31

Platoro is an old mining town sitting at ten thousand feet above sea level in southern Colorado. Because the scenery is so beautiful, more than a hundred families have built summer cabins up there, including us. The place looks like a setting for a John Wayne movie, with its log houses, rough dirt roads and smoking chimneys. The people are friendly and supportive if someone needs help, and they interact with each other in old-fashioned ways, such as throwing potluck suppers every now and then for the entire town.

Another thing they do is hold outdoor church services every Sunday where everyone is welcome, no matter what their religious background. The "pews" are planks bolted to logs. Three large wooden crosses loom on a nearby bluff, anchored by heavy chains. Behind the crosses, on top of the bluff, are bristlecone pine trees, said to be the oldest living things on the earth. Some bristlecones have been found that are more than two thousand years old. When I look at those trees on the bluff, I wonder, "Have you been growing there since before Jesus was born?"

The service this past weekend was particularly moving. Our song leader led us first in "God Bless

America" and then in "America the Beautiful." As we sang, I looked up into the deep royal-blue sky that you see only at high altitudes. Then I looked at the rugged mountains that encircle the town. High above us that day soared an eagle. My heart swelled with love for the world and for God Himself. All I could say was, "Thank You."

> *Lord, I will pick up trash, continue my recycling efforts, conserve our city water as instructed and urge others to live "Green."*
> —Madge Harrah

THIS I KNOW

Mon 2 *Be content . . . and let thine heart be merry.* —Judges 19:6

A GIFT AT PARTING

After David and I were married, we went to serve a remote Appalachian parish. For everyone involved, there was a huge learning curve. David was a thinker, fresh to the faith, while I was a young, naive do-gooder, used to a comfortable life. The people in our new world were uneducated and desperately poor. But we gave each other a chance, and things happened.

While the men schooled David in real faith, the women taught me to make stack cake and rhubarb cobbler. They shared their stories with me and showed me how to be content with simple living. And as poor as they were, they joined me in serving the poorest. But finally, after two-and-a-half years, it was time to leave.

When the women insisted on giving "the preacher's wife" a going-away party, I went with a heavy heart, knowing how little they had to give. Yet there on the table amid cakes and pies and Jell-O, was an elegantly wrapped package bearing the seal of an upscale store in a distant town.

Suddenly they were all talking at once: "We rode the bus all that way. . . . We've all been saving our money."

Inside the box was a pair of red crystal candlesticks.

For years, the candlesticks made me sad. I saw only a sacrifice that made the givers poorer. And then one day, as I was polishing the candlesticks and remembering, truth descended. It had been written across their faces. It had sung through the lilt in their voices. Giving all they had to a young woman who had come to love them for a time hadn't diminished their meager resources. Giving had made them rich.

Father, let my heart be merry and my soul
content with what I have given away.
—PAM KIDD

Tue 3

Above all else, guard your heart, for everything you do flows from it.
—PROVERBS 4:23 (NIV)

Rush had been my best friend for years. He had been the "buddy" assigned to me on my first day of elementary school. Over the next eight years, even though he became class president and I stayed awkward and shy, we grew closer and closer. But he went away for high school, and we barely saw each other anymore.

Now it was summer, and he was visiting me in Maine. We had kayaked to a small island off the coast and were now sitting around a fire, alternately warming hot dogs and roasting marshmallows.

We'd passed the time pleasantly enough, but I was ready for him to leave. I had had a hard time adjusting to high school, too frightened around new people to make friends. Knowing this only heightened how inferior I felt to Rush.

"Look at that," Rush said, pointing out to the ocean. It was a circle of moonlight on the water, concentrated as if a spotlight was shining from the sky.

"Do you think we could paddle out to it?" I asked. "To be in the light?"

We paddled for ten minutes, but the light seemed no closer. We kept going, faster and faster, thinking we could catch up with it that way. But we never did.

So we let our arms rest and the kayak drift in the gentle Maine sea. And there, surrounded by nothing but ocean, we really talked for the first time in years, about high school and where our lives had gone in our time apart.

Finally Rush said, "School's hard, being alone with no one you know. It's really, really hard."

I knew something now. I had a friendship here, strong and enduring, and in my unease with him before, I'd just been chasing moonbeams.

> *Dear Lord, thank You for revealing*
> *what is truly important.*
> —SAM ADRIANCE

Wed 4

Now the Lord is the Spirit; and where the Spirit of the Lord is, there is liberty.
—II CORINTHIANS 3:17 (NKJV)

Tonight my family is being treated to a fireworks extravaganza that surpasses any we've seen elsewhere, thanks to the neighborhoods surrounding us. We live on Sunset Pond in Mandeville, Louisiana, and its wide-open landscape of water and sky makes our backyard the perfect theater in which to watch the show.

At dusk we turn our lawn chairs toward the pond, the children and grandchildren full of anticipation.

Then, it begins: *Boom!* The first of hundreds of fireworks launch into the sky, exploding into red chrysanthemum sprays, blue strobes and flaming silver-and-gold clusters that flash over us like a gallery of flickering lights. We *ooh* and *aah* and cheer the bottle rockets, the strobes and the spinners that light up the night sky.

My grandson Indy can hardly contain his excitement. He's jumping up and down on the backyard trampoline, shouting as loudly as he can between each jump, "This is incredible! This is incredible!"

I dash inside to get my camera, hoping to capture the Fourth of July sky over Sunset Pond. Once inside, I look out through the large windows that frame a perfect picture of my backyard. I see fireworks exploding into the air, with the pond mirroring it all, and my kids and grandkids cheering on this magnificent show.

Then I notice the ceramic plaque hanging next to the windows. Painted on it is an angel flying through the sky, draped in red, white and blue ribbons, with stars and stripes on her wings. A banner flies above her head that reads: FAITH, FAMILY, FREEDOM.

A feeling of gratitude rushes over me for the blessings offered by this angel-patriot. I have a joyful faith in the Lord, a family to cherish and the freedom to celebrate the independence of my country tonight.

*God of liberty, thank You for freeing my heart
to love and to be loved.*
—MELODY BONNETTE

Thu 5   *"The Lord gave, and the Lord has
taken away; Blessed be the name of the
Lord."* —JOB 1:21 (NKJV)

I'm at the age where my brain is approaching the
"full" mark. If I want to put something new in it,
I have to be ready to give up something I've known
for a long time. For example, I recently decided to
memorize the name and size of my truck motor so
I don't have to look it up at the auto parts store. My
brain had this conversation with me:

1. Brain: *So, you want to learn the name of your truck
   engine?*

2. Me: "Right, I need to remember it's Duratec,
   Three-Point-Oh Flex Fuel."

3. Brain: *Well, what are you willing to forget so I
   can make room for this?*

4. Me: "Forget? I don't want to forget anything."

5. Brain: *How about your name? You don't use it
   much any more.*

6. Me: "My name? Well, okay, whatever."

And that's how it happened that when the lady at the license bureau asked me for my name, I replied, "Duratec." And when she looked puzzled, I added, "Three-Point-Oh, Flex Fuel."

The loss of memory is only one of many losses in middle age. I can no longer run, due to bad feet, but I can still ride my bike. I don't multitask well any more, but then multitasking was never a good idea. I can't get through the day without a nap, but if I had known how wonderful naps are, I would have started taking them long ago.

I could rage about the losses I feel, but that's exhausting and pointless. It's far better to embrace them and find the humor in them. It's the only way to be at peace. "The Lord has taken away; blessed be the name of the Lord."

I thank You, Father, for all the good things I have left.
Help me to enjoy them and not to dwell on
what has slipped away.
—DANIEL SCHANTZ

Fri 6

As a fair exchange—I speak as to my children—open wide your hearts also.
—II CORINTHIANS 6:13 (NIV)

Jojo arrived last Sunday, cute and fluffy and white. He's a loaner, a test case; we'll be boarding him for two weeks while his owners are in France. The kids have promised to walk him and feed him. I have my doubts, but so far they've done their part.

Deep down, I like dogs. I grew up with them: Gulliver, a basset hound I wheeled in a baby stroller; Gretchen, a German short-haired pointer who wagged her entire rear end; and little Gretel, who jumped the six-foot fence and was hit by a car. I cried into the fur of Ding and Penny, the dogs who helped me make it through adolescence. But I haven't ever owned a dog as an adult.

Jojo is an apartment-size dog, small and decorative. He yips when the doorbell rings and needs to be shampooed and brushed regularly. I did not think I would like him, but I do. The latent teenager in me is pleased that Jojo wags for me. He wants to curl up on my lap and to greet me when I walk in the door. Except for a few nights at the beginning, Jojo has demanded very little of me beyond physical affection. And the kids love him.

I'm still not sure if we'll get a dog; it's a lot more work than I care to supervise. But my heart has opened to the possibility. And an open heart counts as progress, even if it's only about dogs.

Jesus, open my heart so I can love more fully.
—JULIA ATTAWAY

Sat 7   *The shame of my face hath covered me.*
        —PSALM 44:15

Who doesn't love receiving a thank-you note? Who doesn't purr a little receiving a few words of recognition for a kindness? Usually I save my notes to read when I feel unappreciated; however, this one that just arrived upsets me—I did nothing to deserve it.

Oh, my intentions were good: bake brownies for the funeral reception of one of our elderly parishioners. I gladly signed up to help with such a simple request. Besides, I truly admired George and his devoted wife, who called him "dearest." What a privilege to offer a final tribute to the sweet man.

That Saturday morning, I duly baked the brownies, and while they were cooling, flopped on the couch for a quick nap. The recent heat wave had zapped me, so I hadn't been sleeping too well at night. When I awoke, the funeral—and reception—were long over. Later I would hear that the church was packed, so no one would have noticed that I wasn't there. Even if my friends were aware of my absence, they would forgive me, I'm sure. Still, I look at this gracious, unwarranted thank-you from the church ladies who hold me in such high regard—and feel awful.

I may have lost one opportunity to serve; however, I can redeem myself by finding others, perhaps smaller and less visible. For example, instead of signing up for events (and risking an unwarranted thank-you), I just show up. Wherever there's food, I can always help by serving, wiping tables, laundering tea towels and washing dishes. Almost any time, I can drop off canned goods and paper products at the church Food Pantry. I don't need a thank-you note. God knows.

Gracious Lord, forgive me for the times I've neglected to help. Give me more chances to get it right.
—GAIL THORELL SCHILLING

Sun 8

"He will wipe every tear from their eyes. There will be no more death or mourning or crying or pain, for the old order of things has passed away."
—REVELATION 21:4 (NIV)

One summer Sunday morning after the early service, I was in the side garden of our church pulling up a few weeds when I noticed a fiftyish woman new to our congregation. She was studying a plate-sized, cloud-white bloom on a sturdy vine.

"What is the name of this flower?" she asked with an urgency that drew me to her side.

"It's a moon flower," I said. "It only blooms once and always at night. It has the most wonderful fragrance," I added, bending down to breathe its perfume.

"Oh," she said, "moon flower! That's it! All these years I'd forgotten. But just now this wonderful memory's come back. I was about three when my mother planted one of these. She waited and waited for it to bloom. Every night she'd go out and check and come inside disappointed. Then one night she rushed into the house all excited, pulled Dad and me out to the garden, and pointed to this exquisite white flower standing out against the darkness.

"I can still see Mom's face that night and hear her saying over and over, 'It was worth the wait.'"

The woman touched the flower. "Isn't it amazing how a memory can bring someone back?"

She left with a spring in her step. I went back to my weeding, pondering this gift from a fragile moon flower on its way to dust.

Thank You, Father, for sudden blooms of memory that, while they cannot last, refresh me on my journey toward my everlasting home.
—SHARI SMYTH

Mon 9

Giving thanks always for all things unto God and the Father in the name of our Lord Jesus Christ.
—EPHESIANS 5:20

When it came time for Vacation Bible School, the children looked forward to being led by Uncle Al. The sanctuary was crammed full of kids when he bounded in saying, "Good morning, boys and girls!" They all shouted back, "Good morning, Uncle Al!"

Al had a bag of tricks up his sleeve like none other, and a unique way of motivating the kids to memorize the scripture verse for the day. On one occasion the verse was Proverbs 15:1 (TLB): "A soft answer turns away wrath, but harsh words cause quarrels." I was helping out that day, and we decided that bottles of bubble mix would work. Al enlisted the help of several volunteer college kids. They stood in the balcony of the sanctuary and on cue blew thousands of bubbles down on the children.

"These are the words you speak," Al said. "Now gather up the bubbles and put them back in the bottles!" Chaos ensued as hundreds of little hands tried catching bubbles. "See, once you say something, it's almost impossible to take it back."

Behind Uncle Al's cheery disposition was his unswerving gratitude to the Lord for all his blessings. During the last year of his life, wrestling with a devastating illness, Uncle Al rallied his family around Romans 12:12, which tells us to be joyful in hope, patient in affliction and faithful in prayer. When the Lord took him home, his memorial service was filled with two generations of his VBS kids. His smiling face lit up the front of the program. On the back page was Al's spiritual watchword: "Live each day with an attitude of gratitude!"

As he entered Your presence, Lord Jesus, I can hear
the angels shouting, "Good morning, Uncle Al!"
—FAY ANGUS

Tue 10

I dwell in the high and holy place,
with him also that is of a contrite
and humble spirit, to revive the
spirit of the humble, and to revive
the heart of the contrite ones.
—ISAIAH 57:15

I was in the office, trying to tie a bow tie and having no luck. My father always wore bow ties; he looked splendid in them, elegant and debonair. I don't remember him ever having problems tying them. His ties were all perfect butterflies.

I stared into the mirror in the bathroom, trying to remember how to do it. Dad had taught me once years ago: "Take the loose end over the top and then go around the back and through the knot . . . "

The loose end of silk looked pretty foolish dangling around my neck. Every time it was supposed to make a neat bow, I'd have one long wing sticking out and a sliver of something else on the other side; a very lopsided butterfly that would never have made it out of the cocoon.

I'd picked up the tie as I dashed out of the house, convinced it would go with my jacket. Carol could have helped me tie it at home, but I was in a hurry. Now I had nothing. Just as I was about to give up, I remembered that my colleague Amy used to help our boss Edward with his bow ties.

I dropped by her office and asked, "Could you help me, please?"

"Sure," she said. She undid the mess hanging around my neck and started over. In less than a minute she created a masterpiece: a perfect butterfly at my throat, making me a dandy for a day.

"Maybe God likes me to wear bow ties," I suggested to her, "so that I'll know how to ask for help."

Clothes might make the man, but humility is even more important. Next time you see some guy in a bow tie, just ask him who tied it.

Make humility my most important garment, O God.
—RICK HAMLIN

�֍ A GRACE-FILLED JOURNEY

Wed 11

Yea, he did fly upon the wings of the wind. —PSALM 18:10

LED BY THE WIND

Our schedule is interrupted today because of gale-force winds that prevent us from docking at Delos. So we have an exciting day on the sea and arrive at Mykonos after dark.

What a magical sight! As we stroll unhurried along the waterfront, Robert calls my attention to the lights of our ship anchored some distance from the shore. She looks like scattered diamonds on black velvet! As we wander through narrow streets, restaurant owners beckon us to "sit down and have something."

"No thanks. We're just enjoying the walk." Holding hands, we amble around the quaint but very much alive little island town to the tune of a Greek love song playing at a sidewalk café.

When it's time to get back to the ship, we realize we've lost our way. So we ask a couple of young men how to get to the waterfront. "Just follow the breeze and it'll take you there." This good advice gets us back to our floating home.

Did you know that the Hebrew word for *wind* *(ruach)* means *spirit?* And the Greek word for *breath* *(pneuma)* also means *spirit?* From now on, when I hear the wind blowing, I'll not complain. Instead, I'll let the streaming air remind me that the Holy Spirit is with me, guiding me in the direction of home. And I'll let myself be led.

Holy Spirit, make Your presence known to me in the flowing wind, so I can follow You.
—Marilyn Morgan King

Thu 12

For behold, I will save you from afar.... —Jeremiah 46:27(NKJV)

During the 1950s, money—or the lack of it—was a worry for Ruby and me. I was working forty hours a week, but we needed to buy furniture. Even a Saturday job couldn't close the gap between our income and our needs. I tried depositing a dollar a week in a bank-sponsored vacation club, but I never accumulated more than a few dollars; something always took it away. I didn't know what to do.

Then a co-worker told me about his summer vacation in a small town in Maine. "The people there have little money, but they have a great way of saving. They call it 'quartering.' Each quarter they receive in change is slipped into a piggy bank. At the end of the year, they have about a hundred and eighty dollars for birthdays, vacation and Christmas." I liked the idea, so I bought a glass piggy bank. It was fun to deposit the quarters from my change. It reminded me of slipping pennies away years ago.

I applied the same discipline to my church pledge. I found that when I took the pledge money out first, we never missed it. And doing that helped us control impulsive spending. Quartering brought me a sense of financial peace.

I still continue quartering, but now, thank the Lord, it's just for fun.

Gracious Spirit, when I took the first step, You were there to lead the way and to guide me always.
—OSCAR GREENE

Fri 13   *But You, O Lord, be not far off; O You my help, hasten to my assistance.*
—PSALM 22:19 (NAS)

We spent two weeks last summer with our son Nathan, his wife Jessica and our fifteen-month-old granddaughter Ella Grace on an idyllic lake in New Hampshire. Grandma and Grandpa rented the cabin, and Nathan and Jessica provided the granddaughter—the perfect recipe for a magnificent vacation.

Ella was walking everywhere into everything and just learning and using her first words. And, with credit to Nate and Jess, Ella is about as happy, curious, friendly, independent and obedient as a toddler can be. One of the best things they have taught her is to ask for help. If a toy needed winding or a glass needed filling, Ella would hold it up to the nearest adult and say, "Hep."

One early morning while everyone else slept in, she and I walked down to the sandy spot on the lake next to our dock. Self-driven and determined, Ella was speeding ahead, leaving Grandpa to follow. Along the way were obstacles: a closed door, steps on the path and, finally, a retaining wall near the water just higher than her little legs could manage. At each one, without looking back, she reached her little hand toward me and exclaimed, "Hep!"

Sitting on the dock, watching her splash in the shallows as the sun warmed the morning, the thought came to me of how like Ella I'd like to be. She just started off into her day, knowing I would be right there when she needed me. When a problem arose, she didn't fret, whine or quit; she simply raised her hand and asked for help, fully expecting I would have the ability to handle whatever obstructed her. Once past the obstacle, she rushed ahead to the next one, confident I would be there every time she needed me.

Hep, Lord, hep.
—Eric Fellman

Sat 14

"I proclaim to you new things from this time...." —Isaiah 48:6 (NAS)

Rick and I married right out of high school. After thirty years together, we still love each other, but we've settled into a rut. Up at six, work, eat dinner, and then TV for him and reading for me.

As we sat in the den together one night, I felt far away from Rick. While he watched an ESPN special, I said, "Do you ever miss me?"

"How can I miss you? You're right here."

"Do you ever feel that things are sort of humdrum? You know, 'same old, same old'?"

"I guess so."

The following Saturday afternoon, Rick bought two hummingbird feeders for the front corners of our wraparound porch. For the past few years, the birds had arrived in April and left in late September, eating at the two feeders we'd put out back. We'd had no hummingbird sightings this year. Rick whistled as he put up the two new feeders and filled all four with food.

You're wasting your time, I thought. *They're not coming back. Our best times are over too.*

"Tomorrow morning we're having a porch party," Rick announced. "Six fifteen. Just you and me."

"What's a porch party?" I asked.

"You'll see."

As we sat on the porch the next morning, ahead of the Georgia heat, we seemed to be covered in a lavender-shaded mist.

"Look over your shoulder," Rick whispered. Two hummingbirds were at one of the new feeders!

"Can you believe it?" I said. "They came back."

"Maybe they were waiting on us."

Hallelujah, Lord! You do make all things new.
—JULIE GARMON

Sun 15

The righteous will be remembered forever. —PSALM 112:6 (NAS)

A plaque among attractive flowerbeds on the grounds of a church I once attended read, "She saw beauty in flowers." And in the children's courtyard another inscription said, "She loved children." As I read these brief words describing two women I had never met, I began to think about how I might want to be remembered in a simple sentence:

"She saw the courage in every elderly person."
"She liked to kick in autumn leaves."
"She needed God."
"She cried over the wonder of words."
"Her favorite name for Jesus was Morning Star."
"She befriended her neighbors."
"She always wanted to live in a tree house."
"She loved her name: Carol, song of joy."

One sentence can tell a magnificent story. Condensing my life in this way is much like reducing a sauce by simmering it on the stove. I get the fullest, richest flavor of who I am—and I can offer this to God for His good work.

Why not try it?

Lord, help me concentrate on the essentials—
the beautiful, simple, truthful things.
—CAROL KNAPP

READER'S ROOM

I'm so thankful to have been born in a country where I can worship my Lord freely, where I'm able to pray to God daily and to pray with friends without any fears.

—*Carolyn Malion, Fairmont, North Carolina*

Mon 16

While I was with them in the world, I kept them in thy name: those that thou gavest me I have kept.... —JOHN 17:12

My grandsons Rome and Kodi and I slowly made our way toward the shore. Rome was letting the tide carry him in on a lime-green inner tube we'd found; Kodi and I were splashing through the rising current beside him, calling out the jellyfish we spotted and the crabs that came floating upside down on the tide. I'd brought them to Boundary Bay because I knew the sunny weather and the tide would create a rare and perfect combination to replay days from my own childhood: heated sandbars and bath-temperature water.

Boundary Bay is a large but shallow and sheltered bay on the Canadian-American border in the Pacific Northwest, and here, years ago, my father had built Grandpa's beach house. Here, the moon can carry the tide out a mile, right out to the stone-and-concrete marker that separates the two countries. I'd taken this walk a thousand times with my grandfather and cousins; now I was taking it again with my grandsons.

My thoughts splashed back and forth in time as I treated Rome and Kodi to their heritage. Grandpa had actually put it into his will to give this to them, but it was up to me to provide it. And this is the gift I was giving his great-great grandchildren, unknown but anticipated: not just a day at the bay, but the knowledge of Grandpa's—and my own— provision and love for them.

Dear God, I stand as the bridge between my grandfather and my grandsons. Keep me faithful to the heritage of Grandpa's love for You—and his love for the generations to come.
—BRENDA WILBEE

Tue 17   *This is to my Father's glory, that you bear much fruit, showing yourselves to be my disciples.* —JOHN 15:8 (NIV)

Last summer I set out three tomato plants. Two promptly disappeared in the night, dug up by some mysterious animal who left craterlike holes to mark my loss. On the sole surviving plant I hung all my hopes for growing fresh tomatoes. Finally, a tiny green ball appeared, one tiny green ball that grew into one midsized tomato—my entire crop for the season.

This morning, I planted three tomato plants . . . again. I placed them in a different spot, in the corner of my big flowerbed. I'm hoping my nocturnal creature with a penchant for tomato plants won't find them. I'm hoping they'll get better sunlight. I'm hoping for more than one tomato.

My mother used to say, "Anything worth doing is worth doing well." So as a child I was taught to do my chores with an eye toward perfection—whether it was ironing pillowcases, washing hundreds of cobwebby jars at the start of canning season or choosing raspberries to freeze for my annual 4-H project. It was all to be done . . . well, *well*.

But I'd like to amend that aphorism of Mother's: "Anything worth doing is worth doing . . . again . . . and again, if necessary." So what if you don't succeed? That's what second attempts were made for! Practice may not make perfect, but it does make practicing a habit. And that's a good thing.

I like to imagine that even now my tomato plants are putting down roots that will let them stretch toward the summer sun flooding that bit of yard.

I want to stretch, too, beyond the comfort of things I do well. I think that the God who created second chances—and tomato plants—would be pleased with that.

Give me courage to grow in new and exciting ways—and to bear much fruit.
—MARY LOU CARNEY

Wed 18

Blessed are your eyes, for they see: and your ears, for they hear.
—Matthew 13:16

One time many years ago I was bustling along an alley in Rome when a lady who looked to be about five hundred years old stared at me and grinned and said quietly, *"Cosa c'è?"* I didn't know what it meant, so I stopped, thinking that maybe she needed assistance. *"Cosa c'è?"* she said again, very gently.

"No Italian," I said, smiling but feeling stupid. Her face was so attentive and solicitous, though, that I started to pour thoughts out, in my own language, and I bet we stood in that alley for twenty minutes as I explained my muddled love life and dull job and bleak prospects. All the time she was gazing up at me with the sweetest care, as if I were her own son.

Finally I finished, feeling silly that I had unburdened myself so, and she reached up and patted my face and said tenderly, *"Stai zitto."* That broke the holy moment, and off we go down the years.

For a long time I thought she'd granted me benediction of some kind, offered some subtle prayer in her language, until a friend told me recently that *Cosa c'è?* means "What's the matter?" and *Stai zitto* means "You're crazy." But maybe I'm a little wiser now that I'm ancient, because I believe with all my heart that she did grant me an extraordinary blessing that hot day in the alley near Via Caterina. She listened, she paid attention, she was wholly present as I opened a door in myself. Isn't that an enormously powerful and haunting form of prayer, to listen with all your might? Isn't that one of the greatest gifts we can possibly give each other?

Dear Lord, for our eyes and our ears that sometimes open to the astounding gift of Your music, grazie.
—BRIAN DOYLE

☀ RUNNING FOR MY LIFE

Thu 19

Turning around, Jesus saw them following and asked, "What do you want?"... —JOHN 1:38 (NIV)

DAY 1: CHANGING MY LIFE EXPECTANCY

I wanted to do something meaningful to celebrate my sixty-fifth birthday because it was a birthday I hadn't thought I'd live to see. Almost five years earlier, I was diagnosed with Stage 4 ovarian cancer, with a life expectancy of only two years.

Yet here I was, still very much alive, a cancer survivor—but in some ways, I was still allowing that grim diagnosis to shape my expectations of life. So one morning as I checked my e-mail, I eagerly read one about a half-marathon scheduled for the day before my birthday in Colorado Springs, a couple of hours from our home in Boulder.

What if I tried to do something I didn't think I could do to mark a birthday I didn't think I would reach?

I immediately filled out the registration form, paid the fee with a credit card and pushed the Send button. That's when reality began to sink in. *What was I thinking? I haven't so much as run around the block in years. The 13.1-mile distance is daunting—and I'm old!* But I couldn't change my mind now; the registration fee was nonrefundable.

So I bought some real running shoes and found a training program online for run/walking a half-marathon. I filled my iPod with pulsating praise music so I could turn the rhythm of training into praise to God for life itself and for my new expectation to cross this finish line.

I began telling people that I intended to do a half-marathon. Most responded with a smile that seemed to say "Seriously? You?"

Yes, seriously, I thought, more determined than ever to reach my goal—against all odds.

Jesus, I want to live with a new life expectancy and mark that goal by crossing the finish line in this half-marathon.
—CAROL KUYKENDALL

☀ RUNNING FOR MY LIFE

Fri 20

Let us run with perseverance the race marked out for us. Let us fix our eyes on Jesus, the author and perfecter of our faith....
—HEBREWS 12:1–2 (NIV)

DAY 2: TRAINING IN PERSEVERANCE

My six-year-old granddaughter Karis joined me on one of my first short training runs around the neighborhood. She started off explosively fast but soon slowed down and then slowed some more. "Oma," she panted. "My brain is telling me to stop." A half block later, she said, "Now my whole body is telling me to stop." And so she stopped.

I smiled, because Karis had just summed up the challenge of training for me—and the definition of *perseverance*.

Earlier that morning, I'd equipped myself with a verse from Hebrews 12 about "running with perseverance . . . the race marked out for me . . . fixing my eyes on Jesus." I decided to make that my signature verse as I trained, learning to persevere through the obstacles by fixing my eyes on Jesus. And I faced plenty of obstacles.

Like wanting to stop while running—or not even wanting to start. Or wanting to sit on the couch and eat cookies in an air-conditioned house instead of going out for a run in the midsummer heat. Because I hate hot.

Perseverance is about pushing through hard places and making myself do what I don't feel like doing, so that on the day of the race, I'll have whatever it takes to get all the way to the finish line. Perseverance means I won't quit before I'm done.

So now when I go out to run and my brain or my body tells me to stop, I force myself to go a little bit farther . . . and then a little bit farther—practicing perseverance.

Lord, talking about my half-marathon
goal is easy; training is harder. But I'm
fixing my eyes on You, Jesus, and trusting
that will help me keep going.
—CAROL KUYKENDALL

☀ RUNNING FOR MY LIFE

Sat 21   *Run in such a way as to get the prize.*
—I CORINTHIANS 9:24 (NIV)

DAY 3: CROSSING THE FINISH LINE

Race day was predicted to be the hottest day of the summer. Friends promised to pray for clouds. But not a single one was in the bright blue sky as I made my way to the starting line amid hundreds of young, fit-looking runners, including my son Derek, daughter Lindsay and son-in-law David.

I'd been sick the day before—an intestinal complication from my cancer surgery, which pops up every few months. I wasn't going to let that keep me from starting this race, but I feared it might keep me from finishing it.

The gun sounded, the racers took off, and I kept in step with Derek for the first couple of miles. But then we turned a corner and faced a long, steep hill. "Oh no," I moaned, "I didn't train for hills like this!" Little did I know that the course was filled with steep hills. I began to get lightheaded and slowed to a walk, but Derek stayed right with me.

I tried to remember my word-picture Scripture, something about keeping my eyes on Jesus, and I wondered if I might actually see Him face-to-face before the end of this race!

Slowly the mile markers mounted up: 9, 10, 11, finally 12.

"You're doing great, Mom! Almost there!" Derek kept urging. I walked to the top of that monster hill, turned a corner and, up ahead, I could see my family, including seven grandchildren, cheering. I sprinted across the finish line—against all odds—at three hours and fourteen minutes.

Lord, knowing You and keeping my eyes on You enables me to run the race that You set before me—and always cross the finish line.
—CAROL KUYKENDALL

Sun 22

Thou hast left thy first love. Remember therefore from whence thou art fallen, and repent. . . .
—REVELATION 2:4–5

Last Sunday was one of those Sundays when going to church seems more of a burden than a privilege. We sang only a couple of verses of the hymns I liked, while the ones I didn't like seemed endless. I hadn't remembered to pick up a service book, so I had to strain to hear the lessons, unable to follow along in the text. I struggled to get the gist of the sermon, and the bits I could pick up only increased my confusion.

The problem, of course, wasn't with the singers or the reader or the preacher; the problem was with me. Over the past few months I'd been stressed by changes at work and troubles at home. I'd become withdrawn, hiding from my problems. And in the process, I'd been hiding from God.

July

In the afternoon I walked Maggie and Stephen to play rehearsal and then headed north to the very tip of Manhattan. I sat on a bench in the park, drinking a cup of coffee and looking out over the salt marsh, with a wooded hill on my left, and beyond it, the Palisades. For some reason, lines of poetry started floating through my mind. And I thought back, for the first time in quite a while, to a long-ago evening in a college dorm, where my friend Kevin and I read the whole of Revelation out loud, and through the mysterious images and in the rhythm of the King James text, my heart was touched by a Presence I'd never felt before.

I took a sip of coffee and watched the birds wading in the marsh. And for the first time in quite a while, I started to pray:

Lord, blow with Your Spirit on the embers You lighted so many years ago and set my heart on fire.
—ANDREW ATTAWAY

Mon 23

On my bed I remember you; I think of you through the watches of the night. —PSALM 63:6 (NIV)

A story in the news recently caught my attention: Using electronic imaging, a university researcher had made a surprising discovery.

Contrary to previous thinking among neuro-scientists, the images showed that when we're daydreaming—zoning out, not thinking about anything in particular—our brain is actually working harder than when we're concentrating on a particular task. In this "default mode," a particular network of synapses lights up, maintaining our identity, keeping us subconsciously aware of our environment and circumstances and recalling our history and relationships: a kind of internal map of who we are. We might be remembering scenes from childhood, envisioning a favorite vacation spot, or anticipating the arrival of a friend or relative.

As I get older, my brain seems to go into that default mode more often than it used to. Is that good or bad? In some ways I think it's good. I experience something deeper when my brain is idling; in that mental state I'm reminded of who I am in Christ, how He revealed Himself to me and how safe I feel in His presence. In those moments, my heart renews its hunger for His touch and signals my brain: "Hey, it's time to pray."

Would you excuse me now? I think I'd like to spend a little time in default mode.

Jesus, it's so good to experience the peace I have with You when I free my mind from the burdens of the day.
—HAROLD HOSTETLER

July

Tue 24

For I will give you abundant water for your thirst and for your parched fields.... —ISAIAH 44:3 (TLB)

My husband Don didn't promise me a rose garden when we married, but he did promise me water.

Water was a scarce commodity when I was growing up. As a young girl living on my grandparents' ranch in southeast Oklahoma, I thought bathwater was supposed to be rusty red with occasional chunks of dirt. When we moved to the central part of the state, Dad hauled drinking water from a windmill a mile away because our gypsum-laden water wasn't drinkable. Even gyp water was precious, though, so showers were brief and baths were taken in no more than five inches of water.

Southwest Kansas, my home for over forty years, looks dry and bare to most people. To me, it's like the Garden of Eden! Our house well provides cold, pure drinking water, and I can enjoy the occasional luxury of a hot soak in a full tub. When rains don't come, the deep irrigation well ensures that the growing corn has enough moisture to produce a crop.

I'm grateful for God's precious gift of water. I'm grateful for Jesus, who offers Living Water "springing up into eternal life" (John 4:14), a well that will never run dry. And each time I walk through the front yard, I'm grateful for the lovely, fragrant roses Don planted and tends—a bonus blessing, made possible by water.

Thank you, Jesus, for the water that sustains earthly life, for the Water that is ours for eternity and for roses that remind me how greatly I'm blessed by both.
—PENNEY SCHWAB

Wed 25

He who dwells in the shelter of the Most High will abide in the shadow of the Almighty.
—PSALM 91:1 (ESV)

Tom Parrish is ninety-two years old and a dear friend. He is one of the wisest people I know. Across the span of his long life, he has played many roles: a sailor and survivor of Pearl Harbor, a public school superintendent, an attorney, an ordained minister and director of development at Baylor University. Long retired, he spends hours in his library reading history and literature with the same eager curiosity he possessed as a young man. If you want to engage in a meaningful and animated conversation, visit with Tom. You will always leave enriched.

July

Recently I returned to Waco, Texas, from my new home in Macon, Georgia, and dropped by to see Tom. He had recently returned home from a two-month stay in a nursing facility due to injuries from a serious fall. Now recovered, he was bright-eyed and ready to take on the world.

As we discussed his long convalescence away from home, Tom exclaimed, "It's so good to be back in my library. I love my books, my easy chair and the quietness of this place. But you know something, Scott? While I was away, I discovered that no matter where I am, I'm at home with God. I learned this once as a young man at war in the Navy; I've learned it again as an old man struggling to walk. I had to leave home for eight long weeks to rediscover that wherever I am, I am at home with God."

Tonight I gazed at a framed quote that I keep on my desk, written by the nineteenth century English poet and priest, John Keble:

Thou Framer of the light and dark,
Steer through the tempest Thine own ark:
Amid the howling wintry sea
We are in port if we have Thee.

Father, may I feel Your presence no matter where I am today and know that "I'm at home with God."
—SCOTT WALKER

Thu 26

If anyone is never at fault in what he says, he is a perfect man. . . .
—JAMES 3:2 (NIV)

When Kendall, our first grandchild, was born, there were the usual discussions about whom she looked liked. Did she favor our son Jeff, our daughter-in-law Leah or her other grandmother, Leonie? When Leonie saw Kendall, she proclaimed, "She has Leah's nose and Miss Karen's mouth!"

As I looked at Kendall's beautiful little face, I saw that she indeed had a cute rosebud nose like Leah's. Fortunately, my mouth is one of my features that I haven't wished was a little more attractive, so I was satisfied that Kendall had inherited my lips.

Then I got to thinking a little more about mouths. Would I want the kinds of words that come out of my mouth to also come out of Kendall's? Sometimes, without thinking about it, I say negative things. If my husband Gordon and I are planning a cookout, I'm sometimes quick to point out that the weather report predicts a chance of rain. When Gordon reminds me that there's a good chance that it won't rain, I defend myself by saying I'm just being practical and prepared.

So I decided to make a list of the kinds of words I'd want my granddaughter to say. On top of the list are words of blessing: It's so easy to say "God bless you" to the people we meet or at the end of e-mails. Next on the list are words of encouragement: I want to make an effort to be positive in what I say to others and to point out their good attributes. And finally there are words of thanks: How easy it is to overlook thanking fellow church volunteers or service people who've gone out of their way to help.

It's quite a responsibility when someone inherits your mouth. Thankfully, it's never too late to give it a serious makeover!

Father, thank You for our incredible ability to speak words that affect other's lives. Make the ones I speak today words of blessing.
—KAREN BARBER

Fri 27

Go . . . and tell them how great things the Lord hath done for thee. . . .
—MARK 5:19

Guess what, Mom?" Jeremy asked. I shook my head, hoping it was something good. Sometimes I doubted God's goodness. "At Celebrate Recovery, they ask some of the guys to give testimonies."

Oh no! I remembered the first time I had given mine, decades ago. I had shaken uncontrollably and nearly fainted. And there had been a time in

Jeremy's life when his shyness had almost been social phobia.

"They asked me to speak, and I said okay. It'll be this Thursday evening on a street corner in downtown Athens. Don't feel you have to, but if you and Gene . . ."

"Oh, Jeremy, of course we'll be there! May I call your sisters?"

"Okay, but it's a long way for them."

Nevertheless, in that sweltering just-before-sunset July heat, Gene and I, Jennifer and her husband Charlie, their nearly grown son Alex, Julie and her husband Rick and their teenage son Thomas sat in folding chairs waiting. Many of our friends, who'd prayed for Jeremy, had also found the busy street corner. First there was loud, joyful singing, accompanied by guys on guitars. The crowd mostly consisted of homeless, hurting or addicted people. Meanwhile, a stream of college students and busy shoppers rushed by us. Some glanced our way; others deliberately looked away; most stared straight ahead.

Then Jeremy stood to speak—with no notes, nothing even planned. He spoke slowly, carefully, choosing his words thoughtfully. He seemed comfortable with occasional silences. He began, "I had to lose everything in order to gain everything. I finally found my own Jesus, not my parents', but to do that I had to hit rock bottom."

Father, through all those dark, scary years,
You knew the plans You had for Jeremy.
—Marion Bond West

Sat 28

And, behold, all the earth sitteth still, and is at rest. —Zechariah 1:11

Heat waves are a fact of summer in New York. When one hits, Manhattan turns into a concrete desert. A lethargy settles over the populace; even my dog is affected. The minute Millie steps outside our building and senses the temperature hovering above ninety, she does an about-face.

"Come on, Mil," I snapped at her one steamy Saturday morning last year before the day became too hot. "You need exercise."

She gave me one of those pleading looks dogs are so good at and then set out in the direction of the dog run, moving slowly, deliberately. I tried to speed up but she was having none of it.

Finally we arrived. Millie greeted her friends, took a long sloppy drink from the communal water bowl, and settled herself for a nap in the shade, under the bench where I was sitting checking my BlackBerry.

Napping was not exercise. I glanced up and scanned the dog run for a ball I could throw. What I saw slowed *me* down.

Dogs were everywhere, relaxing in the shade, wading sedately in the big kiddies' pool we all chipped in for, stretching languidly or just sitting peacefully with their people. And everyone appeared very content. Owners read books and newspapers, sunned themselves, chatted and, yes, even napped, heads lolling to the side. A briny breeze wafted softly from the Hudson, rustling the trees. Otherwise, all was quiet.

Millie was right. What was all the hurry about, especially in this heat? Slow down. Take a break.

I turned the phone off, slipped it into my pocket and closed my eyes. Today was going to be one of those days when nothing happened. And that was good.

Lord, sometimes You need to tell me when to slow down, because I'm not always as smart as my dog.
—EDWARD GRINNAN

Sun 29

David encouraged himself in the Lord his God. —I SAMUEL 30:6

Back in my small childhood church I heard one question nearly every Sunday evening: "Does anyone have a testimony this week?" The request invited parishioners to share impromptu thanksgivings or spiritual lessons, sometimes learned while working through difficult situations or watching through sleepless nights. Gray-haired saints spoke up most often, but youngsters also participated.

I remember the specifics of only one testimony I gave. It was the summer between high school and college. My parents had moved a hundred miles away, and I had accepted a hard-to-find job back in our old neighborhood. Though I lived with my older brother and worshiped with family friends, I was homesick for my folks and their household routines.

One midsummer evening during testimony time, I stood to speak. With minimal explanation, I quoted what seemed to me as an amazingly relevant verse I'd discovered tucked away in a psalm: "When my father and my mother forsake me, then the Lord will take me up" (Psalm 27:10). As I sat down, some of my parents' friends chuckled at the hyperbole. Forsaken? Hardly. But we all knew that wasn't the point. I had found sustaining strength in Scripture, and to fortify my faith, I'd accepted an opportunity to share my assurance of God's guardian care.

It's been years since I've heard anyone ask for testimonies. The noun may be out of fashion, but the principle stands. In proclaiming God's good Word to us, we encourage ourselves in the Lord—and a few onlookers besides.

*Lord, today I am encouraged by the promise of
Your guardianship. Give me an opportunity
to share this good news with someone else.*
—EVELYN BENCE

Mon 30

[The Lord] has sent me to bind up
the brokenhearted. . . .
—ISAIAH 61:1 (NIV)

In the weeks following Dad's death, I took long walks around my neighborhood, exploring new paths in an effort to erase the memories of old ones. One afternoon my husband Brian suggested we take a bike ride together, a departure from my usual routine.

We put on our helmets and headed out into the Atlanta heat. As we coasted downhill, I felt my heart lift, but on the harder uphill climbs, my spirit sank. Spiraling into my own private world of sorrow, I began to cry.

Brian, helpless as he navigated the quickest path home, kept trying to talk to me, but I couldn't bring myself to answer for fear my sobs would utterly consume any energy I had left.

Suddenly, the skies opened and a torrential rain flooded down. I slid on the pavement as I tried to follow Brian to the shelter of an ancient oak tree, leaving a pedal-shaped gash in my calf.

Brian held me as I sobbed, "It's not the bike. It's not the bike." He squeezed me tighter and simply said, "I know."

Soon the rain eased and we were able to pedal home. Throughout the entire ride back, I never felt alone. I had Brian, who had held me, and God, Who had heard my cries and cried right along with me.

Lord, You bring me comfort in my times of need. Help me to keep my eyes on You as I seek peace and joy again.
—Ashley Kappel

Tue 31

You made all the delicate, inner parts of my body. . . . Thank you for making me so wonderfully complex! Your workmanship is marvelous—how well I know it!
—Psalm 139:13–14 (NLT)

During the summers preceding first through sixth grades, my mother stitched four dresses for me to wear during the coming school year. I loved choosing figured fabrics from hundreds of hypnotic, *pick-me!* bolts at the dry-goods store; sniffing the new material's scents; watching Mom position tissue-paper patterns, just so, atop the cloth; and finally, hearing the exciting *clickity-clack* of her treadle sewing machine.

The two dozen photos she snapped of me in my finished dresses are glued in a now-dusty album. Although these photos are black-and-white, I can still recall the dresses' colors and patterns, because, when she cut out their various pieces, she also snipped a fat little "Sunbonnet Girl" from each cloth's remnants to appliqué atop a white block. She carefully joined the twenty-four squares—each containing a miniature "me"—into a quilt now hanging on our living room wall.

One day a plumber who was just finishing repair work at our house pointed to the quilt. "Where'd *that* come from?" I explained, adding, "It's a treasure."

The man shrugged. "An antique dealer might buy it. Along with lots of this other old stuff you have around here."

That *stuff*—some from before I was born—included items my mother had tatted, knitted and/or stitched while bent over an ancient sewing machine whose pedal power was hers. None was mass-produced; every thread, every color came with *me* in mind. Its value wasn't in its function, but in its maker!

> *I, too, may appear to be "old stuff" to many.*
> *But not to You, my Maker.*
> —ISABEL WOLSELEY

July

MY PATHWAY TO PEACE

1 _____

2 _____

3 _____

4 _____

5 _____

6 _____

7 _____

8 _____

9 _____

10 _____

11 _____

12 _____

13 _____

14 _____

15 _____

16 _____

17 _____

18 _____

19 _____

20 _____

21 _____

22 _____

23 _____

24 _____

25 _____

26 _____

27 _____

28 _____

29 _____

30 _____

31 _____

August

Therefore being justified by faith, we have peace with God through our Lord Jesus Christ.

—ROMANS 5:1

❧ THIS I KNOW

Wed 1

*So that we may boldly say... I will not fear.... —*HEBREWS 13:6

FEAR NOTHING

My husband David had served Hillsboro Presbyterian Church in Nashville, Tennessee, for thirty-seven years when he felt led to leave. The good of the church and the love of its people had been at the forefront of every decision he made, and this was no different.

Over these years, David's signature phrase, "Go out into the world and fear nothing," had become a benediction. Church members had put it on everything from bumper stickers to church signs to needlework samplers. David's greatest hope was that the bold spirit these words expressed would continue to define Hillsboro.

But somewhere between leaving the church and redefining ourselves, a nagging doubt had been planted inside me: "Oh, God," I'd pray, "we gave it our all. Did it matter?"

God's answer did, of course, come in time. Almost a year after David left Hillsboro, we were back in Zimbabwe with our family. On our arrival, Paddington, the father of Village Hope, seemed especially eager to get us out to the farm. There, painted boldly on the long white stucco wall of Village Hope where the hungry gather to be fed and where the gate swings wide open to welcome orphans with AIDS to their new family, were the words that answered all my questions and pointed me forward: "Go Out into the World and Fear Nothing."

What more did I need to know?

> *Father, heal my trust deficit. I want to step out*
> *fearlessly into the world.*
> —PAM KIDD

Thu 2

As a mother comforts her child,
so will I comfort you. . . .
—ISAIAH 66:13 (NIV)

For months I'd been taking a Bible verse from the Scripture basket at our local YMCA. I could hardly wait to get to the car to read "my" verse. Then I'd sit and digest those words like spiritual comfort food:

The Lord is my shepherd; I shall not want. (Psalm 23:1)
I can do all things through Christ which strengtheneth me. (Philippians 4:13)

Do not fear for I am with you; do not be dismayed, for I am your God.... (Isaiah 41:10, NIV)

But one evening I got this: "Return to me . . . and I will return to you. . . . " (Zechariah 1:3, NIV). The words flew up at me like a rebuke. I laid the verse on the passenger seat and drove off. "Lord, what are You saying to me?" I asked. But I heard only silence. The unsettling verse followed me into the supermarket for a quick grocery shop.

The store was crowded with people and carts, including a mother with a small child squirming to get out of his cart. She put him down and briefly turned her back. He darted ahead; I saw him just a few feet away, lost in the crowd. His face crumpled. "Mommy!" he cried. She was there in an instant, scooping him up, covering his face with kisses.

Return to me and I will return to you. Now I heard those words as they were meant to be heard: God's joyful invitation to me to "return" to Him each time I step away and look to something or someone else as my source of strength and hope. Like that child, I'm assured of an exuberant welcome each and every time. No judgment. Just joy.

Father, again and again I return
to the One Who loves me.
—SHARI SMYTH

Fri 3

By your endurance you will gain your lives. —LUKE 21:19 (RSV)

My mom has often said she's not a very patient person. I can attest to that and I would say it can be an admirable thing. She has tremendous energy—"a life force" a friend calls it—and fills her days with tennis, bridge, visits with friends, reading for her book group, dinners for the family. All the while she is Dad's primary caregiver. "I pray for patience," she tells me on the phone. Dad has a host of ailments that have slowed him down and leave him in much pain. Mom helps him get dressed, gets his breakfast, reads to him, makes sure he takes his pills, drives him to doctors' appointments, takes him to church, gets him to do his physical therapy. "He moves so slowly," she says.

I mostly hear about these things long distance because I live three thousand miles away, so I was glad to be with Mom and Dad for a ten-day vacation. I watched her do all those things that she says come so hard to her. I even pitched in a bit, helping Dad get dressed—a curious reversal of roles—and assisting him with his physical therapy. But I was touched mostly by Mom.

"You know, Mom," I said to her, "you never complain. You never even sit down and sigh. You just keep doing. You're very patient."

"You'll have to ask Dad about that," she said modestly.

"I think your prayer has been answered." She had acquired a virtue she never thought she could have. Love had made the impossible possible, and faith had done the hard work.

> *Lord, work through me to give me*
> *the spiritual gifts I lack.*
> —RICK HAMLIN

Sat 4

"Your gift will return to you in full.... Whatever measure you use to give—large or small—will be used to measure what is given back to you."
—LUKE 6:38 (TLB)

Laguna Beach has always been one of our family's favorite spots in Southern California. We love the exhilarating crash of waves against the rocks, the whirlpools of churning foam and even the seagulls inching closer and closer to our picnic feast spread out on a blanket on the sand.

The only irritant is having to climb a steep ramp up from the beach every couple of hours to feed the meter where our car is parked. That was usually my job when the kids were boogie boarding, diving through the waves or crouched down looking into tide pools, mesmerized by starfish, sea urchins and tiny crabs.

We weren't quite ready to head back home one day when I started up the ramp. *Bother*, I thought. *The meter is running out; better give it four quarters for another hour*!

A lady was feeding the meter next to mine. "Ah, so that's your car," she smiled. "You can relax. The time had expired but I fed it a couple of quarters for another half an hour."

"How very kind of you. I would have hated to get a ticket."

"I know the feeling. Two years ago I got a ticket on my expired meter. It was horrible; not only expensive, but a nuisance. Ever since, whenever I notice an expired meter close to mine, I feed it a few quarters."

I added quarters to my meter and offered her the couple she had fed into it. "No, no," she said with a laugh. "Just use them to help out someone else."

I now carry extra quarters and am a meter maid on the watch. Small, seemingly insignificant generosities sometimes make all the difference to someone's happy day.

Open my heart, Lord, to the let-me-do-this-for-you opportunities of my daily encounters.
—FAY ANGUS

CAMP HOPE

Sun 5

I will praise you among the nations, O Lord; I will sing praises to your name. —PSALM 18:49 (NIV)

DAY 1: A MOTHER IN ZION

I call Lizetta Williams my "roomie." She's hardly ever still, and it's hard to catch more than a glimpse of her silver hair as she whizzes by in her motorized golf cart. For the past few summers, she has shared her home with me while I volunteer at Bible Witness Camp in Pembroke, Illinois. She is ninety-four years old now, and the walls of her home are almost completely covered with pictures of her six children and more grandchildren and great-grandchildren than I can keep track of. In a special place there's a picture of her late husband Marshall, whom the people at the camp affectionately refer to as "The Rev."

My roomie is candid when she tells the story of how she and her family came to be at the camp. There had been a rift in the congregation Marshall pastored, and he was turned away from the church they both loved. Then she and her husband were invited to take over the direction of Bible Witness Camp. The founder, Mrs. Jewel Pierpont Ford, had prayed for a minister with a wife and children to serve the African American families in rural Pembroke Township.

It was the 1950s, and Lizetta's mother and family were against it. "They thought it was dangerous. They thought I was sacrificing my children." In time, her mother came around and became one of the camp's biggest supporters. The people embraced her family, including the set of twins born on the campgrounds a year after they arrived.

Lizetta still teaches the women's Bible study on Sunday mornings. The people at the camp look at her as an honored mother.

*Thank You, God, for Your faithfulness and grace
and love, even in unexpected places.*
—SHARON FOSTER

CAMP HOPE

Mon 6

As Jesus was getting into the boat, the man who had been demon-possessed begged to go with him. Jesus did not let him.... —MARK 5:18–19 (NIV)

DAY 2: THE MISSION FIELD

Becky and Dave McMillan, a white couple, spend their days and lives among Black people. Becky is counselor, teacher, mentor and head cook at Bible

Witness Camp; Dave pastors the chapel and works as the camp's fix-it man. The children at the camp bury their faces in Becky's apron and swing from Dave's arms like they were tree limbs. Becky and Dave are happy people, but sometimes they are wistful. Around them there is a thin veil of regret.

Becky is the daughter of Lizetta and Marshall Williams, who ran Bible Witness Camp for several decades. Growing up at the very rural camp, Becky dreamed that she would devote her life to missions in a land far away. She met her husband Dave when they were in college. Dave's father was martyred in 1965 in the Congo; Dave still dreamed of returning to Africa. Sharing their dreams, Becky and Dave married, intending to spend their lives in Africa.

They never got there. Instead, they were sent to a mission in France. Becky didn't feel at peace there; it wasn't where she belonged. She sometimes feels that she caused her family to fail on the mission field.

I smile and say the same thing to her that I say every year: "You're on the mission field that God intended for you." God meant Becky and Dave for missions right here at home.

*Lord, help me to find the place where
You can use me best.*
—SHARON FOSTER

❀ CAMP HOPE

Tue 7   *As apostles of Christ we could have been a burden to you, but we were gentle among you, like a mother caring for her little children.*
—I THESSALONIANS 2:6–7 (NIV)

DAY 3: CREATING FAMILY

"Mary, are you ever going to take a vacation?" I ask. She and I laugh as we fantasize about the cruise we'll take someday.

Mary Williams and her twin brother Mark were born in Pembroke, Illinois, at Bible Witness Camp. They both work there full time; he is the director and she runs the camp programs. Mary is amazing! Every summer she creates a new curriculum, with games and shows and songs and outings for the campers. Her energy is boundless—she's up in the morning for chapel and is still awake late at night, leading scavenger hunts and listening to prayers. Always dressed in pink, she moves so quickly sometimes all I see is the blur of her tennis shoes.

The girls, teens and preteens, hang on to her every word. She mediates their squabbles and visits them at the public schools they attend. She's like an aunt or big sister. They tell her their joys and their struggles; they even text-message her. For some of the girls, she's the closest thing they have to a mother.

After she graduated from Wheaton College, Mary could have gone anywhere. But she chose to come back to the place where she was born to serve the people who need her. She creates family wherever she goes, including people she invites into the fold—like me.

> *Lord, bless all those who stand as mothers and fathers for Your children. Bless them with joy, good health, long life and sweet rest.*
> —SHARON FOSTER

CAMP HOPE

Wed 8   *"Come, follow me," Jesus said, "and I will make you fishers of men."*
—MATTHEW 4:19 (NIV)

DAY 4: MISS TRUDIE

This past summer, I met Miss Trudie at Bible Witness Camp.

Miss Trudie is the kind of woman I remember from church when I was a girl: gray-haired, brown-skinned, always neatly dressed, with eyes that twinkle from behind bifocals. But those twinkling eyes can quickly turn to a stern look that's sure to put the most wayward child in his or her place. Like many of the churchwomen I remember, Miss Trudie plays the piano.

She played for me last summer in her upstairs apartment. "What made a young girl from Chicago just pick up and go to Trinidad?" I asked her. Miss Trudie has been a missionary there for more than sixty years.

"They needed missionaries, so I went," she said. There were people—children—who needed to hear about Jesus. But what she does not say is that it was not easy for her to go. She was one of the first young people at Bible Witness Mission in Chicago in 1948. When the mission bought land in rural Illinois so that city children could experience life in the country, she was among the first to attend the camp. Inspired, she took classes at Moody Bible Institute and learned about missionaries.

Most organizations at that time had no use for a single African American woman. But she kept at it until she found an opening. "I practiced and I practiced," Miss Trudie told me, "and I became the church pianist." She played for many churches in Trinidad and Tobago.

Miss Trudie invited me to the piano. As I fumbled over the keys, trying to remember a tune I had learned as a child, I smiled, thinking of how many lives she has touched.

Lord, help me always to be open to Your calling.
—SHARON FOSTER

🌀 CAMP HOPE

Thu 9

"Go home to your family and tell them how much the Lord has done for you, and how he has had mercy on you."
—MARK 5:19 (NIV)

DAY 5: QUASHANA

QuaShana never planned to return. She had got a good education and made a home for herself in Virginia. But at thirty years old, she returned to the rural Illinois community where she was raised and works as a supervisor at a mental health facility. Many of the people she serves live hard-knock lives: unemployment, drug abuse and teen pregnancy are commonplace in this African American community. She credits Bible Witness Camp, especially Marshall "The Rev" Williams, with starting her on the right path.

"All through college, Mary sent letters to encourage me," QuaShana says, referring to Williams' daughter, who runs the summer camp for girls. "But it was the Bible verses and the Rev's encouragement that really did it." Every year, from ages eight through eighteen, QuaShana and her fellow campers memorized Bible verses and were taken to a competition in Bloomington-Normal, Illinois—a Super Bowl of Bible memorizing. No one expected much of them, but each year the camp team had the most members to "quiz out" (correctly repeat the verses assigned to them).

"When we returned, the Rev would brag on us!" she said, beaming. The Rev seemed to know just how much the kids needed that boost, how much they needed someone to believe in them.

Now QuaShana wants to share those seeds of healthy esteem with others. "I want to help them make their lives better. I want them to have hope."

Lord, help us to tell the simple story of
how good You have been to us.
—SHARON FOSTER

🌺 CAMP HOPE

Fri 10   *Thus they gave to the children of Aaron the priest Hebron with her suburbs, to be a city of refuge....*
—JOSHUA 21:13

DAY 6: ON THE SWINGS

A swing set on the playground of Bible Witness Camp holds the memories of many children.

Painted a plain, metallic gray, it has survived for almost fifty years. Many of the adult volunteers who come back to work at the camp look at it longingly; they were once campers themselves and played on it.

The town of Pembroke, Illinois, from which most of the children come, is a place that offers them little hope. Their parents try their best, but there is little opportunity for employment, drug use is rampant, and poverty is all around them. In the summer, if the children have attended classes and learned their Bible verses, they are invited to come to camp for free.

The sounds of gunshots and sirens are not heard in the camp. Nestled among trees and hidden from the roads outside, there are arts and crafts, skits, games, a weekly swimming trip, and a field trip to pick blueberries. There are mosquitoes, hot dog roasts, sloppy joes, sugary treats and scavenger hunts with flashlights. There are Bible quizzes and chapel.

And all of the children love the swing set. They hang on it barefoot and swing high in the air. The swing set is also the place for tearful, nighttime confessions. It's a cradle that comforts them, a refuge from all their cares.

Lord, give each one of us a place of refuge and help our hearts to be a refuge for others.
—SHARON FOSTER

❀ CAMP HOPE

Sat 11

"This brother of yours was dead and is alive again; he was lost and is found." —LUKE 15:32 (NIV)

DAY 7: HOLY GROUND

The week of boys' camp is over, and the young minister sitting next to me is enjoying the final lunch. "I love this place! This place is holy ground to me," he says, speaking of Bible Witness Camp. "They kicked me out. I had to go home."

His family was troubled; summer camp was a refuge for him. But something happened. "It was craft time and I was in wood shop with the other boys." There was a contest, and he was certain he had won. The camp leaders didn't agree. Angry, the boy took things into his own hands—literally. He went outside and with a large object began to beat on one of the camp counselor's cars. He damaged it badly. Marshall "the Rev" Williams spoke to him kindly, but said there was no choice but to send him home.

"I knew he was right," the young minister said to me. "I felt so bad for what I had done." Several years passed, but he never got over the shame. He no longer came to the camp.

When he was seventeen, he got a job at a local store. "I was working, and suddenly there she was...Mary." He was referring to the Rev's youngest daughter. "She asked me to come back and if I would like to be a counselor." The young minster's eyes fill with tears that quickly begin to roll down his face. "This place is holy ground," he repeats. "You don't know what it means to me to be forgiven, to know that they loved me even after what I did. I will never forget. That's why I come back. I will never forget."

Lord, help me always to remember the joy of being forgiven, the joy of being welcomed home.
—SHARON FOSTER

Sun 12

He will love you and bless you....
—DEUTERONOMY 7:13 (NIV)

Our early church service during the summer is held outdoors in the woods just behind the sanctuary. A cozy fire and birdsong accompany the gathering. Ancient trees reach heavenward, creating a green canopy that shelters our slightly sleepy congregation. Each Sunday we take communion while guitars strum the old, familiar hymns. A giant cross forms the backdrop for our speakers, elders who bring us a variety of homey spiritual insights.

But last week it was the lady sitting across from me who really preached the sermon, and she did it without opening her mouth. The dress code for this early service is casual—capri pants for women and khaki shorts for men are not uncommon. T-shirts are welcome too. Still, I was surprised to see this gray-haired woman sporting a shirt that said, "Jesus likes you. But He loves me best."

What? I thought, just slightly offended. Then I began thinking what that might really mean.

If I had that T-shirt, I'd wear it too. Because I'm the one Jesus *really* loves best. And so are you. Jesus loves each of us as though there's no one else. His love doesn't have to be divvied up—like a grandmother at Christmas when all the grandchildren clamor for her lap. You are the center of His universe and so am I. The Creator of the universe loves me! Oh, and you, too, of course.

I left that service with a happy heart, knowing I was loved. Greatly.

This week I want to love others as You, God, love me.
—MARY LOU CARNEY

Mon 13

His mother kept all these things in her heart. —LUKE 2:51 (NKJV)

Everyone looked different. My cousins, a normally sweet but rowdy group, all watched my mom with rapt attention. My dad smiled lovingly from the end of the dinner table. Some of my uncles and aunts even started to tear up.

This happens every summer on my mom's birthday. It's the only real tradition my family has. No matter what has happened in the twelve months between, we all—four families, all told—make sure to be in Maine for her birthday party. We buy local lobsters and eat them on the beach as night falls and the gray tide rolls out, always keeping an eye on our black Lab Nellie, who can be sneaky when there's food to be had. Then we hunt for sticks and roast marshmallows over the fire and yell indulgently at Nellie as she chews on lobster carcasses that have been thrown into the sea.

When we've eaten, we return to the house, where Mom gives each cousin, all seven of us, a present. There's always a theme—one year it was books illustrated by N. C. Wyeth, this year it was boxes to hold our treasures—but each gift is uniquely chosen for the recipient.

Then she makes a speech. She acknowledges everyone in the room and lets them know the ways in which they touch her life. The speech invariably ends with her crying in gratitude—and all of us thanking God that she was born.

Thank You, Lord, for showing me that the best birthday parties are the ones where you celebrate everyone else.
—SAM ADRIANCE

❀ A GRACE-FILLED JOURNEY

Tue 14   *For this cause I bow my knees to the Father of our Lord Jesus Christ . . . that Christ may dwell in your hearts by faith. . . .* —EPHESIANS 3:14, 17

ECHO OF HIS WORDS

I can hardly believe I am now standing at the top of a long street in Ephesus, facing the spectacular ancient library. Nearby is the amphitheater, where the apostle Paul confronted the worshipers of Artemis, the goddess whose great temple in Ephesus was one of the Seven Wonders of the World.

From prison in Rome, Paul wrote a letter to the church he left behind in Ephesus. Though I've read it many times and quoted it often, I've never before felt as if Paul's prayer was for me. It seems now as if I've stepped backward into New

Testament times. Paul places his hands on my head as he speaks his powerful words directly to me: "For this cause I bow my knees unto the Father of our Lord Jesus Christ . . . that he would grant you . . . to be strengthened with might by his Spirit . . . that Christ may dwell in your heart by faith: that ye, being rooted and grounded in love . . . [may] know the love of Christ, which passeth knowledge, that ye might be filled with all the fullness of God" (Ephesians 3:14–19).

Could anyone ever ask for a greater blessing? Can you hear the echo of the gifts Paul is asking God to give you and me? Listen! He asks for us: inner strength, Christ in our hearts, knowledge of all dimensions of Christ's love and the fullness of God.

With joy, I give thanks to the Holy Spirit through which Paul's prayers are fulfilled.
—MARILYN MORGAN KING

Wed 15

If it is possible, as far as it depends on you, live at peace with everyone.
—ROMANS 12:18 (NIV)

My wife Rosie and I recently celebrated our fortieth wedding anniversary, and yes, we're still working on living at peace with one another.

When she walks into the house, Rosie loves to pull off her shoes and leave them wherever she takes them off. She can sit down to do something, pull off her shoes and leave them where she's been sitting. Whether it's the den, living room, kitchen or bedroom, a pair of dress shoes, slippers or walking shoes might be there. Then, when Rosie needs them, she'll ask me, "Have you seen my shoes?" Well, I've learned how to give her a gentle answer or simply ask, "What was your last stop?"

When we were first married, Rosie's shoe-leaving habit irritated me. But eventually I learned to step over, around and sometimes on her shoes without getting upset.

In Romans 12:18 (NIV), Paul tells us to "live at peace with everyone," but we ought to start with the people closest to us. Peace, like charity, begins at home.

Lord, help me not only to talk about living at peace with everyone, but to practice it as well.
—DOLPHUS WEARY

READER'S ROOM

My husband became disabled in 1992, and he has learned—and I have learned along with him—to appreciate the simple things: a walk with our dog, a beautiful rainbow, watching the moon rise over the mountain. I am able to press on because I know God has a plan; life is good because He is with me.
—*Sharon Adams, Williamsport, Pennsylvania*

Thu 16

But thanks be to God, who always leads us in triumph in Christ, and manifests through us the sweet aroma of the knowledge of Him in every place.
—II CORINTHIANS 2:14 (NAS)

My husband Rick and I established a few guidelines for our porch parties:

1. No nagging or criticizing.
2. Avoid discussing problems.
3. Notice something beautiful in our surroundings or in each other. Comment on it.
4. Speak only positive things.
5. Ask for prayer.

The rules sounded simple enough to follow, but one day I broke every single one of them.

On one hot summer morning, I plopped into my rocking chair and said to Rick, "How am I going to meet my work deadline?" Speaking that one sentence opened the door for negativity and the tangled knot of worries that clamored for my attention. Ignoring our porch-party guidelines, I kept talking. Then I reminded Rick to clean the garage.

"Hey, look," my husband said. "The gardenias are blooming." I glanced at the thriving bushes. After last February's ice storm, I'd assumed they were gone.

For the first time that morning, I acknowledged something positive. "They sure smell sweet, don't they?" I said.

> *Oh, Lord, Your sweet aroma is so*
> *close—only a praise away.*
> —JULIE GARMON

Fri 17

For he will command his angels concerning you to guard you in all your ways. —PSALM 91:11 (NIV)

They were everywhere, those little reminders of Dad. I'd pass a golf course and think about the backswing that once sent him head over heels, landing on his back in the tee box. Seeing the roasted-nut vendor at the fair reminded me of Dad pulling up a chair and making that man very rich over the course of an evening.

But the hardest reminders came when I wasn't expecting them. The first time I walked into the grocery store and saw Peeps, the little sugarcoated marshmallow treats, took my breath away. Dad would always ask Mom to buy him a few at the store, and then he'd go out and get at least a dozen more. Once when I found them half-off after Easter, I asked how many he wanted. His quick reply: "If they're the big ones, thirty-six packages; if they're the little ones, get everything they've got."

As I walked the aisles, I was continually bowled over. There was Diet Mountain Dew, a drink Dad loved so much we mentioned it in his obituary. And Diet Peach Snapple—he once asked me to "pick up forty-eight," prompting the cashier to say, "You must be Dr. Johnson's daughter." But for once, I found myself smiling instead of tearing up. The reminders of Dad were no longer instant tear-starters but rather the beginning of fond memories.

Now when I go to the store, I think about what Dad might like and sometimes even pick up some. There's nothing like a little Diet Mountain Dew toast while watching a sunset at the end of the day to bring back memories of Dad—and feelings of peace.

Lord, keep me in Your heart as I journey through mourning to find joy once again.
*—*Ashley Kappel

Sat 18   *Serve God with all your heart and with all your soul.* —Joshua 22:5

The final exam for the spiritual-direction program involved supervising a retreatant for a weekend. My class had been studying for three years, and the weekend would be the culmination of all our studies.

"We'll assign each of you a room," said the instructor, "and you're free to decorate it any way you like."

I gulped. A few weeks earlier I'd have been able to create a lovely space, but Keith and I were moving out of Los Angeles in three days. Everything I owned, except for the barest necessities and the trash, was already packed, waiting for the moving van. And it didn't seem right to buy things to decorate the room; new things wouldn't be part of me.

I raided the "To Be Discarded" pile, taking out a mostly burned-down Yankee candle, a worn sheet with a swirly pattern, a chipped vase and a sprig of plastic flowers. I added a box of tissues and drove down to the campus, where we were given a page of rules for decorating our rooms. One of the rules was "No fire," so I couldn't even light the candle.

When I got the decorations to my room, they looked makeshift, but at least I'd done something. I hoped my retreatant wouldn't be too choosy.

When she walked in, she didn't even seem to notice the room. She introduced herself, sat down and burst into tears. I moved the box of tissues to the side table by her chair. For the next hour, she talked and I listened, hoping I was saying the right things in the pauses.

When that session was over, I suggested she spend time by herself until the next hour we would spend together. She smiled at me and said, "I really like how fresh the flowers look."

"They're plastic," I said.

Her smile widened. "What matters," she said, "is that you're real."

Help me, God, to know that what is within is much more important than appearances.
—RHODA BLECKER

Sun 19

Lord, you have been our dwelling place throughout all generations.
—PSALM 90:1 (NIV)

We had a tree-housewarming celebration last Sunday afternoon. Seven grandchildren, three sets of parents, my husband Lynn and I circled the trunk of a tree in the waning sunshine as my son Derek pounded the final nail in the wooden structure he'd been constructing for the past several weekends. We took pictures and gave loud cheers for the tree-house builder.

I grew up on this land, and when I was a child, my grandfather built a tree house in a huge cottonwood tree at the bottom of the hill below our house. A farmer owned the property, but he was happy to have a tree house there because nobody lived anywhere near that tree—except a bunch of cows.

That tree house became my place of sacred solitude. I remember lying on my back on the planks of wood and looking up through the huge green leaves at the panorama of sky. I'm sure that's where I learned how quickly clouds can change shape and move across the sky. It's also where God became real to me. I felt His nearness and I didn't have to use words to talk to Him. I believed He could hear me and He cared about me. No wonder I went to the tree house when I felt lonely or sad.

When our children were growing up on the same land, they, too, visited the tree house, but eventually the land was sold and new homes sprouted up. New children discovered the tree house, and over time, the boards in the branches of the tree disappeared.

So as I stood, looking up at this new tree house, I prayed that it might become the same kind of place for some of these grandchildren as the old one had been for me: a place to look up at the sky and realize, maybe for the first time, that God is real.

Father, bless this tree house and all the sacred places where we discover ourselves in You.
—CAROL KUYKENDALL

Mon 20

God is our refuge and strength, a very present help in trouble. Therefore will not we fear, though the earth be removed, and though the mountains be carried into the midst of the sea. —PSALM 46:1–2

The scenes seemed almost post-apocalyptic: To my right, the front of a clothing shop had been sheared off and the legs of a mannequin had been amputated, leaving her head and torso lying on the floor halfway across the room from her limbs. To my left, an apartment building had shed half the tiles on its façade. None of its windows were intact, and a bush was growing on the second floor where a chunk of wall had given way.

Street after street in the town of Huayang, in China's Sichuan Province, testified to the shattering power unleashed here during the great and tragic earthquake of 2008. As I walked these abandoned roadways, many of them still piled with debris from that disaster, I thought of the families who had once made their homes here, the shopkeepers who had sold their wares here, the children who had lived and played and grown up amid this now-crumbling asphalt, brick and tile.

I saw a sign next to one pile of debris: Ruins generate hopes. It was an odd phrase. But then, while I don't think this is exactly how the writer of the sign meant it, it occurred to me that this place, these buildings, these creations of man in their destroyed state did generate hope—by reminding me of what really matters.

Lord, no building code in the world can give us the security that we crave. No mortar can hold the bricks in place with the surety that we want. No human construct is capable of providing the framework that we need. Only You can.
—JEFF CHU

Tue 21

In quietness and confidence shall be your strength.... —ISAIAH 30:15

When my son Jeremy applied, after a three-year suspension, to have his driver's license reinstated, he was ecstatic. Me too: no more chauffeuring. Our state patrol office directed him to another office in a nearby town—something about a list.

There he was told, "Sorry, Mr. West. Your name appears on a list of possible terrorists in our New Jersey office."

"But I'm not a terrorist. I've never even been to New Jersey."

Still, he was sent on a scavenger hunt for essential credentials such as his birth certificate and original Social Security card. He could only leave voice messages in New Jersey, and it took nearly a week for his messages to be answered by a voice message from New Jersey.

Several weeks and a stack of tedious paperwork later, a kind woman in the New Jersey office spoke with Jeremy—live! "You aren't supposed to be on the list. It's a mistake, but it's difficult to remove names from the computer. They should do it at your local office. I'm calling them and sending a letter."

Jeremy reapplied, feeling confident. "Sorry, Mr. West. Your name's still on the list. It must be removed in the New Jersey office."

On the way home, as I fumed, Jeremy said, "I need to pray more."

On the third attempt, six weeks later, he was told at the window, "Sorry, Mr. West. Your name's . . ."

Gene and I sat there stunned. I complained loudly; Gene looked grim. Jeremy sat down with us, bowed his head and prayed for about fifteen minutes.

Suddenly, the loudspeaker announced, "Mr. West, if you are still in the building, will you return to the window?"

Leaning forward toward the window and listening, we heard, "Your name was just deleted. Let's get you a license. Congratulations!"

Father, I want to learn to quietly persevere in prayer.
—MARION BOND WEST

Wed 22

I have set before you life and death, blessing and cursing: therefore choose life. . . .
—DEUTERONOMY 30:19

My sister died recently. She was a quadriplegic. For the past forty-five years, my sister would wake up to the knowledge that her paralysis—the result of a sledding accident at age twelve—hadn't left her overnight, that the pleasant dreams where she walked or ran or climbed trees would become nightmares upon waking, that she would face another day with a full and active mind but with legs oddly bent, uncontrollable arms, relying on others for even the simplest of actions—for a drink of water, for a crust of bread, for compassion.

Every minute Cindy spent reading or watching TV or taking classes at Pitt or writing e-mails (using a pencil between her teeth) took three minutes of prep. And, to paraphrase Jackson Browne, when the morning light came streaming in, she'd get up and do it again. And her first question, her very first question every time she'd see us? "How *are* you? How are *you* doing?"

Each morning my sister made a choice. A random fracture of the C3/C4 vertebrae all those years ago left her with seemingly few choices, save the most crucial one of all: We can live this life as it comes, meeting others *where* they are and *who* they are, and not what they can do or what they look like or what they could be if only. We can meet tragedy on its own court: We can choose to play—outmatched, outmuscled, except where it counts—or take our ball and go home, safe in our own suffering. Cindy chose the former, difficult, tenacious path: to get up and do it again. I'd love to tell you she did so without complaint, but she was human. She did so with remarkable courage that was also human, which means it's available to us as well. It's our choice.

Lord, help me always to choose life.
And may Cindy rest in You.
—MARK COLLINS

Thu 23

Strengthen the feeble hands, steady the knees that give way; say to those with fearful hearts, "Be strong, do not fear; your God will come...."
—ISAIAH 35:3–4 (NIV)

Somehow my husband Andrew, our son John and I snagged a three-seater on the subway at rush hour. We were on our way to a meeting about John's residential placement. It has been a rough summer.

The car filled up with people who appeared to have uneventful lives. I knew this was an illusion:

Surely in a crowd this size someone was grieving, someone was just diagnosed with a serious illness, someone was severely depressed. You can't tell from the outside. They couldn't tell what was tearing at my heart, either.

But then I began to cry, and anyone looking up from an iPod or a newspaper or a book would have known all was not well. Andrew reached over and took my hand.

After seventeen years of marriage, we don't hold hands much anymore, and when we do, I don't sit gazing at how our fingers twine.

I stared at Andrew's wedding ring and remembered going to the concourse of shops on 47th Street in Manhattan to buy it. I thought of Andrew as a newlywed, tapping his ring on the subway pole, a subtle call that said, *Look at me! I'm married!*

I looked at my husband's fingernails, cut crooked (he's never learned to do it right), and at his small, gentle hands. The skin is a little more wrinkled now, the veins a bit more prominent. The same is true of mine. Given how much I feel I've aged through John's crisis, our hands look surprisingly youthful.

Andrew worries about getting older, but I don't think of him as old. I think of him as my spouse, the man given to me for always, the man I love. The man who will hold my hand when I cry on the subway in the middle of a crowd that doesn't know what is in my heart.

Lord, hold my hand, hold my heart, and teach me to hold the hearts of others ever so gently.
—JULIA ATTAWAY

Fri 24

Thus he continued slowly southward to the Negeb, pausing frequently.
—GENESIS 12:9 (TLB)

Just before his seventh birthday, our grandson Caden and his dad went for a twenty-mile bike ride on the Poudre River trail in Ft. Collins, Colorado. "It took about five hours," Mike said. "We drank lots of water, ate a ton of snacks and made frequent stops. We had fun, and Caden was proud that he finished the whole trip."

I thought about that bike ride when I was slogging through projects I couldn't seem to complete. I was sure I could dismantle my tuneless upright piano in a day; I'd taken one apart before and it was easy. Only this one weighed a ton and was full of wires that had to be individually unwound and bolts that hadn't been loosened for nearly a century.

It was the same with a grant I was writing. A month-long task stretched to forty-five days and then to sixty because I couldn't get needed information and my writing time was limited by other obligations. And after three months, the outside doors we'd ordered still weren't installed!

Eventually, though, everything was finished. My husband Don helped take apart the piano. I submitted the grant before the deadline. The doors were in place before the first winter snow. And in my devotional time, I read this beautiful reminder that "keeping on keeping on" is an integral part of God's plan for our spiritual growth:

Faithfulness means continuing quietly with the job we have been given in the situation where we have been placed...a lot of the road to heaven has to be traveled at thirty miles per hour. (Evelyn Underhill)

Thank You, Jesus, that whether we're seven or seventy, it's okay to travel life's road at a slow but steady pace.
—PENNEY SCHWAB

Sat 25

[Jesus] said to his mother, "Woman, here is your son." Then he said to the disciple, "Here is your mother." And from that hour the disciple took her into his own home.
—JOHN 19:26–27 (NRSV)

Not long ago, I spent the early morning hours of a Saturday packing our car for a day trip. I carried duffle bags of shirts and blue jeans, a suitcase of linens and piles of books and compact discs down a flight of stairs and loaded them into the back of our 1999 Toyota. My wife, my son and our dog Max all piled in beside my daughter Celia, who we were driving to college.

I still can't believe I have a daughter in college. It seems only a few years ago that I was the one in that dorm room. Moving a child on campus isn't easy, and I don't just mean the physical work of it. The emotional work is much greater, and I knew it would be. Once again, I have to learn to let go.

Imagine the letting go Jesus did from the cross as He saw His best friend and His mother standing below. He loved them. He was concerned for their future, knowing the loss each would feel when He was gone. Most importantly, He reminded them of something He'd been teaching all along: Family is more than biology.

Ever since the boy Jesus was twelve, sitting in the temple while his parents searched for Him, He made it clear that a reordering of things was going on. And later, as He looks around at His friends and disciples, He declares: "Here are my mother and my brothers! Whoever does the will of God is my brother and sister and mother" (Mark 3:34–35, NRSV).

Family is more than biology. My daughter will be fine. This is her time to shine, and it's my time to care for others. If I take seriously what Jesus taught about family, my family will always increase.

I need You today, God. Bring me peace.
—JON SWEENEY

Sun 26

He who finds a wife finds a good thing. . . . —PROVERBS 18:22 (NAS)

Our son Philip decided it was time to marry and so began an intense Internet dating search. He met Ashley, an African American Texas jewel, fifteen years his junior. They had a whirlwind courtship and engagement. Then Phil informed us that they'd like to be married in Minnesota—in two weeks!

Sixty years after his grandparents married on a Sunday afternoon in August, Phil married Ashley in a tiny chapel at our church with space for only one at a time in the aisle. Twenty people packed into the pews. The flower girl, our three-year-old granddaughter, said she was too shy and backed out the door. Vows were made, rings exchanged and their union prayed for in ten minutes. The lime-and-purple gladiolas and white lilies on the altar came from a local farmers' market. The reception meal was homemade by Mom—me—with the help of two friends.

The bride, who'd never lived outside of Texas, chose to move to Alaska with Phil, although he was willing to relocate south. When I called him at work one day to ask how it was going, he answered, "I rush home to Ashley every night." Now that's what I call well and truly married!

Father, it's not how big the wedding but how big the love. Keep us loving one another in our marriages.
—CAROL KNAPP

Mon 27

For thou Lord, hast not forsaken them that seek thee. —PSALM 9:10

This is Harrison's year," my mom announced over dinner one Sunday. "It's time to take him to Africa to meet his Zimbabwe family."

"Mom, there's no way I can take any more time away from work."

My mom smiled across the table at Corinne. "So, Corinne, what do you think?" she asked.

Looks like Harrison and I are headed to Africa, I thought. Winning an argument with my mom was difficult enough, and now that she and my fiancée were joining forces, there was no way!

I was amazed at how well Harrison weathered the twenty-four-hour flight and how quickly he warmed to his African brothers and sisters and to Paddington and Alice, their foster parents.

One day we visited an orphanage that had no sponsors. Paddington had taken us there hoping we might find some way to help. One child, deaf and unable to speak, had been introduced to art as a means of expression. He made it clear that he wanted to draw Paddington. Paddington posed proudly.

When the boy finished, Corinne smiled at Harrison and then at the boy. "I would love to buy this beautiful drawing." The boy's brother made a few signs to him as a look of pure joy spread across the boy's face.

A while later, the boy found us again. He lifted up his arm; on it, lightly scratched out on his skin, were the words *Thank You.*

Seeing the tears in Harrison's eyes, I thought back to my mom's announcement a few months earlier and then remembered the knowing look on Corinne's face as she backed my mom up. I saw the circle coming together.

Father, in the days of my deepest disappointment,
when the only prayer I knew was "God help me,"
I could never have imagined just how good
Your answer would be.
—BROCK KIDD

Tue 28

"And underneath are the everlasting arms."
—DEUTERONOMY 33:27 (NIV)

I'm not a very adventurous person. I don't like heights, and I don't like to go fast. And I'm definitely not an adrenaline junkie. But I was on vacation on a cruise ship and something looked fun about the six-story-high zip line—an inclined cable with a pulley attached—that went across an open area in the center of the ship. "Look," I told myself, "twelve-year-old kids are doing it, so it must be safe. You'll never have another chance. And it's free."

The next thing I knew I was on the top deck with a member of the crew fastening me into a sturdy harness. I strapped a helmet on my head and stepped up onto the platform. As the attendant hooked my harness to the zip line, I grasped the handlebar. Suddenly the whole thing felt like a very bad idea. I looked down at the deck so far below and told the attendant nervously, "My arms aren't strong enough to hold me."

"Your arms don't have to be strong," he said. "Let the harness hold you."

When the attendant counted to three, I gritted my teeth and lifted my feet off the platform. I didn't look down as I sat in the harness, letting it hold every bit of my weight. The ride was over in a matter of seconds, and I made a safe landing on the far deck.

As a second attendant unhooked me from the zip line, I was shaking like a leaf. But I was also a little proud of myself. And I'd learned that when I'm scared that I'm not strong enough to hold on, I can call on God. I can always rest on Him.

Dear Father, when I don't have the strength to keep myself from falling down or falling apart, I give myself up wholly to the security of Your everlasting arms.
—Karen Barber

Wed 29

Let your speech always be with grace, seasoned with salt....
—Colossians 4:6 (nkjv)

It's 5:00 AM when the sirens awake me. We're on the last leg of our vacation, staying in a motel in South Bend, Indiana, near the tollway. I peek out the window to see round after round of police cars and ambulances screaming by.

I can't get back to sleep, so I take a walk in the warm morning air until my wife Sharon awakes at six o' clock. Together we walk down the street to a little restaurant.

The restaurant seems dead; only one waitress is in sight. We order, but it takes twenty minutes for our order to arrive. I am starved, irritable. Forgetting my manners, I shove biscuits into my mouth and force them down with cranberry juice, but the biscuits are doughy. The eggs are slimy, the bacon is rubbery, the hash browns are not brown. Everything needs seasoning!

"This food is awful," I mutter to Sharon, and she nods her agreement. "This is supposed to be a name-brand restaurant. There's no excuse for this kind of service. This is the last time we ever eat at this place."

At last the waitress arrives with our ticket.

"Was everything okay?" she wants to know.

I feel my jaws clench, and my eyes are stone. "I've tasted better."

She blushes. "I'm sorry. There was a big accident on the tollway, and my help hasn't arrived, not even the cook. I'm having to do everything myself. I'm so sorry."

Suddenly my anger turns to shame, and then to compassion. I leave an extra-large tip, and as I exit the restaurant, I'm thinking, *Everything needs seasoning, especially me.*

Lord, forgive me when I put my own feelings ahead of the needs of others.
—Daniel Schantz

Thu 30

"Lord, how long?"....
—ISAIAH 6:11 (NAS)

The family had decided we should celebrate my seventieth birthday in style by eating dinner at Pine Ridge Hollow, a quaint little restaurant out in the country. Reservations were made, and on the appointed day we all piled into our son Lyle's van for the twenty-mile drive. Lively conversation and laughter bounced back and forth as each passenger took great delight in teasing me about my advancing years, discussing all the challenges associated with aging.

About five miles down the road, an uncharacteristic lull descended on the conversation. At that point, Brent, our fifty-year-old son, suddenly broke the silence with a whiny "Are we there yet?"

A burst of laughter and then a stream of complaints followed, reminiscent of our family trips when the children were young. "I hafta go to the bathroom!" "I need a drink of water." "I'm hungry!" "Mom, he's teasing me again." "Dad, he's hogging all the space." Coming from these now middle-aged men, the comments created more ripples of laughter, until all too soon we were at our destination.

Back in those early days, we discovered that the way to maintain peace among impatient little travelers on a long trip was to keep them constantly occupied with quizzes and books and games and singing. A similar solution seems to work for us seniors and middle-aged folk. The busier we keep ourselves, the less time we have for murmuring and complaining on this long journey of life.

Father God, keep me peacefully and joyfully focused on worthwhile activities until the day I reach my destination.
—ALMA BARKMAN

Fri 31

The trees of the field shall clap their hands. —ISAIAH 55:12 (NKJV)

From my upstairs windows, I look out on a cluster of oaks and maples. Their gnarled canopy is the first thing I notice when I awake. I'm aware of them throughout the day, framed by the windowpanes above my computer screen.

Over decades the trees have weathered seasonal wear and tear: a record-breaking snowstorm, a summer drought, a nor'easter's windy deluge. Nature's knocks and breaks have left their marks in forked trunks, knobbed branches, split limbs. Thomas Merton noted that the tortuous "gestures" of the orchard outside his window had become part of his prayer. I'm beginning to understand what he meant.

Last week I heard a commotion, looked up and saw a squirrel fall out of an oak. She scampered off unharmed, but she left behind a lawn littered with a dozen torn-off twigs. The new scars on the overhanging branches will make for even more knotty bends, what some might call tangled disrepair.

But that's not what I see in my present state of prayer. The trees remind me that yesterday's nicks and rips shape today's praises and petitions. The artfully twisted boughs give me permission to meander in my conversation with God: a request for guidance, a confessed fault, a colleague's irritating habit, a friend's crisis, a perplexed "Why?" I interject a *Thank You, Jesus*, before naming a family worry or a world crisis.

This morning the dangling twigs of "my" trees are swaying in a gentle breeze. Their fleeting gestures, this way and that way, provide another prayer connection for me: The tree limbs rustle hallelujahs. In response I whisper *Amen*.

> *Lord, through Your creation I can learn*
> *to commune with You.*
> —EVELYN BENCE

MY PATHWAY TO PEACE

1 _____

2 _____

3 _____

4 _____

5 _____

6 _____

7 _____

8 _____

9 _____

10 _____

11 _____

12 _____

13 _____

14 _____

15 _____

August

16 _____

17 _____

18 _____

19 _____

20 _____

21 _____

22 _____

23 _____

24 _____

25 _____

26 _____

27 _____

28 _____

29 _____

30 _____

31 _____

September

*And all thy children shall be taught of
the Lord; and great shall be
the peace of thy children.*

—Isaiah 54:13

September

Sat 1

Those who hope in the Lord will renew their strength. They will soar on wings like eagles.... —ISAIAH 40:31 (NIV)

Why me?

After a frantic first week of classes, this was supposed to be my free morning of a long-anticipated three-day weekend. We were supposed to go to Mom's lakeside cottage. In fact, Trina will begin the drive there in just two hours. Now at nine on this brilliant Saturday morning, my brother calls to say that the cottage has been rented. Moments later, my phone dies, disconnected. How can I tell Trina of the change of plans? I can't even call my brother.

I sputter all the way to the wireless store, wait in line, pay the overlooked bill—and try again to call Trina. Still no service. The patient store manager lets me use his own phone. No answer. I leave a message. Just to be on the safe side, I'll have to drive twenty-five minutes to Trina's to tell her in person; so much for my free morning. I fume all the way to my car.

My heart still pounds as I merge onto Route 4. At least traffic is light, so I can scan the woodsy landscape lining the road. Soon, I spot a hawk—perhaps an eagle—wings outstretched as it catches an updraft and glides, seemingly forever, over the highway. No flapping here. This majestic bird, the essence of grace, trusts the air and its invisible support. Imperceptibly, the tension in my neck and shoulders disappears. I remember the hymn about the security of eagles' wings and begin to hum it, then sing all the verses.

By the time I arrive at Trina's, I'm totally calm and better able to help her get over her initial disappointment at the botched plans. We share coffee, create Plan B, and ultimately enjoy a restful weekend—lifted up by grace.

Heavenly Father, thank You for the ways You lift me up and help me glide when I start flapping.
—GAIL THORELL SCHILLING

Sun 2   *For everything created by God is good, and nothing is to be rejected if it is received with thanksgiving.*
—1 TIMOTHY 4:4 (ESV)

For many years I was a good piano player. I accompanied instrumentalists when they performed in recitals, played floor routine music for gymnasts, and composed and arranged the music for two full-length musicals about New Mexico, written in conjunction with my friend Paula Paul.

Things were going well, but then I developed rheumatoid arthritis, a crippling disease. My hands twisted into claws: I could no longer play the piano; I could no longer type seventy-two words a minute.

Finally I was reduced to typing with one finger on my left hand and two fingers on my right hand. I became depressed, mourning for my lost skills.

Then one Sunday at church I heard a sermon saying there are many ways to serve God and lead a productive life. If one door closes, other doors can be opened. Ignore the skills you don't have and look for the skills you do have. Use them with joy and thanksgiving to the glory of God.

That advice changed my life. I can no longer play the piano, but I enjoy other people's playing. I can't type fast, but I can still type, and I have written and published twelve books as well as articles and short stories.

> *Lord, today I will encourage someone else who is physically or emotionally challenged, and share with them the good news that there are many ways to serve You and enjoy life.*
> —MADGE HARRAH

Mon 3

> *"Do not work for the food that perishes, but for the food that endures for eternal life, which the Son of Man will give you. . . . "*
> —JOHN 6:27 (NRSV)

The summer I turned fourteen, I worked longer hours than I've ever worked since. At 6:30 each morning I'd rise and, after a quick breakfast, begin the seven-mile bike ride to a golf course in a nearby suburb, where my brother Doug and I worked as caddies. We'd arrive at about 7:15, and by 8:00 we'd be on the course, carrying two heavy golf bags each, "double-caddying" for two people at once. These early-morning golfers liked to walk fast, and we'd be back in the clubhouse by about 10:30, having walked eighteen holes and about six miles.

By noon, we'd be back out on the course, this time carrying the really heavy golf bag of a more serious golfer or sprinting beside a golfer in an electric cart. The latter was called "fore-caddying"; we had to run ahead of the cart and find the ball in the tall grass before they arrived on the spot.

I worked hard that summer, but I rarely felt very tired. I was only fourteen. No wonder!

More recently, my toughest days of work have left me mentally, spiritually and physically exhausted. I began to wonder why—until I recently figured out that I was missing something essential: I was forgetting to stop for a moment every now and then to rest my mind, think a fresh thought, walk around the block, pray for a friend or look up in the trees and admire the songbird just outside my office window.

I wasn't more easily refreshed at fourteen simply because I was fourteen; I was less tired then because

I was more easily distracted. Today I'm good at focusing. But too much focus leads to too much stress, as well as exhaustion.

It's Labor Day. Take a break today. But don't forget to take a break on your working days too.

> *Lord, we work hard. Teach us to rest*
> *as well as we work.*
> —JON SWEENEY

THIS I KNOW

Tue 4

He that loveth silver shall not be satisfied.... —ECCLESIASTES 5:10

THE SILVER CRAYON

I'm scouting through the school supplies in our local Kmart, searching for ink cartridges, when I'm greeted by a familiar smell. My husband David says that smell is the most primitive trigger in our brain and easily brings us vivid memories. I find that to be true as I stand in the store aisle, breathing in the smell of rainbow-colored happiness.

I see myself now, a child again, carefully opening my prized yellow-and-green box of crayons. My fingers run over the sixty-four luxurious hues until

I touch my beloved silver crayon. I pull it from its place and add a bit of sparkle to my coloring book Cinderella. Then I quickly return the crayon to its special spot.

My brother Davey reaches over for a crayon to finish off a Mickey Mouse fireman, but he keeps his hands off of silver, knowing how jealously I guard it. Part of me is pleased, knowing I have this power over my brother. Still deeper, another part of my heart feels a bit tight, a little greedy and a lot dissatisfied.

The memory becomes complicated, as it offers a truth I've known for a long, long time: Hoarding will never make us happy. Keeping the best for ourselves dulls the shine of all we possess. Refusing to share makes abundance seem paltry.

Someday I hope I might look back and see my life as a luscious box of crayons: sixty-four beautiful colors, each with a special name like sky blue, eggplant, dandelion, indigo—and yes, silver. Nothing held back, everything shared to spread shades of hope and happiness out into the larger world.

Father, show me how to let go and use my gifts
to brighten the lives of others.
—Pam Kidd

Wed 5

He hath made every thing beautiful in his time: also he hath set the world in their heart, so that no man can find out the work that God maketh from the beginning to the end.
—ECCLESIASTES 3:11

Yesterday I was on a commuter train at eight o'clock in the morning, hurtling my way to Manhattan. Surrounded by fellow passengers, I had my head down, consumed by a folder of work papers, readying myself for my day.

The people around me seemed equally involved in their own worlds. Some sipped coffee, some seemed lost in the newspaper, others were already responding to e-mail, listening to music, even surfing the Internet. Each of us was engaged with our own thoughts and activities, yet all together in the same shiny silver train car on our shared excursion into the city.

No one spoke to anyone else; each person sat on this train as an individual, delineated by profession, personal circumstances, attire, attitudes and activities, even the seats they'd chosen. Yet among us there was also an unspoken, perhaps less-than-conscious companionship of people on a shared journey to a common destination.

As the train neared the tunnel into the city, it slowed, and the change in velocity nudged me back into an awareness of my surroundings. I lifted my head and glanced out the window to a marshy scene alongside the tracks. I had looked up just in time to witness the largest blue heron I'd ever seen lift off from the water. It extended its long, graceful body and gently flapped its broad, beautiful wings at a pace exactly in sync with our train.

How magnificent is this life that puts a great gray bird in sync with a silver train, that allows us all to pursue our journeys in our own way, yet somehow all in the same direction.

Dear God, thank You for putting me on a path with so many companions and so much at which to marvel.
—ANNE ADRIANCE

Thu 6

I was sick and ye visited me....
—MATTHEW 25:36

Dad had moved full time into a skilled nursing facility. By Mom's account, it sounded like a good place, with compassionate caregivers, lovely gardens, good food and a welcoming atmosphere. I was flying across the country to see Dad in his new home for the first time. What would I do? "Sing for them," Mom suggested. "They would like that."

Dad could never carry much of a tune but always liked it when I sang. I sang at family weddings, in school musicals, with my college friends and in church choirs, but this would be different. Dad was in a new place, with a roommate, wide institutional halls and a group of complete strangers to eat his meals with. I printed out some words to songs I thought they might like, but wouldn't it be odd to stand there in the room where they watched TV, me singing as though I were back in the living room at home?

"Hi, Dad," I said, kissing him on the cheek.

"Hi, honey," Mom said, coming around to the back of the wheelchair to push him down the hall.

"Hi," I said to the group assembled there, many not even meeting my gaze. "I'm Thornton Hamlin's son, and one of the things I've always done for Dad is sing. I thought I might sing for you too." Feeling very much alone, I opened my mouth and sang an old big-band dance tune that Dad always liked.

He beamed. Others swayed in their chairs. One woman, who'd seemed completely out of it, smiled at me and mouthed all the words. "East of the sun and west of the moon," she sang along, "we'll build a dream house of love, dear."

They made one of the best audiences I'd ever had.

I will take myself, Lord, where You need me.
—RICK HAMLIN

Fri 7 Lord I believe; help thou mine unbelief.
—MARK 9:24

Over the years I have come to realize how much we need to pray for our kids as they leave the protective covering of home and church and move on to college, where frequently the faith and moral values with which they have been raised will be vigorously challenged.

I had watched a friend's daughter grow from a gangly teenager into a beautiful young woman. She aced her way through high school and earned a scholarship to a prestigious college. Now, just over a year later, she was sitting at my kitchen table having a cozy cup of tea.

"I've dumped the faith." Her tone was defiant. I raised my eyebrows and waited for her to continue. "All that stuff they taught me in Sunday school . . . I've chucked it. I don't believe in God anymore."

"Pity," I said as I added tea to refill her cup.

"What do you mean, 'pity'?" She was itching for an argument.

Lord, give me the right words. I thought of all the wonderful Scriptures on faith that I could fling at her; she knew them better than I did. I decided all I could do was share from my heart. "I don't know how people get along without the Lord, without a higher power to Whom they can pray." As I spoke, she was looking at me intently.

September

"What would I do if a call came in to pray for a friend who was critically injured in an accident, and there was no one to whom I could pray! In the final moments before she died, I held my mother in my arms. 'Mummy darling, don't be afraid, you're going from my arms into the arms of Jesus,' I told her. She gave a little smile and gasped her last breath. What would I do if at the end of their lives, all I could say to my loved ones was 'good-bye,' without the hope of everlasting life? More and more, I need the Lord."

"I hadn't thought of that." She had tears in her eyes. "I guess I need Him too." We held hands and prayed.

As our children leave home and move on with their lives, Father, protect and steady them in the faith.
—FAY ANGUS

Sat 8

A fool gives full vent to his anger, but a wise man keeps himself under control.
—PROVERBS 29:11 (NIV)

It was late afternoon at the Nashville Zoo, and my five-year-old grandson Frank had his favorite place all to himself. It has nothing to do with the animals: It's the wall-to-wall tumbling mats in the playground area. He'd just finished building an obstacle course with every one of the uniquely shaped pillows.

"Watch this action, Granny," he called to me, knees bent, arms spread.

But his takeoff was interrupted by a mother and her young daughter striding across the mats. To my shock, the mother snatched the biggest and best pillow right out of Frank's obstacle course. "Do you mind if my child plays with this?" she asked brusquely.

She can't treat my grandson like that, I thought, and in anger I rose from the bench ready to let her know it. But Frank beat me to it.

"Would you like to play with me?" he asked the dark-haired little girl peering around her mother.

The girl nodded, giving Frank a wide smile. Sheepishly the mother handed back the pillow. Quietly, I sat down. The pillow debacle had ended before it began. The children came together to put on a tumbling show for two chastened adults, who were reminded that playing together is what it's all about.

Lord, when friction divides, help me to still my tongue and sit on my anger long enough to see what's really important.
—SHARI SMYTH

Sun 9

And may you live to see your children's children. . . . —PSALM 128:6 (NIV)

When my sister Anna was a child, Grandma would come over to our house a few times a week to play games with her. Though they were separated in age by some seventy years, they would sit together on the floor and laugh and giggle like best friends.

Once, Grandma looked down at my young sister and said, "Anna, you're so cute I could just eat you up!"

Worried, Anna said, "But Grandma, if you ate me up, then you wouldn't have anyone to play with you!"

Over the years, Grandma has recounted that conversation many times, usually on holidays when the family is gathered around the dinner table. She always concludes by looking each of her grandchildren in the eye and saying, "Someday, when I'm on my deathbed, if you see me smile just before I pass from this world, you'll know that I'm remembering that story and thinking of each of you."

Fortunately for the grandchildren who love her, Grandma is still very much with us. But hearing her say those words has shown me that at the end of my time here, the earthly thing I'll care about most is my family. And if that's true at the end, it should be no less true today.

I try to thank God each day that He's given me my family; and not only that, He's given me Grandma, who's taught me how to love them.

Lord, thank You for my family. Please give me the grace to love and care for them each and every day.
—JOSHUA SUNDQUIST

Mon 10

"I will refresh the weary and satisfy the faint."
—JEREMIAH 31:25 (TNIV)

Our calico cat Thelma and our thirteen-year-old black Lab Cooper faithfully attend our porch parties. Cooper never leaves my husband Rick's side. Cooper lies beside his feet, happy to be included. But Thelma keeps a tight schedule. Somehow she manages to squeeze in porch parties despite her busy ways. Always in a hurry, she arrives late. She has so much to do, such a long list. Like me, I guess.

One morning, Thelma was wired. She didn't stop for a second. Usually she'd rub against our legs, but she had no time for play that day. She zipped across the porch, chasing a lizard; Rick helped it escape. Then she balanced on her hind legs on the railing and stretched up to paw at a hanging basket. The basket began to sway, and a few dried fern leaves fell from it. "No, Thelma!" I said. "Stop it!"

Momentarily satisfied, she hunted the crispy fern sprigs as though they were prey.

"Thelma, rest a minute," I said. "Like Cooper. See? He never leaves us." Hearing his name, Cooper wagged his tail.

"Wonder what that cat's thinking," Rick said.

"No telling. Come here, kitty." Ignoring me, Thelma leaped off the porch and landed in the gardenia bush. "She runs from one emergency to the next," I said.

"They're emergencies of her own making," Rick observed.

That's when it hit me: I'd allowed busyness to crowd my days. Unimportant duties had distracted me from spending time snuggling beside the ones I love.

Lord, I've been so busy chasing silly things. This feels better—resting by Your side.
—Julie Garmon

Tue 11   *God is not unjust; he will not forget your work and the love you have shown him as you have helped his people.... —Hebrews 6:10 (niv)*

Shortly after we moved into our townhouse in Carmel, New York, we learned that our next-door neighbor's husband, a firefighter, had been killed on September 11, 2001. Like so many, we were deeply impacted by events of that day.

In our first year in the community, Elba and I felt we wanted to show our support to our neighbor. We wanted to let her know that her husband's sacrifice was not forgotten. Elba suggested giving her an angel figurine, but we didn't know how she might react to our gesture. We chose not to do anything.

The second year, we were still uncertain how best to express our thoughts to our neighbor. Early on the morning of 9/11, we watched the ceremony from Ground Zero on television and listened to the roll call of those who had died at the World Trade Center. Elba turned to me and said, "I want to do something for our neighbor. I have a tugging in my heart to give her a gift, maybe flowers or a plant."

I said, "Follow your heart and just do it."

Elba decided to go out to pick up a gift. On the way, she remembered her original idea: an angel. At the store the salesperson pointed out the Angel of Remembrance. Elba thought to herself, *This is the perfect angel.* She put the angel in a gift bag and left it at the door of our neighbor's townhouse.

Several days later, we received a card from our neighbor. "Thank you for the gift," it said. "I've put the Angel of Remembrance beside my husband's photo."

Dear God, give me the courage to follow the tugs of my heart and show others that I care.
—PABLO DIAZ

Wed 12   *Write: for these words are true and faithful.* —REVELATION 21:5

I resisted signing on to a social network because I'd heard the sites were full of negativity and gossip. Besides, I couldn't possibly keep up with the five hundred–plus "friends" lots of people had. But eventually I joined, and I discovered a world of bewildering one-liners, personal insights and inspiration. Here are some of my favorite posts:

He was okay when the helicopter came. It took a phone call to discover that our grandson David's friend Collin was bitten by a rattlesnake while they were hunting.

Other than our team losing, someone throwing green liquid at the car, and a fight at the drive-in, I'd say today was all right! Grandson Mark, fourteen, has a unique ability to find the positive in every situation.

All thirty-three Chilean miners and the rescue workers are on the surface. To God be the glory for such a dynamic exhibition of teamwork! Marsha Douglas

Gordon, a Texas woman of great faith, wrote this on October 13, 2010. Her posts remind me of the power of prayer and thanksgiving.

Spirit of Peace, fill us this night so as the morning comes we may be your Peace in the moment, in the place, and in the Sacred Space where we are. Pastor Kent Little, Wichita, posts morning and evening prayers—reminders of God's grace and presence in a world of turmoil.

Sometimes I come across negative and disturbing statements. Overwhelmingly, however, the daily writings delight, encourage and lift my spirits.

Thank You, Jesus, for the blessings my fifty-five (and counting) social network friends add to my daily life.
—PENNEY SCHWAB

Thu 13   *He that hateth his brother is in darkness, and walketh in darkness, and knoweth not whither he goeth, because that darkness hath blinded his eyes.* —I JOHN 2:11

One time I was on the other side of the planet, where the birds and trees and stars and heroes are different. I was waiting for a friend under an enormous clock, and I got to talking to a woman who had grown up in the middle of that country, in a red desert, where there was "no police law," she said. "There was people law, the law our people had lived by for maybe fifty thousand years, very good law."

"Then the police law came," she said, "and pinned our law to the ground like you would pin something down with a stake. The old law couldn't get loose and the new law damaged the people. Children were stolen, and worse. A lot of hate got built up. Hate has to go somewhere, you know, like lava has to go somewhere. It's like that.

"My grandmother, she was very wise, and she gave me a hat, and I told every word of hate out of me and into the hat, and then we buried that hat so deep you couldn't dig it up in a week. 'So much for *that* hate,' said my grandmother, and you would be surprised how right she was.

"So there is a story for you to carry home to your country. How do you get hate out of you in your country? I bet there are a lot of ways to get hate out but we don't know them all. What if there were more ways to get hate out of us than there is hate in us? That would be fine. We would certainly need a lot of hats, though."

Dear Lord, thank You, most sincerely and heartfelt-fully, for hats. You know what I mean.
—BRIAN DOYLE

Fri 14

He himself bore our sins in his body on the tree, so that we might die to sins and live for righteousness; by his wounds you have been healed.
—I Peter 2:24 (NIV)

For years our son Stephen hadn't slept in his own bed. We'd read a bedtime story, brush teeth, say prayers . . . and then, no matter where Stephen lay down, five minutes later he'd be up again. "Mommy, I need a snuggle," he'd whisper.

When I'd tell Stephen to go back to bed, he'd appear again in a few minutes. He was willing to face all consequences, including my wrath, because he couldn't fall asleep. So each night I held him until he drifted off; snuggling my youngest for half an hour was easier than dealing with meltdowns from a sleep-deprived child the next day.

I'd always assumed Stephen was just one of those kids who have a hard time getting to sleep. Then his older brother John moved to a residential facility. That week Stephen suddenly decided to sleep in his own bed—the bed he'd slept in perhaps once in his life, in the room he theoretically shared with his brother. My six-year-old climbed into his bunk and was asleep within five minutes.

And then I knew: Stephen's restlessness at night was based on fear. The kind of fear that slithers out of the dark corners of the heart at night, infecting reason, distorting hope, daring morning to ever come. The fear that makes us cling to the few things we know are safe and true and good.

I looked sorrowfully at my child, overwhelmed by the damage I was unable to prevent or even see. I grieved for his brokenness and wondered: How did Christ manage it, up there on the cross? How could He have stood to look on all the brokenness of all the people of all time—and take it upon Himself?

Jesus, You bore what we cannot; when suffering overwhelms me, teach me to join my suffering to Yours.
—Julia Attaway

Sat 15

"See that you do not look down on one of these little ones. For I tell you that their angels in heaven always see the face of my Father in heaven."
—Matthew 18:10 (NIV)

The Crimson Tide, the University of Alabama's football team, roared onto the field for the season opener. Early fall was just starting to creep into the stadium, giving the cheering crowd of nearly a hundred thousand a brief reprieve from the sweltering heat of summer.

The cheerleaders wore their familiar crimson outfits, the stadium announcer led the crowd in the traditional cheers, and we recognized the people around us from previous falls, but one thing was different: For the first time in years, Dad wasn't there.

As the crowd swayed along to the national anthem, I wondered at how something that was so familiar and so routine could feel so utterly foreign. Without Dad, the stadium somehow seemed bigger, as if I were a little girl again, struggling to navigate the turnstiles. But when the announcer began to play a highlight video of the Crimson Tide's victories, it seemed to me that Dad was right there, cheering on the team.

The Dallas Cowboys may say they have a stadium with a roof that opens so that God can watch His favorite team, but I guarantee you that on that first game day after his passing, Dad had the best seat in the house.

Thank You, Lord, for reminding me that with
time comes healing and the return of our
fond memories and smiles.
—ASHLEY KAPPEL

READER'S ROOM

I was a shy and quiet university student who noticed the many couples walking to classes hand-in-hand. Wistfully, I prayed that God would send someone to me, so we could be one of those couples. Very soon after this Ed and I met. He was a veteran studying under the GI Bill. Now, although we have completed six decades of marriage, he continues to be my gift from God for whom I am thankful every day. And, yes, we still hold hands during our daily two-mile walks.

—*Natalie Barber, Green Valley, Arizona*

Sun 16

My dear brothers and sisters, be strong and immovable. Always work enthusiastically for the Lord, for you know that nothing you do for the Lord is ever useless.
—I CORINTHIANS 15:58 (NLT)

I've long believed that God sends people into our lives. Sometimes I don't recognize them as quickly as I should; at other times it's so obvious I can't ignore it. This past year I had the privilege of meeting Kent Annan, a missionary to Haiti.

I first heard about Kent from a friend, an avowed agnostic who'd read Kent's book *Following Jesus*

Through the Eye of the Needle and knew I'd enjoy the story. I ordered the book and started to read it in fits and starts.

Then a month later someone else mentioned Kent's name and mailed me a second copy of the book. By this point I'd gotten the message: God wanted me to read the book. I did and was deeply touched by the powerful message. Then to my surprise I discovered that Kent Annan lived just a few miles from me. I got in touch with him, and the two of us met for lunch.

As we shared the meal, Kent told me that his father was a pastor. Kent had lived a pretty normal life before his call to the mission field. He'd never rebelled against his family or his God. His spiritual life, Kent said, had been filled with "little conversions," small steps of faith that drew him closer to God and lit his own life path.

I thought about what Kent shared that day and realized I've had little conversions too. They were the quiet mornings when I prayed and felt His presence and His love, guiding me, urging me to step forward in faith and assuring me He would always be at my side.

Thank You, Father, for Your presence and peace,
and for the confidence in knowing that
You are always with me.
—DEBBIE MACOMBER

Mon 17

*"If you have faith the size of a
mustard seed, you will say to this
mountain, 'Move from here to
there,' and it will move; and
nothing will be impossible to you."*
—MATTHEW 17:20 (NAS)

Tucked away in a tiny museum at the Peale
Center in Pawling, New York, is a mustard
seed. The first time I saw it, I was going through
a hard time, living in a new town and looking for
work. I had been through the help-wanted ads and
filled out job applications while keeping a close
watch on my checking account and going over my
budget to find ways to cut corners.

My mind filled with worry, I walked to a nearby
bakery, ordered a cup of coffee and began reading
the newspaper I found on the table. In the classified
section was an advertisement for a museum only a
few blocks away. *Why not?* I thought. *Maybe it will
make me feel better.*

The building that housed the museum was easy
to find; a receptionist guided me up the stairs to the
exhibit and turned on the lights for me. I walked
through the room, looking at tapestries and arti-
facts, and then turned a corner. At the end of the
aisle was a glass case. I almost walked by it, thinking
it was empty, but from the corner of my eye I could
see something on a pedestal inside it—a seed. A

card explained that it was a mustard seed that had traveled to the moon on one of the *Apollo* missions.

I looked at the case for quite a while, captivated by such an extraordinary symbol of faith: as small as a mustard seed, yet open to every possibility— like the once-impossible journey to the moon and back.

Dear Lord, even though things may seem impossible, my faith in You will always see me through.
—SABRA CIANCANELLI

Tue 18

"But God meant it for good...."
—GENESIS 50:20 (NAS)

After my son Jeremy's driver's license was re-stored, Gene and I helped him look for a truck. He'd received an unexpected, long-overdue check, had the money he'd been saving for three years and had gotten a job in a restaurant. He didn't want to buy anything flashy like the sports cars he once drove (much too fast). Week after week we searched, to no avail.

"Hey, Marion," Gene suggested, "what about that dealership nearby? You know, the one where you rear-ended one of their salesmen."

I frowned, embarrassed. "I don't want to see him again. That was a bad day."

"Never mind. You've got his card, don't you?" Gene asked.

I handed it over, grumbling. Jeremy looked at it. "Maxie Price in Loganville. I've bought from them before!"

At the dealership, Jeremy asked for the salesman I'd slightly rear-ended about six months before. The young man appeared and smiled—even at me. Jeremy explained what he needed and exactly what he could pay.

"Trucks like that are very popular," the salesman said. "Unfortunately, we don't have one on the lot. We can't keep 'em."

As we were leaving, the salesman called us back. "Hold on. We just got a truck in from South Carolina today. They're still detailing it out back."

We waited, and soon a mighty fine truck appeared: a Dodge Ram, 2002, clean as new, four-door, fully automatic. I saw a slight smile playing on my son's face as he stroked the hood ornament as he would a good dog. Sure enough: his truck, his price.

"I'll never take having a driver's license for granted again," Jeremy said. "It's a privilege. God's so good to me; He knew all along where that truck was."

Father, help me learn to expect Your goodness
to redeem even bad situations.
—MARION BOND WEST

Wed 19

Now it is required that those who have been given a trust must prove faithful.
—I Corinthians 4:2 (NIV)

Last year I met two teenage boys whose father had been killed for teaching about Jesus in India. For a few years, he had been a traveling preacher and often got Bibles in the local language from our staff and carried them on the back of his bicycle into distant villages. Caught by an angry mob one evening, he was beaten unconscious and then thrown onto a pile of burning rubbish, where he perished.

I'd arrived in their town with representatives of three other organizations who were working together for the first time. Two of us have a mission of providing Scriptures, and two have missions of providing relief supplies and help. We came together because it seemed ridiculous to bring spiritual encouragement without practical help, and giving practical help without spiritual encouragement feeds only the body and not the soul. Here were people whose homes had been destroyed and who had been run off the land where they had grown food to survive. The government had finally contained the violence, but the people were returning to villages that were now just piles of rubble.

September

The boys had ridden their single-speed bicycles for many hours to join the group gathered in town. We were introduced and tearfully embraced. Then they stepped back and, with faces shining, exclaimed, "Brother Eric, you will not believe what has happened. Many neighbors were saddened by Father's death and they want to know what is in that book he died for. So please, please, Brother Eric, give us two boxes of Bibles each to take home!"

They got their boxes and I got a lesson in faithfulness, the faithfulness of a father passed on to his sons.

Lord, let me be found faithful today, using everything You have put into my hands.
—Eric Fellman

Thu 20

You knit me together in my mother's womb. —Psalm 139:13 (NIV)

I stood outside the door of my daughter Kendall's surgery-delivery room with my nose pressed against the small window. I'd been in on the last several C-section births of my grandchildren, but this hospital had suddenly changed the rules and now allowed only one other person in the delivery room with the mother during a C-section.

After Kendall's first C-section two years earlier, I told the world how much I loved witnessing the miraculous sight of a baby popping right out of a mommy's tummy. I didn't get the least bit weak-kneed and took pride in my masterful videotaping of the delivery. It was the same with my other daughter's three C-section births.

But on this day, I stood outside Kendall's delivery room, dressed in scrubs and holding a camera, in hopes they might let me in to be with Kendall after her husband David carried their newborn baby out to another room to be cleaned up. I squeezed to one side of the window, watching and waiting—and then suddenly, I heard a cry and saw the doctor lift a perfect, flailing little body up in the air so Kendall and David could see him: a boy! All at once, tears ran down my face and I could hardly breathe.

Within seconds, someone opened the door and beckoned me to come in, earlier than the policy usually allowed. I was able to take some pictures of Daddy holding the baby, cutting his umbilical cord and then putting his little body up close to Kendall's face so she could touch him for the first time. Soon the baby was whisked away, and I sat down beside Kendall while they finished the procedure.

And I thanked God that once again I'd been given the privilege of witnessing the most sacred and miraculous earthly hope-bringer: the birth of a baby.

*Lord, what a miracle You give us in the creation and
birth of a new life, which astounds and infuses
a whole family with hope.*
—CAROL KUYKENDALL

Fri 21

*For whom the Lord loves he
chastens....* —HEBREWS 12:6 (NKJV)

My mother and father did not rear six good
children without having to practice corrective
discipline from time to time. If I was doing something that needed to stop immediately, my mother
might apply her wooden mixing spoon to the back
of my thigh with a sharp rap. "Ouch," I'd respond,
but it was harmless, and it served to get my attention. Actually, I preferred that form of discipline,
because it was simple and quick.

If my crime was more serious, she would put a
chair in the middle of the living room and say,
"Now, Danny, you will sit on that chair for one
hour, and I mean one solid hour." I hated that form
of discipline. One hour is one year in the life of a
restless boy. By the end of the hour, I was utterly
limp and compliant.

If these two modes of correction did not work,
the third one always did: She would cancel my
allowance until I learned to behave. Money talks,
and I would promise anything to get back on the
payroll.

When I became a dad, I quickly learned that dispensing discipline truly is harder than submitting to it. There is always the risk that children will interpret discipline as meanness or a lack of love. In reality, discipline is a form of love more real than kisses and hugs, because a parent is putting his or her own popularity and image at risk to administer it.

Discipline is a godly thing, and I have no resentment toward my parents for their efforts to help me grow up strong and wise. I wish more parents were like them; the world would be a safer place than it is.

Thank You, Lord, for my parents, who loved me more than their own popularity and peace. Help me to be as unselfish as they were.
—DANIEL SCHANTZ

Sat 22

There she shall respond as in the days of her youth. . . .
—HOSEA 2:15 (NRSV)

I was an autumn equinox baby; when I was young, the end of summer reminded me that I had a birthday coming. I grew up in Pennsylvania, where autumn was an occasion. We could watch the leaves change color, feel the crispness in the air and watch the markets begin selling school supplies, pumpkins, gourds and ears of colored horse corn.

September

My husband Keith and I lived in Los Angeles for so long that I forgot those things. Perhaps it would have been painful to think I was missing them. Autumn was so like the other seasons that my birthday's arrival always surprised me, especially as I grew older and birthdays seemed less important. Besides, Southern California was deeply enamored of youth, so birthdays were inconvenient reminders of aging.

Our move to Washington State brought back the seasons, and I recaptured what autumn had meant all the time I was growing up. The bright leaf colors against the dark green of the pines, spruce and cedar brought back memories. Honeycrisp apples showed up on the supermarket shelves, crisp and tart-sweet rather than mealy-fleshed and flavor-challenged. The pumpkins and squashes were grown down the road, not hundreds of miles away. The gutters needed cleaning out in preparation for the rain. Like the squirrels, we put in supplies of food; we had the heater checked. We were all lining our nests.

My birthday became an occasion again. And I saw that it had less to do with growing older than with celebrating life.

Thank You, Lord, for showing me that autumn can be a time of brightness and birth.
—RHODA BLECKER

Sun 23

When Job's three friends heard of all this adversity that had come upon him, they came each one . . . to . . . comfort him . . . with no one speaking a word to him, for they saw that his pain was very great.
—JOB 2:II, 13 (NAS)

We had scarcely become acquainted with a new couple in our congregation when their only son Barry was diagnosed with an aggressive brain tumor. Within two weeks, this young man with the physique of a top athlete was in a hospital for the terminally ill.

At the time, our little church was without a pastor, but my husband Leo had made himself available as a lay minister in case of emergencies. When the phone rang one evening and Barry's mother introduced herself, I could sense the anguish in her voice even before she explained the situation. "Would your husband please come?"

Feeling inadequate, Leo nevertheless drove to the hospital that evening and continued to visit for the next several weeks.

One evening I decided to accompany Leo. Barry's mother spied me at the end of the long corridor and came hurrying to greet me, her arms enfolding me in a welcoming hug. "Oh," she said, "you've no idea how much your presence means!"

I had worried about what words of consolation I could bring, so I merely sat with her, "with no one speaking a word," for I saw that her "pain was very great."

> *Lord, let me not underestimate the importance*
> *of merely being there.*
> —ALMA BARKMAN

❊ A GRACE-FILLED JOURNEY

Mon 24

But I say unto you, Love your enemies, bless them that curse you, do good to them that hate you, and pray for them which despitefully use you, and persecute you; that ye may be the children of your Father which is in heaven. . . .
—MATTHEW 5:44–45

A SONG IN THE NIGHT

Here is a story told to our group at Gallipoli, the site of one of the most famous battles of World War I. British forces were facing Turkish resistance in a situation of very close combat. The trenches in some places were no farther apart than the width of a two-lane highway.

From a soldier's diary comes this account: During the day the troops were shooting and throwing grenades at each other, but at night, they would sometimes throw candy and packs of cigarettes across to each other. One night, a Turk was heard singing and the British responded by singing back. Even in the thick of war, this interaction continued for several nights as the men were actually relating to one another as fellow human beings! Then came the night when there was no singing and the British troops concluded the singer had probably died in the fight of the day.

That soldier might not have called himself a Christian, but he followed one of Christ's most important teachings.

Help me, Lord, to follow the example of that Turkish soldier who learned to love his enemy.
—MARILYN MORGAN KING

Tue 25   *"I am the Lord, the God of all mankind. Is anything too hard for me?"* —JEREMIAH 32:27 (NIV)

I'm not sure when I fell in love with hydrangeas. Growing up, I never saw them in our yard—the closest thing we had was the lowly snowball bush. But when, as an adult, I finally discovered this lush, lovely plant, it was love at first sight.

Then, in March sixteen years ago, my mother died. I was grief-stricken, devastated, numb. My faraway friend Aline sent me a lovely pink hydrangea, top-heavy in its small clay pot, and I vowed to keep this plant alive. For weeks it bloomed on my desk before I thought the ground was warm enough for outdoor planting.

Slowly, flowers began to appear: the first year, only one; the next year, two. Some years I'm blessed with more blossoms than I can count; other times the bright pink blooms are sparse.

Recently, I mentioned to a master gardener friend that I'd like to keep the bush growing, to make sure lots of flowers appeared regularly. He looked at me as if I were crazy. "That thing should never have survived even one winter! It's a hothouse florist's plant. It was never meant to face up to this frigid Midwest weather!"

Today I walked around my flowerbeds, noting the bareness of impending fall. Then I caught a glimpse of my hydrangea bush. The magenta blossoms had faded to a mottled mauvy green, but they were still lovely.

I picked a handful and brought them inside. They will dry quite well and last through the snowy months, a lovely reminder of Mother—and of miracles.

Open my eyes, God, to the miracles around me.
—MARY LOU CARNEY

ON THE ROAD

Wed 26   *You shall love your neighbor as yourself....*
—LEVITICUS 19:18 (RSV)

DAY 1: THREE WHO CARE

It's not the way you want a monthlong trip to begin. We'd set out from our apartment outside Boston on September 2. The next morning, leaving our motel in New Jersey, we spotted a dent on the right side of the Camry. No note, no name, no phone number. No, no one had reported the damage to the front desk. Some irresponsible person had hit the car, indifferent to the welfare of others.

So John and I did what we've done many times before when confronted with an uncaring person: asked God to show us, that very day, three very different people.

I met the first even before we left the motel. As I headed for the car from the breakfast area carrying two Styrofoam cups of coffee, a young man literally ran from his table to open the front door for me.

An hour later, filling the tank before leaving New Jersey's cheaper gas, John asked a fellow driver if there was a grocery store in the area. "Yes—but it's complicated to find from here," the stranger said. "I'll lead you there."

And pulling into a picnic area in Pennsylvania with our lunch makings, we watched a mother and two youngsters running from table to table with paper bags, making a game of picking up the litter other visitors had left behind. A responsible citizen raising two more!

God had shown us our three caring people and it was only noon.

Did You put three exceptional people across our path, Father, or did You answer our prayers by opening our eyes to the thoughtfulness that's so much more common than callousness?
—ELIZABETH SHERRILL

❦ ON THE ROAD

Thu 27   *For I am the Lord, I change not....*
—MALACHI 3:6

DAY 2: EXILES ON THE OHIO

On a steep bank above the Ohio river, on our way to visit our son Scott and his family in

Nashville, we stopped to admire a statue of a man and woman. She holds a baby; his right arm wraps protectively around her shoulders, while with his left he gestures at the scene before them.

Today that scene is the handsome town of Gallipolis, Ohio, but what the couple saw in October 1790 was a forested wilderness. They were two of some five hundred well-to-do French citizens fleeing the French Revolution, who'd invested their fortunes in land in America. They came with their fine china and crystal chandeliers, only to discover that the deeds they'd purchased were worthless. Nor was "their" land, as the prospectus promised, in a settled community, but on the raw frontier. The newcomers were lawyers, doctors, professors—not a carpenter or farmer among them.

When President George Washington learned of their plight, he sent woodsmen to construct log cabins for them. For the first few years, the inexperienced settlers struggled simply to survive. But by 1795, they had purchased the land on the Ohio a second time and found themselves perfectly situated on the major artery of trade with the opening West.

Looking at that couple confronting the challenges of 1790, we thought of our son, worried like all country-music writers whose songs are downloaded free on the Internet, that he might lose his home, might have to learn new skills in a new location. And we thought we'd tell him the story of the pioneers of Gallipolis, confronted with an unfamiliar world, who not only adapted, but thrived.

> *In an ever-changing world, Lord,*
> *keep my eyes on Your unchanging love.*
> —ELIZABETH SHERRILL

❧ ON THE ROAD

Fri 28

You are no longer strangers, but . . . members of the household of God. —EPHESIANS 2:19 (RSV)

DAY 3: A ROAD STOP FOR PRAYER

There weren't many customers in the roadside restaurant. Our waitress was a tall, thin, blonde girl who couldn't have been out of her teens. She lingered near our table after she brought our order.

John picked up on her obvious desire to talk. "Have you worked here long?"

"Three years," she said, ever since her second child was born.

Slowly the story came out. She'd fallen in love with a boy who promised marriage and fathered the two children. Then she discovered that he had four other children by three other girls. She worked two jobs, one in a supermarket and this one, which paid $4.19 an hour. The tips couldn't amount to much, we thought, in these remote mountains of east Tennessee.

She wasn't fishing for one now, we felt, just grateful for a listening ear. We finished our meal but lingered at the table; clearly she wanted to say something else.

"I noticed," she ventured at last, "that you said a prayer before you ate. I wondered . . . could you say one for me?"

The three of us held hands. We prayed that her son's asthma would improve, that her car would keep running, that one day she'd finish high school. Then this girl with many problems of her own prayed for us: for our health, for safety on the road. And a roadside place with neon signs in the windows became for a few moments a little church—and strangers were brother and sisters.

Remind me, Father, when I'm self-conscious about saying grace in public, that to You there is no "public," only individuals whose every need You know.
—Elizabeth Sherrill

❦ ON THE ROAD

Sat 29

*You have made the Lord your refuge.... —*PSALM 91:9 (RSV)

DAY 4: SANCTUARY

I spotted the rabbit, half hidden beneath a bush, as we got out of the car at the motel. "Let's see how close we can get," I whispered to John.

As we walked toward him, the rabbit remained motionless. Three feet away, John stooped down. "Hello, little fellow!"

Still, except for the quivering of his nose, the rabbit did not move. Amazed at the small creature's fearlessness and not wanting to break the spell, we headed for the motel office.

An hour later, stepping out to the car to go in search of someplace to eat in this sparsely settled region of eastern Kentucky, we were surprised to see two more rabbits beside the walkway, showing no more alarm at our presence than the first one had. In the morning the same two rabbits, or ones just like them, were peacefully nibbling the grass just outside our window. Checking out at the office, we commented on these remarkably trusting wild creatures.

The desk clerk nodded. There were always rabbits around the motel, he said. "We're in the Daniel Boone National Forest. Foxes, wildcats, owls, wolves—they all hunt rabbits." The defenseless creatures had discovered, he explained, that predators wouldn't venture anywhere near humans. "The rabbits know that when they stay near us, they're safe."

Let me learn from the rabbits to stay close to You, Lord, where the enemy dares not come.
—ELIZABETH SHERRILL

ON THE ROAD

Sun 30   *My times are in thy hand....*
—PSALM 31:15

DAY 5: SAFE AT HOME

After dark on the last day of September, we pulled into the garage at our apartment just outside Boston. We'd been gone nearly a month and driven more than five thousand miles. "Let's unload the car tomorrow," John said. We were both feeling the miles of the final push from the mountains of West Virginia.

Next day John carried the heavier things from the car and then drove to the post office to get the mail they had held for us. He looked tired as he set down a hefty carton of letters and magazines. "I think I'll lie down for a while."

When I checked on him a little later, he said it felt like he had "a heavy weight" on his chest. Apartments here are equipped with emergency pull-cords. Over John's protests, I pulled ours. In three minutes a paramedic team was at the bedside. Fifteen minutes later we were in an ambulance on our way to Boston's Brigham and Women's Hospital, where later that week John underwent quadruple bypass surgery.

As I watched the streets of the city recede through the rear door window of the ambulance, all I could think of was the isolated hamlets of Appalachia where we'd spent the previous week. Suppose the emergency had happened on one of those twisting mountain roads, a hundred miles from some rural hospital . . . ?

And all I could say was:

Our times are in Your hands, Lord Jesus.
And that's the safest place we could be.
—ELIZABETH SHERRILL

MY PATHWAY TO PEACE

1 _____

2 _____

3 _____

4 _____

5 _____

6 _____

7 _____

8 _____

9 _____

10 _____

11 _____

12 _____

13 _____

14 _____

15 _____

September

16 _____

17 _____

18 _____

19 _____

20 _____

21 _____

22 _____

23 _____

24 _____

25 _____

26 _____

27 _____

28 _____

29 _____

30 _____

October

He maketh peace in thy borders, and filleth thee with the finest of the wheat.

—Psalm 147:14

❧ THIS I KNOW

Mon 1   *For thou, Lord, art good, and ready to forgive....* —PSALM 86:5

THE BIGGER PICTURE

My Friend Denver robbed a bank.

It was a long time ago, and he was depressed and desperate and felt he had nowhere to turn. So he walked into a bank and said, "Give me your money." He was caught and went to prison.

When Denver got out of prison, he began to make amends. When I first met him, he had a great job, owned his own home, was happily married, was a customer of the bank he'd once robbed and was working diligently for the rights of former offenders who were trying to make better lives. Then Denver went a step further: He decided to run for a seat on the city council.

I watched the newscasts with trepidation. There was Denver, telling his story honestly, taking responsibility, making no excuses. "I'm running for council because I want to serve the people of my community," he said.

"Denver," I texted him. "I saw the interview. It's difficult to be objective, because I can only see your goodness. I pray that others will see what I see."

The next day, Denver texted me back: "I've heard from many people, former offenders and others who just wanted me to know that they were touched by the interview. They say my story encouraged them. There's always a bigger picture, Pam."

A bigger picture, indeed. Here's the bigger picture of my friend Denver, the picture our heavenly Father sees: He made a serious mistake. He paid his debt and then kept giving. Wouldn't it be something if we all saw each other the way God sees Denver—the way God sees us?

Father, this I know: When You look at us, You see us whole. Let me always see the bigger picture.
—PAM KIDD

Tue 2

"Surely the Lord is in this place, and I did not know it."
—GENESIS 28:16 (NAS)

I'm a college grandma in a fall semester fiction-writing course. One evening I was to introduce an essay on the significance of place in fiction writing. Author Eudora Welty emphasized seeing place through eyes of discovery. The tired and over-looked and familiar setting, newly awakened, can deepen the meaning of the story.

As I drove onto the campus up a long hill, I was dazzled by a sinking sun making flaming torches of red-orange maple leaves. A quartet of girls walked down the grassy slope toward a grove of trees. One broke free from the group and flung herself down on a crunchy cushion of leaves bunched beneath a tree. She lay on her back swinging her arms and legs, making a leaf angel. I'd made snow angels, but angels in leaves were a novelty.

Suddenly I wasn't driving to class on an ordinary autumn evening. I was discovering place—place ablaze in sunset, transformed by a leaf angel, celebrated with youthful exuberance; place possessed of meaning that quickens me each time I revisit or remember it.

I wonder, how might I be revitalized if I began to see my life through eyes of discovery, if I looked for fresh meaning in my daily routine and said, "Surely the Lord is in this place, and I *do* know it"?

Ever-present God who fills "all in all"
(Ephesians 1:23), fill wherever I am with
awareness of You.
—CAROL KNAPP

Wed 3   *They helped every one his neighbour;*
and every one said to his brother, Be of
good courage. —ISAIAH 41:6

I was hiking north on a favorite section of the Appalachian Trail one warm fall day, trying hard to get my mind off some problems I was having, when I passed them coming south: two scraggly guys and a girl in their early twenties. They looked like they'd been out in the woods for some time, which was probably why my dog Millie took extra time sniffing them. Then a while later as I was coming down, I saw the three at the spot where I'd parked my Jeep.

Turns out they were thru-hiking the trail from Maine to Georgia. It was awfully late in the season to be doing that, and they were still only in western Massachusetts and didn't seem very well provisioned. I wished them luck, and they stuck out their thumbs, trying to hitch a ride into Great Barrington.

Normally I don't pick up hitchhikers, but I told them if they didn't mind a thirsty golden retriever slobbering all over them, I'd give them a lift. They gratefully piled in while I opened all the windows for maximum ventilation.

"Is there a McDonald's in town?" one guy asked hopefully.

"I'll drop you there," I answered.

"Great. We can charge our phones and get something to eat."

"And use a real bathroom," the girl added.

They climbed out at the Golden Arches and I went inside with them to get Millie a pan of fresh water while they ordered burgers and fries.

When they weren't looking, I slipped the counter guy enough money to cover their bill, remembering how, when I was doing crazy youthful things, I depended on the kindness of strangers.

I said good-bye while they were plugging in their phones to call their parents to let them know they were okay. And on a day that started with me trying to hike away from my troubles, I was feeling okay too.

> *How often, Lord, You help us by giving us*
> *a chance to help someone else.*
> —EDWARD GRINNAN

Thu 4   *Wherefore comfort one another*
with these words.
—I THESSALONIANS 4:18

I carried my nine-week-old German shepherd puppy Elijah across the church lawn to the brown pavilion where romping dogs and doting humans were gathering for the annual blessing of the animals. A bit of sadness followed me into this happy occasion. Isaiah, our eight-year-old German shepherd, had accompanied me the year before. There was no hint then of the cancer that over the summer was to take my best buddy.

As I carried my sweet pup, my eyes traveled beyond the pavilion to the football-sized field where just a short year ago Isaiah and friends had romped after their blessing, a sort of victory lap it seemed.

At the pavilion, Elijah wriggled his pudgy puppy self out of my arms, eager to make the rounds of his new fans in this dog-devoted crowd. One of them, whose dog Toby had played with Isaiah, made an understandable but to him embarrassing slip-of-the-tongue. "How's Isaiah doing?" he asked, meaning Elijah. Realizing the mistake, his face turned red. But his stammering apology was interrupted by Sean, a big man with a big heart.

"Isaiah's doing fine," he said, petting his own floppy-eared beagle. "He's romping through fields that these dogs can only dream of and digging up heavenly biscuits that melt in his mouth. He's in a land where the blessing never fades."

It was a perfect image. It not only covered our friend's embarrassment but my sadness as well. When, after the blessing, the dogs, loosed from their leashes, raced in the field, I could almost see a certain beloved German shepherd running through those greener fields that have no boundaries, no sickness, no death.

Lord, thank You for celebrations and blessings that are a taste of things to come and for friends, human and canine, who in joy and sorrow walk with us.
—SHARI SMYTH

Fri 5

You have proved yourselves . . . in sharing. . . .
—II CORINTHIANS 9:13 (NIV)

For twenty-three years, my wife Ruby and I ran seven Trash-and-Treasure tables at our church's October fair. It was hard work, yet we loved it.

The items we sold came from the homes of people—usually older people—who were moving. Often our eyes filled with tears as we felt the pain of someone parting with items that were wrapped in memories. We collected all year long. Then we cleaned, priced and arranged fifty-four hundred items.

On Fair Friday, customers rushed to our tables, which groaned with things they could use at half the price of a yard sale. One lady bought so many things we had to help her carry them to the checkout table.

When she left, we discovered that she hadn't taken her table radio, toaster and waffle iron. Ruby said, "Oscar, put these away. She paid for them, and she might return." We put them aside, and then we forgot about them.

At noon on Saturday, the lady reappeared. "I purchased some things yesterday, and in my haste I forgot my radio, toaster and waffle iron. I don't suppose you still have them."

When we handed her the things, her smile filled the hall. Every year she returned to the fair, bringing new—and generous—friends. She'd always tell them about the day we saved her things.

The fair gave us an opportunity not only to serve our church, but also to build trust in our community.

Creator of Light, by a small act of thoughtfulness we built trust for a lifetime.
—OSCAR GREENE

Sat 6

Incline your ear to wisdom, And apply your heart to understanding.
—PROVERBS 2:2 (NKJV)

I'm a senior at St. John's College in Santa Fe, New Mexico, an idiosyncratic school where the entire curriculum is required—we don't have a single elective in four years—and we read the works of the most important thinkers in the Western tradition. This means we read everyone from Aristotle to Einstein, and it's a struggle to understand them even when you're in class every day, working along with everyone else. So what my parents do every year on Parents' Weekend is truly remarkable.

In early October, St. John's opens itself to parents, letting them sit in on classes and giving them a taste of the St. John's experience. After freshman year, attendance is low; the cost of travel is surely a factor, but I suspect most parents come once and are so overwhelmed by the challenge of sitting in on a discussion of, say, Thomson's atomic theory, that they just give up. Frankly, I can't blame them.

But my parents come each year without fail, and come eager not only to see me but also to learn. Once they attended a math class where we discussed what Pascal's triangle (a major mathematical discovery) could tell us about the nature of God. Afterward, they had that look on their faces that new St. John's students sometimes have: wide-eyed and slack-jawed, as if the universe had been opened to them in a new way.

I can't see the awe they experience without being reminded of just how lucky I am to be getting this education and to have such parents. So every time the weekend ends and my parents prepare to head off to the airport, I hug them, say "I love you" and feel my own kind of awe—at parents who've taught me that education never ends.

Dear Lord, thank You for reminding me that
life is a school I'm never done with.
—SAM ADRIANCE

Sun 7 *We conducted ourselves in the world in*
simplicity....
—II CORINTHIANS 1:12 (NKJV)

I was visiting a small country church, and the worship leader invited me to help serve communion. I hesitated, knowing how clumsy I can be.

"It's simple," she assured me. "All you have to do is say a prayer and then remove this cloth and hand the trays to the deacons. They'll do the rest."

I looked at the trays. The wafers were the commercial ones, the kind that look and taste like Styrofoam quarters, not real bread. The trays were covered with a thin white cloth to protect them from dust.

When the time came, I said the prayer. Then I pinched the cloth in the middle and whipped it off, smartly. The effect was swift and dramatic. A strong vacuum created by the cloth sucked the wafers high into the air, where they snowed down on me and the floor all around me. I gasped, and a ripple of snickers rolled through the congregation. So much for dignity. Fortunately, enough wafers were left to serve the small crowd.

Now you know why I am suspicious of the expression "It's simple."

When my boss is showing me a new trick on the computer, he always says, "It's simple," but it never is. He forgets how smart he is.

When I'm traveling and stop to ask directions, the station attendant always says, "You can't miss it," but I always do.

It's good for me, a teacher, to remember that all things are first hard before they become easy. I shouldn't say, "This is easy; you can do this." I should say, "This can be challenging at first, but you can learn it." That way they won't feel stupid when they don't get it the first time. What's easy for one person can be nearly impossible for another, and I need to show more patience with beginners.

Lord, all things are easy for You, but not for us.
Please be patient with us.
—DANIEL SCHANTZ

🔆 A WEEK DOWN UNDER

Mon 8

Now to him who is able to do immeasurably more than all we ask or imagine, according to his power that is at work within us, to him be glory. . . .
—Ephesians 3:20–21 (NIV)

DAY 1: SUN POWER

Here at Eurardy, a bush heritage reserve in Western Australia where I've come to visit my daughter Elizabeth and her husband Matthew, I'm learning about tapping into a source of power that is clean and ecologically friendly: solar power.

Even though we're miles from the nearest town, the homestead is fully equipped with electric light, refrigerator, freezer, toaster, blender, coffeemaker, air-conditioning, television, Internet, telephone—all the amenities of a modern home and all because of solar power! "How does it work?" I ask.

We walk over to the solar panels, and Matthew explains: "The panels catch the sun's energy, which is converted into electricity and sent along an underground cable to a shed where it charges twenty-eight batteries. There, the energy is stored so that even when there is no sunlight, we can still have power in the house.

"To get the most benefit from the sun, the solar panels change their positions throughout the day. At the base of each panel is a pipe with water in it. As the water heats up, some of it turns to steam and forces the remaining water into a pipe that leads to the other panel. With the exchange of water and steam, the panels go up and down like a slow-moving seesaw."

Paul tells us in Ephesians that we have at our disposal the same power that raised Jesus Christ from the dead. But I must position my heart so I can receive that energy from God and make use of it.

> *Thank You, Father, that I can do all things*
> *through Christ Who gives me strength.*
> —HELEN GRACE LESCHEID

🌸 A WEEK DOWN UNDER

Tue 9
> *Many, O Lord my God, are the*
> *wonders you have done. . . .*
> —PSALM 40:5 (NIV)

DAY 2: WILD BOUQUET

I don my hat and let the net fall over my face. I'm wearing a long-sleeved shirt and good running shoes, with a sock protector over my socks. My daughter Elizabeth grabs her camera, binoculars and car keys, and we're off to see some of the wildflowers of Western Australia.

The countryside is awash with pink-and-white heath interspersed with waving smoke bushes. We pass wattle trees decked out in yellow pompoms, trees with bright red bottle brushes, banksia that carry celebration candles, grevillea with flowers like fancy crochet work. In among all of this is a thick carpet of bright yellow flowers peppered with blue pincushions and red copper cups.

Some flowers are round like decorated birthday cakes sitting in the sand. Others, the parakeelya, remind me of ballerinas waiting on tiptoes for their cue to come onstage. Promptly at 9:30 AM, they open up their bright skirts. The patch becomes transformed as though somebody has splashed pink paint all over it. Then, at 3:30 PM, the show is over and the parakeelya go to sleep again.

I'm overwhelmed with so much beauty, and Elizabeth reminds me that I'm seeing only a tiny fraction of the more than six hundred species in Western Australia.

Thank You, Lord, that here among all this beauty, You reveal Yourself as a God Who loves to surprise us with color and design, lavish in generosity and with the sense of humor to create flowers that look like kangaroo paws, lambs' tails, pink slippers and green birds.
—HELEN GRACE LESCHEID

❧ A WEEK DOWN UNDER

Wed 10   *Give thanks to the Lord, for he is good; his love endures forever.*
—Psalm 107:1 (NIV)

DAY 3: GIVING THANKS

We might be in the Australian outback, far from the nearest town, but my daughter Elizabeth and I decided we'd give her husband Matthew a taste of a Canadian Thanksgiving. We'd have an elegant table setting and candlelight, roast lamb and stuffing and pumpkin pie. Matthew got into the festive spirit and made a beautiful candleholder from a piece of driftwood stuck in the blade of a plowshare.

When everything was ready, we dressed in our best clothes, lit the candles and turned off the electric lights. Then I opened a card that a neighbor back home in Canada had given me with strict instructions not to open it until Thanksgiving.

As I opened it, I heard a chorus of children singing, "We are family . . . Everybody sing: We are family." Soon all three of us were swaying to the music and singing along.

Yes, thank God for family. I beamed across the table at Elizabeth. Soon she would be traveling many miles to see her siblings, just as I had done to see her. And Matthew would be going home to his family in South Australia.

My friend back home had signed the card, "Your family at Belmont Ridge."

It doesn't take blood to make a family, I thought.

Dear God, thank You that I may call You "Father" and that all Your children the world over are family.
—HELEN GRACE LESCHEID

❧ A WEEK DOWN UNDER

Thu 11

The Lord God took the man and put him in the Garden of Eden to work it and take care of it.
—GENESIS 2:15 (NIV)

DAY 4: A SPRING IN THE DESERT

When my daughter Elizabeth and her husband Matthew first came to Eurardy Reserve, which borders on the desert, she worried about water. Here in the Australian outback with no rainfall for up to six months and temperatures soaring between 113 and 122 degrees, lack of water is a real danger. In days gone by, their homestead had been flanked by a prize-winning garden. Now it lay in shambles. Fruit trees had died and the lawn had shriveled.

On one very hot day, Elizabeth saw birds splashing in the water she had put out for them. Obviously, they weren't worried about the water running out. Seeing their trust, Elizabeth was determined to care for them. But how?

Then Matthew came up with an idea. Chipping through the hard soil, he dug a trench to a borehole leading to a water table twenty feet down. The water hadn't been thought fit for human consumption, so nothing had been done with it.

With the trench finished, Matthew attached a cable to three unused solar panels and laid it in the trench. Then he fed a pump through a hose forty-nine feet down the borehole. When he turned on the switch, a hissing sound gave way to a spray of water that glistened in the sunshine. Soon the birds were playing in the puddles forming in the sandy soil.

"At this rate we'll be able to revive the lawn and fruit trees," Elizabeth said. "How incredible! The water was there all the time, but it was up to us to harvest it."

Father God, You have given us incredible riches in
Christ. Help me to make full use of them.
—HELEN GRACE LESCHEID

❧ A WEEK DOWN UNDER

Fri 12
   Good people leave an inheritance to their grandchildren, but the sinner's wealth passes to the godly.
—Proverbs 13:22 (NLT)

DAY 5: AIRING THE QUILTS

My daughter Elizabeth, her husband Matthew and I attended the Airing of the Quilts in Northampton, Western Australia. People get together at this annual event to display and sell patchwork quilts and other crafts.

On both sides of Main Street, an exquisite array of colorful quilts hung from buildings and wash lines. Old and new quilts were displayed in every store window and from balconies and other fixtures. Near city hall, a band played rousing music. Then a parade of old cars, costumed people, jolly clowns and Red Hat ladies passed by.

We wandered from stall to stall and from window to window. Suddenly, Elizabeth gave me a poke. She pointed to a store window; in it was a quilt that looked rather ordinary. *Why does it have my name on it?* I thought. Grinning, Elizabeth said, "Read the placard."

"This quilt was made by my grandmother, Agnes Loewen, who died in May 2003, a widow of World

War II. She always did what she could with the little she had. Helen Lescheid, my mother, is Agnes' eldest daughter. Helen will be visiting Australia for the first time this fall, and I am displaying the quilt in her honor."

Father, I want to leave a legacy that will bless my children and show them the way of faith.
—HELEN GRACE LESCHEID

✢ A WEEK DOWN UNDER

Sat 13   *Like cold water to a weary soul is good news from a distant land.*
—PROVERBS 25:25 (NIV)

DAY 6: THE FRIDGE

My daughter Elizabeth and I had spent a day at the Indian Ocean and seen an abundance of sea life: stingrays, which reminded me of kites with their flat bodies and long tails; bulky gray dugongs; sharks of all kinds; dolphins; a sea turtle. A rusty, ragged coastline was catching the ocean waves. Cormorants outlined the seashore like beads on a string.

Before going home to the Eurardy Reserve, we stopped at the Peron Homestead to soak in an outdoor hot tub. A young man from Texas was already in the water. He seemed thrilled to meet up with other North Americans, and soon we were talking the way old friends do.

"Funny thing," the man said. "On my way up here, I saw a fridge standing beside the highway."

"Was it painted with bright red tulips?" my daughter asked.

"Yes," he said.

"That's our mailbox," Elizabeth said with a laugh.

Three times a week she goes to check the refrigerator. The personal mail is neatly tied in a sack; the latest newspaper lies on top. Sometimes, the mail carrier has left a surprise for them, such as a box of very ripe mangoes. I know, because we'd been eating mango jam every day for breakfast.

> *Father, thank You for the thoughtfulness*
> *that adds sweetness to our lives.*
> —HELEN GRACE LESCHEID

A WEEK DOWN UNDER

Sun 14   *The Lord is close to the brokenhearted and saves those who are crushed in spirit.*
—PSALM 34:18 (NIV)

DAY 7: SHELL BEACH

While walking on Shell Beach in the Shark Bay World Heritage Area in Western Australia, I learned that this amazing pure-white beach is composed of trillions of tiny shells gathered and broken by the pounding of the waves over four thousand years. The compacted shells have been quarried for building blocks best displayed in the Old Pearler Restaurant in Denham; broken shells are used to make calcium carbonate and chicken feed.

On Sunday morning, I attended St. Andrew's by the Sea in Denham, also made from blocks of broken shells. The rector met me at the door and warmly invited me to come in. The pianist played "How Great Thou Art" as I took my seat. Other familiar hymns followed. As I sang along with the congregation, I felt I'd found my family in Australia. Later, over tea in the rectory, I learned that people here are experiencing the same stresses and challenges we have back home in Canada. Brokenness is part of our human experience.

On Shell Beach, I learned that brokenness has a purpose in nature, but we may not see it until some time has elapsed. And when I feel broken by the pounding of life's pressures, I can rest assured that God is very close, working out a plan and purpose for my good and His glory.

Father God, thank You for being close to the brokenhearted and all who are crushed in spirit.
—HELEN GRACE LESCHEID

Mon 15

Many are asking, "Who can show us any good?" Let the light of your face shine upon us, O Lord.
—PSALM 4:6 (NIV)

Today as we walked from the car to the grocery store, my four-year-old stopped and looked at the ground. Thinking he had dropped something, I was about to ask him what the matter was when he hugged my legs.

The autumn light shown behind us and cast a beautiful orange glow on the surrounding trees. Henry hugged me tighter, pressing his body close to mine. He looked down at the stretch of pavement in front of us.

"What are you doing, Hen?" I asked.

"Something," he mumbled. He grasped my legs and moved his feet on top of my toes.

I leaned down close to his face. "What? What is it, honey?" I asked.

"Look!" He pointed to the pavement.

I looked ahead. "What am I looking at?"

"Shadow," he said. He glued himself to my legs.

"Yeah, that's our shadow."

"Stay," he said. "See. I just want to be in your shadow."

I hugged him tight and we walked inside holding hands, admiring our shadow the whole way.

> *Dear God, send Your light so the shadow*
> *I cast gives shape to Your love.*
> —SABRA CIANCANELLI

❀ A GRACE-FILLED JOURNEY

Tue 16 *Rest in the Lord, and wait patiently for Him.... —PSALM 37:7*

DAY OF REST

I woke with a digestive ailment today, and the ship's doctor has said I should stay on board and rest while the group spends the day at Rhodes. I don't like this medicine of missing out! Yet I know it's best for my health, so I sigh and agree.

After receiving an injection and spending most of the morning in bed, I begin to feel better and go to the observation deck, notebook in hand. As I sit on the plush wicker loveseat watching the hypnotic movement of the waters, I fall into a dreamlike state. In contrast to the more strenuous tour days of tramping through ruins and climbing skyscraping stone stairways, today feels soothing and I find myself letting go into a simple state of *trusting God*. I decide that just for today I will allow myself to be truly "at sea," mentally, emotionally, physically and spiritually. I'll free-float with the ship, where no mail or e-mail begs for an answer, no deadlines or expectations of achievement can capture me. I fall asleep, gently rocking with the anchored ship.

The sun is slowly sinking below the horizon as the tour group returns, tired and hungry. They've had a wonderful day. And so have I!

> *Thank You, Holy One, for leading me to spend*
> *this time resting in Your arms!*
> —MARILYN MORGAN KING

Wed 17

We, while we were children, were held in bondage under the elemental things of the world. But when the fullness of the time came, God sent forth His Son....
—GALATIANS 4:3–4 (NAS)

One of the joys of returning to my native central Georgia is to rediscover the beautiful countryside and agrarian culture of this fertile land. I'm particularly enjoying riding my bicycle down country roads and seeing the peach trees in bloom and the tall, green grandeur of the pecan orchards.

One of my teenage buddies, Charles (Chop) Evans, is now one of the largest pecan growers in the United States. Recently I asked Chop how his pecan crop was doing. "We've got a great crop in the trees if the weather will only cooperate," he replied. "We must have enough rain and cold weather for the nuts to drop."

Not sure what he meant, I asked Chop to explain why pecans need cold weather.

"Well, Scott, for the pecans to fall from the tree, the thick husk or pod that holds and protects the thin-shelled pecan has to split open and allow the pecan to drop to the ground. The pod won't crack until there is enough moisture and cold weather to split it and release the nut. And we can't harvest pecans until they are on the ground. I sure hope it gets cold real soon."

Life is a lot like harvesting pecans. Sometimes we have to wait for the right conditions to come together before "things drop into place." A wise farmer understands the need for correct process, planned growth and infinite patience.

When contemplating the slow course of human history, the apostle Paul thought about the birth of Jesus and wrote the verse above. God alone understands the fullness of time for each individual and for human history.

Father, grant me the gift of patience.
—SCOTT WALKER

Thu 18

He made darkness his canopy around him—the dark rain clouds of the sky. —II SAMUEL 22:12 (NIV)

The evening before we were to settle Dad's estate left me in a funk. Mom and I, along with one of my brothers, had planned to get everything signed and taken care of that day, and none of us was looking forward to it.

I puttered around the house, releasing my grumpiness on anything in my path before deciding to take a shower in hopes that it would calm my nerves.

It didn't. I stepped into the shower and began to sob, the sounds muffled by the stream of water, letting the ache wash over me.

But then a funny thing happened: My mouth completely filled with water, startling me and causing me to close my mouth. Surprised, I spit the water out and kept crying. Again, I was choked by the water.

Finally I had to laugh. "Okay, God," I said. "I get it. You can't sob and stand under a heavy-flow showerhead."

Once again, God had shown me that everything has a time and that tears are a perfectly acceptable form of mourning—just not in the shower.

Bless You, O Lord, for bringing laughter into my darkest moments, and for reminding me that after the hardest rains come the prettiest rainbows.
—ASHLEY KAPPEL

READER'S ROOM

I am thankful that as I enter God's temple of prayer each morning, I am able to quiet my mind and my thoughts to listen for Him speaking to me and filling me with His Holy Spirit. This prepares me for the day ahead, and I am able to feel God's presence throughout the day.
—*Carole Nace, Mifflintown, Pennsylvania*

Fri 19

"If anyone would come after me, he must deny himself and take up his cross daily and follow me."
—LUKE 9:23 (NIV)

As I was driving on the main road near our sub-division one mid-October day, I saw that the homeowners down the road had once again put up a six-foot-tall wooden cross as a seasonal decoration, surrounded by hay bales, pumpkins and artificial flowers.

It was still dark at 6:15 the next morning as I eagerly set out toward the cross as a special destination on my morning prayer walk. When the cross first appeared a few years earlier, I discovered that if I made a detour and walked on a short sidewalk along a busy road, I could take a "cross walk," meditating on the many meanings of the cross as I moved toward it. The only problem was the cars that zoomed by on the road at forty-five miles an hour. I worried about my safety, and the hurrying cars chilled me with their back draft as they whipped by. I rarely got to walk toward the cross in the kind of peace I longed for.

I'd waited all year for the cross to return, but as I turned the corner to walk along the busy road, I was dismayed to find that it was still too dark for me to see it. As I strained my eyes longingly down the road, several cars whizzed by, and I suddenly glimpsed the faint gray outline of the cross reflected in their headlights. More cars passed. I kept my eyes glued on the cross, able to see it, not *despite* the traffic, but *because* of it.

Lord, Your cross stands in an imperfect world.
Help me to understand that these imperfections
only make the cross more beautiful.
—KAREN BARBER

October

EDITOR'S NOTE: *Monday, November 19, will be Guideposts' annual Thanksgiving Day of Prayer. Please plan to join all the members of our Guideposts family in prayer on this very special day. Send your prayer requests (and a picture, if you can—but remember that we won't be able to return it) to Day of Prayer, PO Box 5813, Harlan, Iowa 51593-1313, fax them to (845) 855-1178, phone them to (845) 704-6080 (Monday through Friday, 7:00 AM to 10:00 PM EDT) or visit us on the Web at Our Prayerg.org.*

Sat 20

He comes alongside us when we go through hard times, and before you know it, he brings us alongside someone else who is going through hard times so that we can be there for that person just as God was there for us. —II CORINTHIANS 1:4 (MSG)

I'd recently encountered an old friend, and I hadn't shared my story with her about the One Who changed my life. I'd just about convinced myself it was okay as I folded clothes warm from the dryer when Jeremy popped by. His expression was difficult to read. He looked stunned. *Is he in trouble?*

He stood there silently staring at Gene and me. Finally he said, "Something unusual happened to me today. It was the first time. Never thought I'd be able to do it. Mostly I believed that preachers got paid to share God and His love. But today I bumped into a buddy. He looked terrible. Somehow he began asking me about my life turnaround and Celebrate Recovery. The thing is, I seemed to be way up above it all, looking down on him—and me. Right there on the sidewalk, with people walking by us, I, Jeremy West, told this guy how, with God's help, I turned my back on my longstanding addictions. The words just came out of my mouth. Man, did he listen. Then he said, 'Jeremy, the Holy Spirit's all over you—and me. You have found the answer.'

"Gene, Mom, I thought meth was the highest high in the world. But it's nothing—absolutely nothing—compared to seeing an addict grab on to God. Whoever thought I'd have something worthwhile to share with anybody? It's worth everything I've been through to be able to help someone else."

Oh, my Father, give me that amazing enthusiasm again for sharing the good news.
—MARION BOND WEST

Sun 21

The Lord will guard your going out and your coming in from this time forth and forever.
—PSALM 121:8 (NAS)

A conservation area about four miles from our house serves as a staging ground for thousands of Canada geese getting ready for their annual migration south. Beginning about the middle of September, their V-formation flight patterns fill the sky, some flocks consisting of only six or eight birds, others made up of fifty or sixty, always with a lead goose out in front.

When the lead goose tires and slows down, it drops to the back of the flock, where the slipstream from the wings of the other geese gives it a flight advantage, and another goose gracefully takes up the lead position. Ornithologists calculate that the geese can fly 70 percent farther by doing this. The ever-changing formations are fascinating to watch. And even in the dark of night or when a low cloud ceiling obscures our view, we know the geese are flying because of their loud honking. It's as if each one is so eager about the prospects of the journey that it can't contain its enthusiasm.

It occurred to me one fall Sunday morning that church is a kind of staging ground for heaven. As "birds of a feather," believers flock together week by week, strengthening our spiritual wings and encouraging one another in preparation for that final flight. When one of us becomes weary, another steps in to take the weary one's place. I fully believe that the prayer support of fellow believers has often provided the wind beneath my wings.

Thank You, Lord, for letting me team up with Your followers wherever my journey happens to take me.
—ALMA BARKMAN

Mon 22

Children are a gift from the Lord; they are a reward from him.
—PSALM 127:3 (NLT)

When I was a child and my father traveled out of town, I remember asking him to bring me a surprise from wherever he was going. I looked forward to his return eagerly, wondering what he was bringing back for me. In fact, unlike some people I know, I actually enjoy surprises . . . well, most of the time.

A number of years ago my daughters Jody and Jenny decided to throw me a surprise fiftieth birthday party. They spared no expense. In fact, they rented a hall, hired a catering company to serve a buffet dinner and planned an elaborate program that included speeches by teachers, editors I've worked with and high-school friends.

Because the details of arranging the party became too much for them, they asked for my help. They brought the guest list to me to go over and needed some guidance on the decorations and music. Actually, I was a bit taken aback when the invitation announced it as a surprise party, because by this point I knew practically every detail.

"Why are you calling it a surprise party?" I asked. I certainly wasn't going to appear shocked when I'd personally selected every name on the invitation list. In fact, I'd chosen the dinner menu and helped order the cake.

"Mom," Jenny said, beaming me a smile, "the surprise is you get to pay for it."

> *Thank You, Jesus, for the joy of my children*
> *and the surprises they bring.*
> —DEBBIE MACOMBER

Tue 23

You will go out in joy and be led forth in peace. . . .
—ISAIAH 55:12 (NIV)

August was a busy month as we helped our daughter Elizabeth get ready to go to college. Then all too abruptly we were on a bus headed to Massachusetts. We stayed with friends, visited the robots at the MIT museum, ate ice cream in Harvard Square, moved Elizabeth into her dorm, went to church and bought college-logo T-shirts for the entire family. Then we climbed on the bus and came home, leaving our eldest behind.

Back in New York, there was soccer practice and ballet, homeschool co-op and play rehearsals. Life felt more or less normal, though the kids were sad and missed their sister. I kept catching myself thinking that Elizabeth would soon be walking in through the door to chat with me. Then one sunny October day I realized that the funny feeling inside my belly wasn't recurring indigestion but a longing for someone I've loved every minute of her life.

On that day I cried a bit and spent a while cradling memories of my girl. I remembered her as a newborn, as a toddler, as a math-obsessed tween and as a growing-in-confidence high-schooler. I thought of tender snuggles and goofy songs, of first words and first sleepovers. I wrestled my heart into thankfulness and pondered the gift of all the years I've been given to relish Elizabeth.

She's out in the big world now. That's where I am. That's where God is. I think we'll be okay.

Father of all, pry my fingers from all that I clasp
fearfully to my heart, and teach me to let go and
let things rest in Your gentle hands.
—JULIA ATTAWAY

Wed 24

My flesh and my heart faileth....
—PSALM 73:26

For months on end my life moves at a rapid pace, my faith rumbling along half-invisible. Then something happens to shake me up: an e-mail from a friend, an irritating phone call, a plan that seemed to fall apart before it had even been made.

All at once, I feel like storming the heavens. And when I read the Bible, I do it ravenously, seeking help that is far outside of myself or my own resources. These times of shattered confidence aren't necessarily fun; I wouldn't recommend them to anyone. But every time I hit one, I think of a prayer I read years ago and turn to again in the pages of a well-thumbed book:

> Our Father, who has set a restlessness in our hearts and made us all seekers after that which we can never fully find, forbid us to be satisfied with what we make of life. Keep us at tasks too hard for us that we may be driven to thee for strength.

According to the notes, Eleanor Roosevelt said this prayer every night, especially during the difficult early days of the United Nations, in which she played an important role. Taking in the words, I remind myself that my restlessness is there for a reason, the doubts serve their purpose. They take me back to a faith that seemed to have been put on hold.

Nothing is too hard for me, Lord, as long as
it takes me back to You.
—RICK HAMLIN

Thu 25 *They ate angel's food! He gave them all that they could hold.*
—PSALM 78:25 (TLB)

Harvest cake, I decided, would be the perfect dessert for the October meeting of my church women's group. The picture looked scrumptious, and the recipe—which called for apples, cinnamon and dates—seemed simple. But when I turned the cake onto a platter, it came out in six chunks and a pile of crumbs.

The nearest bakery is fifty miles away, and I had no cake mixes on hand. But less than five minutes into my pity-party, I remembered the Very Good Cake. I've had the recipe for at least forty years and it's never failed. It came to the rescue when I forgot I'd promised a cake for a bake sale. It came to the rescue when my grandson Caleb tried a red velvet cake for the county fair, only to have it sink in the middle. (The Very Good Cake he made as a substitute won a blue ribbon!) It would have to come to my rescue one more time.

I topped the cake with berry sauce and whipped cream. It was delicious! So for any cooks who need a foolproof recipe or who just like pound cake, here's how:

Very Good Cake

6 eggs	2 cups sugar
2 cups flour	2 teaspoons flavoring
2 sticks margarine, softened	

Blend the sugar and eggs. Add the margarine, flour and flavoring. Beat the cake for fifteen minutes. (Yes, fifteen minutes. A stand mixer is helpful.) Pour batter into a greased Bundt pan. Bake at 325 degrees for forty-five to sixty minutes. Turn onto a cake plate when cool.

Thank You, Jesus, for the Very Good Cake, for the long-forgotten person who gave me the recipe, and for the haphazard cooks it has rescued through the years.
—PENNEY SCHWAB

Fri 26

My burden is light.
—MATTHEW 11:30

The road that stretches through the area surrounding Village Hope is rocky and sometimes very steep. Today my son Harrison and I are following Paddington, the director of this project founded to give a safe home to newly orphaned children in rural Zimbabwe.

As we walk from one mud hut to the next, Paddington introduces us to some of the people who have benefited from these projects. There's the Pass It On program that provides villagers with animals, and Seed to Sadza, which supplies families with seeds to plant their gardens and enough meal to keep them fed until their crops come in. There's a poultry project and also a lunch program that feeds all the students at two schools.

"Our people," Paddington says as he pats the head of a huge cow, "are benefiting from our work in many ways."

I put my hand on Harrison's shoulder. *If only he can take the joy that comes through giving back home to America,* I fretted as we approached an old woman on the road. The woman was small and frail, yet she was carrying a huge bundle of firewood on her head.

"Having enough wood for the evening fire is everything to our people here," Paddington was explaining as we drew nearer.

Ahead, Harrison had caught up with the woman. She paused, looking at him, her face filled with surprise.

"I was just asking if I could help carry her wood," he explained simply.

As it turned out, the tiny lady's load was a challenge for both Harrison and me, but together we struggled down the road, balancing the wood between us as best we could. The load was heavier than I anticipated, but the burden inside my heart had become notably lighter.

> *Father, You turn our burdens into joy.*
> —BROCK KIDD

Sat 27

You anoint my head with oil; my cup overflows. —PSALM 23:5 (NIV)

I'd told myself it was a drive to enjoy the fall colors, but in the privacy of my car I knew I was running away from too many people making demands. My desk was buried under half-finished assignments, my answering machine filled with unreturned calls, e-mails multiplying faster than I could respond, family members clamoring for attention.

I turned the wheel automatically, not headed anywhere, just away from the pressures at home. It was in the little town of Delhi, New York, that I passed a small stone church, its bright red door invitingly ajar. Maybe inside I'd find an answer to a hectic schedule.

I did find it, before I ever reached that door. The flagstone walkway that led to it was blocked by the sagging branches of a large crabapple tree heavy with fruit. A small, hand-lettered sign apologized for the inconvenience. "These apples come from the apple blossoms we enjoyed so much last spring."

Blossoms. Beginnings.

I remembered how eagerly I'd applied for the job that led to the work now waiting on my desk. Those phone messages and e-mails—with what hopes and plans I'd originally contacted most of these people. The needs of children and grandchildren: This was the family my husband and I had prayed to have. What I called pressure was in fact abundance, hope fulfilled, prayer granted! I hurried to the car, impatient to get back to a life overflowing with the fruit of spring flowers.

Help me to be as quick with my thanks,
Father, as with my requests!
—ELIZABETH SHERRILL

Sun 28

Take away from me the noise of your songs. . . . —AMOS 5:23 (NRSV)

I have been leading a men's Bible study for the past two years. Our pastor attends, and one day he shared a story about a former Bible study participant, Rick. I learned that he had been deaf until late in his life, when a new kind of hearing aid enabled him to hear. "I'll bet he was thrilled," I remarked.

"Not right away," our pastor said. "I mean, eventually he was thrilled. But Rick told me that at first he hated being able to hear. He couldn't make sense of the noise and kept his hearing aid off most of the time. After a life of silence, it was a long time before he could sort through all the sounds bombarding him."

I could understand Rick's reaction. When I tried to study God's Word as a young man, the Bible seemed like so much noise to me. I gave up and "kept my hearing aid off" for more than twenty years.

Then my younger brother gently and, thank God, persistently persuaded me to focus on the themes most often repeated throughout the Bible: "Love your neighbor as yourself" (Leviticus 19:18, NRSV); "You shall love the Lord your God with all your heart, and with all your soul, and with all your strength, and with all your mind; and your neighbor as yourself" (Luke 10:27, NRSV); "What does the Lord require of you but to do justice, and to love kindness, and to walk humbly with your God?" (Micah 6:8, NRSV); and "Be kind to one another, tenderhearted, forgiving one another, as God in Christ has forgiven you" (Ephesians 4:32, NRSV).

Rick learned to love what he heard and so did I.

*Oh, God, thank You for teaching me to hear
your Word!* —Tim Williams

Mon 29

*Every good gift and every perfect
gift is from above, and cometh
down from the Father of lights,
with whom is no variableness,
neither shadow of turning.*
—James 1:17

I think of twelve-year-old Mary as our surprising child. She surprised us first by being born in the afternoon, rather than in the small hours her siblings seemed to favor. Then she surprised us by her "They're not able to do that at that age" smile, so different from the solemnity of her sister Elizabeth and her brother John. She surprised us with her beautiful gold-red hair, which—again unlike her older siblings—has resisted turning brown. She's surprised me with her dancer's grace and poise, so different from my own tendency to trip over thin air. But over the past year she's given me another surprise.

Mary loves to cook. She subscribes to *Bon Appétit* and enjoys poring over the recipes and the stunning photographs. She'll discuss the main dishes with her mother, but what really grabs her attention is the desserts. She'll spend hours deciding on what to serve for Christmas or Easter and then consult with Julia about ingredients and kitchen procedures. She's treated us to apple-almond pies and pumpkin pies, chocolate-orange-raspberry cakes, soufflés and custards, homemade ice cream and strawberry tarts. She's studied meringue-making and cake decorating and knows the subtle differences between a half-dozen varieties of chocolate.

In a sense, all this should be no surprise; her mother's dessert creations have dazzled me for years. But Mary is the dancer, who exults in movement and has to keep herself slim. Why is she the one to tantalize the tongue with tastes and textures while creating a beauty that catches the eye—like a photograph in *Bon Appétit*?

The mystery of our gifts is hidden in the mind of the Giver, Who scatters them as and where He pleases. But when I go home tonight for my birthday dinner, I'll give special thanks for the ones He's given Mary.

> *Thank You, Lord for every gift You've given me,*
> *especially for the people in my life.*
> —ANDREW ATTAWAY

Tue 30

"But ask the animals, and they will teach you...." —JOB 12:7 (NIV)

Life as a panda at the Ya'an Panda Research Base is pretty sweet. You sit, you climb, you play, but mainly you eat. And eat. And eat. And eat. Sometimes apples, but mostly it's just bamboo—lots and lots and lots and lots of bamboo, up to thirty pounds a day.

This, to put it bluntly, seems like a boring life. So why are we so intrigued? That's what I thought about as some colleagues and I visited Ya'an while touring China last fall. We had met government officials, enjoyed lavish banquets, visited stunning historical sights, talked with fascinating people—but nothing got us, a bunch of allegedly hardened media types, like those pandas. We were positively cooing.

The most popular panda lolled on the ground, munching on a big stalk of bamboo while lying on his back, vaguely resembling a fat-bellied human dad on the sofa after Thanksgiving dinner. Other pandas were scattered around an enclosure, munching a little and vegetating a lot. And then it came to me: They really were like a family—and maybe that was it. Maybe we were so fascinated with the panda because we could see something of ourselves in them. Not just anything, but the good things. They were cuter, fatter humans, without the arguments, without the flaws...without the sin.

In the story of the panda, we can truly see a little of our own. They are rare and precious creatures. They have come to be beloved by humans, especially in China, venerated as national symbols and brought back from the verge of extinction. In God's eyes, we are much the same, each and every one of us, except even more precious and worth saving.

Lord, I may not be as cute as a panda, but You have created and preserved me and given me Your saving and sanctifying grace.
—JEFF CHU

Wed 31   *"Truly I say to you, wherever this gospel is preached in the whole world, what this woman has done will also be spoken of in memory of her."* —MATTHEW 26:13 (NAS)

Sometimes ordinary people doing supposedly ordinary tasks are rarely noticed, nor do they make the newspapers or have their lives told on-screen.

Let me tell you about an "ordinary" person: a modest, soft-spoken woman—trim, quiet, unassuming, unnoticed in a crowd. Her house, like her, didn't stand out from others. "Everyone has a talent," she used to say, "but I don't. I'm just a nobody."

Then one late October night, groups of neighborhood children knocked on her door. Into each colorful trick-or-treat bag, she dropped a homemade invitation to Sunday school.

However, she hesitated before doing so for two young brothers. *Their father heads a construction company; their mother's a TV anchor. They already have everything. They'll probably laugh at me.* Even so, she told herself, *I'll drop them in anyway!*

The two small boys, aged five and eight, carried the notes home in with their accumulated candy. The following Sunday, both brothers—and their parents—showed up at church, all because of their neighbor's invitation.

Twenty years passed; the former five-year-old was by then a pastor and his older brother a missionary on a foreign field. Their father rebuilt that same church when a faulty furnace burned it; their mother resigned her position to be a stay-at-home mom. As for the self-effacing woman, she never stopped inviting little kids to Sunday school.

I know the above story is true because my husband and I and our two small boys were "Mrs. Nobody's" neighbors.

> *Thank You, Father, that none of us*
> *is insignificant in Your sight.*
> —ISABEL WOLSELEY

October

MY PATHWAY TO PEACE

1 _____

2 _____

3 _____

4 _____

5 _____

6 _____

7 _____

8 _____

9 _____

10 _____

11 _____

12 _____

13 _____

14 _____

15 _____

16 _____

17 _____

18 _____

19 _____

20 _____

21 _____

22 _____

23 _____

24 _____

25 _____

26 _____

27 _____

28 _____

29 _____

30 _____

31 _____

November

But the fruit of the Spirit is love, joy, peace, longsuffering, gentleness, goodness, faith, meekness, temperance: against such there is no law.

—Galatians 5:22–23

Thu 1 *Gather my saints together unto me; those that have made a covenant with me by sacrifice.* —PSALM 50:5

When I washed and folded the church dishtowels after a fifth Sunday dinner, I noticed that a few were getting worn. All were homemade, some from material I recognized from my childhood as chickenfeed sacks. Others were sewn from sturdy white cotton and embroidered with teapots, dinnerware and simple prayers. Several of them had "Methodist Church" stitched on a corner. Those had been made prior to 1968, when my denomination became the United Methodist Church.

Those dishtowels had been on kitchen duty for over forty years!

I thought about the women who made them. A few were still active participants in the church. Although their ages range from eighty to over ninety, Neva, Martha and Lillian all help with funeral dinners and church fund-raisers.

Other women had passed from this life into God's eternity. Ruth suffered a paralyzing stroke but witnessed to Christ's faithfulness from her room in a nursing home. Sue, who'd been a school cook, was famous for her red hair, mile-high angel food cake and sunny smile. Margaret, a teacher and mother of twelve, never missed Sunday school and had keen insights into human behavior. Lucille, who spent her life caring for others, was killed when she failed to see an oncoming truck before pulling into an intersection. "She's in heaven now," her son said, "rejoicing she didn't cause harm to anyone else."

Dishtowel saints: women who lived their lives with fortitude and faith, women whose legacy graces our church kitchen—and us—today.

Thank You, Jesus, "for all the saints who from their labors rest" and for the saints who are still with us . . . and still drying dishes.
—PENNEY SCHWAB

Fri 2

"With pain you will give birth to children. . . . "—GENESIS 3:16 (NIV)

In real life I usually don't associate pain and blessings together. A while ago, I had to speak at the funeral of a man who had been part of our early days of ministry to young people. He was one of our "children," as were his older brothers and sisters. As I sat waiting for my turn to speak, I thought about how young he was and why he had to die at age forty-six. My heart was heavy. But as I listened to testimony after testimony of the impact he had had on the lives of others, God gave me peace. I had peace knowing that God had allowed us to invest in him, and he in turn invested his time and talent in the lives of other young people.

The pain of death is hard, but life spent committed to God and affecting others is a great testimony of joy and peace. Our friend, our brother—our son—worked to point others to the Kingdom and challenged them to stretch beyond their limitations. Knowing that, I've been learning how to walk through pain and count the blessings.

Lord, help me to live blessing others, knowing that even in pain, You enable me to experience Your peace.
—DOLPHUS WEARY

READER'S ROOM

Life is not about what we have and who we know, but who we have and what we know. I have friends and family who love me, and I know Jesus is my Savior, who gave His all for my salvation. I can't ask for any better gifts than that.
—*Betty Crow, Prescott, Arizona*

Sat 3   *Fix your thoughts on what is true and good and right. . . . Think about all you can praise God for and be glad about . . . and the God of peace will be with you.* —PHILIPPIANS 4:8–9 (TLB)

A friend was having a terrible time sleeping. "Brooding thoughts keep coming into my head," he groaned. "Seems like night after night, the memory of every bad thing that ever happened in my life crowds in with the darkness. It's stealing my peace."

"That's rough." I paused and thought for a moment. "This might be helpful: My husband was an avid sports fan and frequently drew on the wisdom of some of the great coaches, especially Woody Hayes of the Ohio State Buckeyes. When the guy carrying the football was having trouble getting through the opposition, Woody used to tell him, 'Run where they ain't!' Try it. When you get into bed at night and dismal thoughts beset you, speed away from them and put your mind on all the good things you can praise God for."

I met him a few weeks later. "What do you know," he said with a grin. "It seems to be working. Before getting to sleep I think about hiking around a lake, fishing and all the fun things that make me happy. When stress-related stuff comes into my mind, I say the Lord's Prayer, sometimes several times over, to help me 'run where they ain't.' I've been sleeping a whole lot better."

Quiet my heart, Lord, through the darkness of the night. May I rest in peace and rise with the morning light, rested and refreshed to praise Your name through another day.
—Fay Angus

🎋 THIS I KNOW

Sun 4 *Grace be unto you, and peace....*
—I Thessalonians 1:1

AMAZING GRACE

For years I've struggled with the concept of grace. Consumed with a longing for justice, grace always threw me for a loop. Grace, you see, isn't fair; you don't have to do anything to get it. But one night grace came to me in person and changed my life forever.

It was the night of my husband David's last communion service at Hillsboro Presbyterian Church. The reception after the service was crowded with people.

Across the way, I caught sight of Sheila. Years before, she and her husband had hurt our family terribly. We were working as hard as we could when they began publicly pointing out all our faults and failures.

Although over time I thought I'd forgiven them, the strain between Sheila and me remained.

Now Sheila was moving toward me. I looked away, and when I turned back, she was there, extending her hand. "Pam, I should have asked for your forgiveness long ago," she said, "I . . ."

I reached out and touched her cheek. "Oh, Sheila," I heard myself saying. "There's nothing to forgive. It's over."

I didn't know it was true until I said it out loud. It *was* over. Now I saw my old enemy as beautiful, a bringer of peace. That's when I saw grace for what it is: something far higher than *fair*, something completely free.

For a time, Sheila had been my adversary. But on our last night at Hillsboro, working together, she and God showed me that beyond all my confusions, I have the ability to receive and to share His grace, and this I know: so do you!

> *Father, how can it be that something*
> *so precious is absolutely free?*
> —PAM KIDD

Mon 5

We give thanks to You, O God, we give thanks. . . . —PSALM 75:1 (NAS)

We had a porch party of grateful tears and thanksgiving one morning a few years ago. Our eighteen-year-old son Thomas had spent the previous few nights camping with friends. We were expecting him home by 7:30 AM to get ready for church. At 7:45 AM, my husband Rick went looking for him. I watched at the window, waiting and praying.

Soon I saw Rick slowly heading up the drive-way with Thomas beside him in the passenger seat, blood covering his face. Rick had found him standing confused on the side of the road that damp gray morning. The guys hadn't gotten much sleep the night before; Thomas fell asleep while driving home and hit a tree head-on a few houses from ours. He had suffered a concussion and needed several stitches near his eye.

The following Monday morning, Rick and I rocked and sipped our coffee on the porch. No words for a few moments. Finally he spoke.

"I can't get the image of Thomas out of my mind—finding him that way. He could have . . . "

"I know." I dabbed tears of gratitude with a corner of my red blanket. "I don't know how to thank God. I can't say enough."

We reached across the space between our rocking chairs and held hands. After thirty years together, my hand slipped easily into the familiar warmth of his.

"Look at the trees," I said. A few orange- and red-blazed leaves dangled in the breeze. "Winter's coming."

Rick's voice was hoarse. "But not today."

Lord, how I thank You for the gift of life.
—JULIE GARMON

Tue 6

*Behold, now is the accepted time;
behold, now is the day of salvation.*
—II CORINTHIANS 6:2

It was early morning on Election Day and most of the races were pretty much settled according to the polls—which was good, because I had a hectic day ahead of me and I was already running late. True, the polls were open till nine, but my vote wouldn't mean anything anyway. So what if I skipped one pointless election?

That's when I ran into Charlie. Charlie is a retired manager for Greyhound who lives on the first floor of my apartment building. "Don't forget to vote!" he called after me.

I cringed. Charlie volunteered every election to help expedite the voter lines and answer any questions people had about the voting machines. I loved seeing him at the polling place in his ubiquitous Yankees cap.

I just don't have the time, Lord, I protested. *Maybe someday when I'm retired like Charlie I can always do my civic duty. But for now I need You to help me through this insane day.*

Charlie's words faded as I sat through a blizzard of meetings and met a dozen deadlines. In fact, I felt quite pleased—and a little surprised—with all I managed to accomplish, and by eight o'clock I was exhausted and ready to head home and grab a late dinner. Suddenly I found myself thinking about Charlie.

Don't forget to vote.

Why did he have to say that? Hadn't I done enough today?

But I hadn't voted, and that was the most important thing I had to do. I checked my watch again. If I hurried I would just make it.

I saw the Yankees logo before I saw him. "They let you wear that cap in here?" I said. "I thought this was nonpartisan."

"The Yankees aren't running for anything," he said with a laugh, and added, "Boy, you barely made it."

Yep. That's because I'd been given just enough time.

> *Lord, You always give us the time to do*
> *the things that really matter.*
> —EDWARD GRINNAN

Wed 7

> *Epaphras... is always wrestling in prayer for you, that you may stand firm in all the will of God, mature and fully assured.*
> —COLOSSIANS 4:12 (NIV)

Our daughter Mary has started taking the subway by herself. It's normal for sixth-graders in New York: The city stops providing bus service to school and hands middle-schoolers a Metrocard instead.

We've been working toward this rite of passage for almost a year. We outlined our family rules: Wait by the clerk's booth until the train comes; board the conductor's car; sit next to someone who looks like a mom; call home when you get back to street level. Autonomy began with short trips of only a stop or two. Then we gave occasional permission for longer forays, as long as no transfers were involved. Finally, Mary started going to ballet class in midtown on her own.

And now my eleven-year-old is transportation-enabled! Whatever occasional worries I have for her safety are offset by the gaspingly rich gift of time Mary's independence has given me. The ballet commute is forty-five minutes each way, three times a week. Now I no longer need to cajole eight-year-old Maggie and six-year-old Stephen into making the best of a boring subway ride. My wallet is relieved not to choke up fares for all of us. I don't have to listen to endless gossip in the ballet studio.

What's more, self-reliance seems to be doing good things for Mary. She organizes her ballet bag, keeps track of her schedule. She makes time to chat with her friends Amanda and Margaret before class. She understands that if she's going to succeed at ballet, it will be because of passion and hard work—not because Mom pushes her. My tween is learning to dance, in more ways than one.

Father, You ask me to trust in You
and yet think for myself.
Help me find the balance.
—JULIA ATTAWAY

Thu 8

Therefore comfort each other....
—I THESSALONIANS 5:11 (NKJV)

Martha Coakley is a neighbor—she lives in our town of Medford, Massachusetts—but I've only seen her on television. Last November, Massachusetts held a special election to fill the Senate seat left vacant by the death of Edward M. Kennedy. Martha was a candidate to fill that seat. She won the Democratic primary, and her chances were excellent to win the November election.

During the campaign I learned that Martha was from Pittsfield in western Massachusetts, only five miles from Williamstown, my hometown. Father and Mother often shopped in Pittsfield. I also learned that Martha was an honors graduate of Williams College in my hometown.

On Election Day Martha was defeated by a newcomer whose rush to victory was unexpected and surprising. During her concession speech, she said, "I am heartbroken." All her hard work hadn't helped her win her goal.

The next day I wrote her a letter to express my regret at her loss and my wish that it would turn out to have been for the best after all. Then I added a few reminiscences about Pittsfield. I mentioned Jack's, a hot dog stand there where hot dogs cost five cents seventy-five years ago.

A month later, I received a formal thank-you from Martha. On it she had written a note saying, "I really appreciated your note! Jack's hot dog stand is still alive and well!"

Martha remains the neighbor I've never seen in person. But to me, she's a friend who received a little comfort from an unexpected letter.

Good Shepherd, written words can touch the heart and cheer the soul. Help me share them always.
—Oscar Greene

Fri 9

I pray also that the eyes of your heart may be enlightened in order that you may know the hope to which he has called you.... —Ephesians 1:18 (NIV)

A good doctor is often more than a doctor in our lives.

At my husband Lynn's recent regular appointment with his neuro-oncologist, we talked about quality-of-life issues. Lynn has been on chemotherapy for more than a year for his recurrent brain tumor, and when the doctor asked how things were going, I confessed that Lynn had been using the word *hopeless* more often.

The doctor swiveled his chair around and looked directly at Lynn. "I treat your cancer, but I also treat you as a person," he said, "and it's important to feel hopeful about something in life. In fact, if you reach the end of a day and can't think of the reasons you are glad you lived through that day, we need to make some changes."

He paused and then asked Lynn, "What feels hopeless?"

"That I may never feel better than I do right now," Lynn answered.

So the doctor outlined an option to cut back on some of Lynn's medications, including his chemotherapy doses. We readily agreed to make those changes.

Maybe even more important, we took the doctor's other suggestion, which had nothing to do with medications but everything to do with finding hope. At the end of the day, at dinner or before we fall asleep, I try to remember to ask Lynn that simple question: "Why are you glad you lived through this day?"

The answers have varied: a grandchild's birthday celebration, voting, the brilliantly changing colors of the trees, accomplishing a banking task or clearing up an insurance snafu. But here's what has been most hopeful: For both of us, that question seems to open our eyes to all the possible answers tucked into each day.

> *Father, may I embrace the grateful-for-life moments You give me each day.*
> —CAROL KUYKENDALL

Sat 10

And we, who with unveiled faces all reflect the Lord's glory, are being transformed into his likeness with ever-increasing glory....
—II CORINTHIANS 3:18 (NIV)

My wife Carol and I are always amazed at the creativity of our grandsons Konner and Brennig, ages eight and six. One evening we took them to a fast-food restaurant and, after the meal, bought them soft ice cream cones. They wandered over to another booth to sit with a young friend they'd met in the play area. A few minutes later they returned, licking their cones into some weird shapes. Looking closer, I saw that the shapes resembled heads, complete with eyes, nose, mouth and ears!

"Where did you get the idea for that?" I asked.

"Our friend," Brennig said through lips dripping ice cream. "He's eight."

"Look!" Konner laughed, holding up his cone. "A monster!" The "head" had taken on a decidedly angry expression, which delighted Brennig, who began reshaping his own cone.

The demonstration lasted only briefly while the ice cream proceeded to disappear into grinning mouths. But for those few moments we were all entertained by the deft shaping and reshaping the boys achieved with their tongues.

I think God does something like that with us. He won't settle for leaving us as He found us. As we soften and become pliable in His presence, He's able to wipe out our self-centeredness and hardness of heart and reshape us for His own use, forming in us new attitudes of love and forgiveness.

It's not time for my life to be set in stone. I want to let the Lord remold me into the shape He desires for me. And I thank my grandsons for a happy graphic demonstration of what it's like to be in the hands of a loving God.

Father, here I am, waiting. Shape me as You will.
—HAROLD HOSTETLER

Sun 11   *You are the children of the Lord your God. . . .*
—DEUTERONOMY 14:1 (NIV)

A few months after Dad's death, Brian and I moved to North Carolina, where we eagerly sought a church family to call our own. We found a local church just a few miles from our home that seemed to have everything we wanted: young couples, volunteer opportunities, and a real community feel.

The service was wonderful and we were both uplifted by the worship and the communion. But the best part came just before the end of the service, when the back doors opened and the pastor called to the children who, having finished kids' church, were waiting in the foyer.

In they streamed by the dozen, holding their completed artwork and lessons proudly above their heads as they navigated the aisle to find their families.

The scene took my breath away: dozens of children running toward the altar, displaying their best efforts. Can you imagine a better image of heaven?

The image stayed with me into my dreams that night, when I thought of Dad making his way toward Jesus with his hands held high and his best efforts showing: a family well-raised, a wife most loved, a community served, and the cause of Christ supported. I can only imagine that Jesus eagerly welcomed him home.

Blessings and praises to You, my Heavenly Father,
for embracing my efforts, no matter how far
I color outside the lines.
—ASHLEY KAPPEL

Mon 12

He makes wars cease to the ends of the earth.... —PSALM 46:9 (NIV)

Our nephew Richie entered the army out of high school, married his sweetheart, had three beautiful daughters, served in Bosnia and then became a drill sergeant, training young soldiers for battle and intelligence gathering. Two years ago, when his class was called up for service in Iraq, he asked to go with them. He was on the downside of thirty-five, had already served in dangerous places and done more than his duty. I called him to see if he could be talked out of it. He said, "Uncle Eric, these are my kids. I want to go with them and see they get home safe."

Those next twenty-four months were tough; e-mail and care packages kept us in touch. Several times in those months we were in airports when men and women either arrived back or departed out for their tours. Once in the Dallas–Fort Worth airport, the long aisle of departure gates was packed with people when a company of troops came walking down a glass-enclosed corridor on their way to passport control. Like a wave at a stadium, people rose to their feet and began clapping as the line of soldiers passed by. We knew he wasn't there, but we kept scanning their faces looking for Richie as tears flowed down our cheeks.

Finally we got the call he was home safe. I waited a few days and then dialed his number. "Richie, it's me, Uncle Eric. I sure am glad you're home. We prayed for you so much while you were away."

"I know, Unc, thanks a lot."

"Well, I'll let you go. Aunt Joy sends her love, and thanks for going over there for us and . . . I love you Richie."

Today is Veterans Day. For all the grandparents, fathers, mothers, sons, daughters, nieces and nephews who have served; find one today and say "Thank you."

*Lord, thank You for Richie and all the others
who serve so we will be safe.*
—ERIC FELLMAN

❋ A GRACE-FILLED JOURNEY

Tue 13   *Pray without ceasing.*
—I Thessalonians 5:17

HOLY MOUNTAIN

Today the plan is to sail past Mount Athos, an island dedicated to a life of unceasing prayer, either as part of a monastic community or alone in a hermitage. I've always wondered what Paul meant when he gave the instruction to pray without ceasing. How could we ever get anything done if we all tried to keep a prayer going every minute of the day?

I've found two prayer practices to be helpful. One involves holding a word or phrase in your heart/mind by repeating it over and over at all times. The monks on Mount Athos say the Jesus Prayer ("Lord Jesus Christ, Son of God, have mercy on me, a sinner") or just the name of Jesus this way. Although this requires an extreme degree of focus and attention, it is quite effective and can become automatic after some time of practice. I practiced this way of prayer for several years, and even after transitioning to another prayer form, I notice that the prayer is still in my unconscious. When I'm brushing my teeth or sweeping the floor or driving some distance, I often notice those words cycling through my mind. It is one way to pray without ceasing.

Another practice I use is *offering prayer*. Whenever I finish one task and start another (making the bed, washing dishes, cooking, writing devotionals), I offer the results to God in prayer. This doesn't mean every task is a huge success. It does mean every job becomes part of an unceasing prayer.

> *When I offer each activity to You, Lord, it's more*
> *likely to bring good results. In the meantime,*
> *I can relax into constant prayer.*
> —MARILYN MORGAN KING

Wed 14

> *Be strong and of a good courage; be not afraid, neither be thou dismayed: for the Lord thy God is with thee whithersoever thou goest.*
> —JOSHUA 1:9

Every time I have a dark day, I meet a kid who cheers me right up again with her or his crazy grace and thorny courage. This morning, for example: I met a girl who told me a story so amazing that I asked if I could take notes.

"I was born in a little town in the woods," she said, "with a mom and a dad. After a while my mom left, leaving me with my dad. My dad gets killed by a tree—he was a logger—and I go to live with my granddad. My granddad dies and I go to live with my youngest uncle, who gets married, and then *he* gets killed in the woods—he was a logger too.

"By now I'm sixteen, and it's clear that the new wife and I are not going to be real close, so I study like crazy and get the best grades I can get and come to college. But oddly enough, you know what I want to study now that I'm here? Forest biology and the science of the woods and stuff like that. I realized the other day that I want to spend my career in exactly the places that killed my dad and my uncle. Is that weird or what? But I figure the best way out is through, you know what I mean? You can't run away from what hurts. You have to walk right into it. Do you think that's so?"

Oh, dear Lord, yes, I think that's so. It's easy to run away, isn't it? And not so easy to walk right into the storm, the deep woods, the country of pain. But You are there; I know You are; I will welcome Your kingdom as this child reminds me to . . .
—BRIAN DOYLE

Thu 15   *Thus saith the Lord, In an acceptable time have I heard thee, and in a day of salvation have I helped thee. . . .* —ISAIAH 49:8

We call it "God's Moment" when suddenly, wondrously, something that's been hard to do becomes easy. We learned about this gift of grace during my husband's years-long struggle to give up smoking. I'd suffered with John through after-meal cravings, smokeless car trips, late-night work sessions. He'd be without cigarettes for a week, a month, once as long as six months, and then the habit would reclaim him.

One morning he seemed to hear God say, *Stop struggling! At My Moment you will quit for good, not in your strength but Mine.* Wondering if he could have heard right, John did stop battling nicotine—and was soon back to three packs of cigarettes a day. It was a few weeks later that he heard an emphatic *Now.* "It's happened!" he told me triumphantly that evening. "I know I've smoked my last cigarette!" I watched somewhat skeptically, but it proved to be true. It wasn't that he tried harder; "It was as if I wasn't trying at all."

Thirty smoke-free years later, both of us have learned to listen for God's Moment in all kinds of situations. The letter I keep putting off writing, the chore I don't want to tackle, the person I dread to go see—I'm learning that God will provide His time for each meaningful endeavor. My part is simply to accept it when it comes. I write that letter, I clean out that closet, I pay a call on the person I've offended, not with gritted teeth but with something that feels very like joy—something that feels like moving for a little while in the rhythm that turns the galaxies.

> *Help me, Lord God, to listen for Your*
> *"Now" throughout this day.*
> —Elizabeth Sherrill

Fri 16

"The Lord is my strength and my song; he has become my salvation...."
—Exodus 15:2 (NIV)

I was out for a walk on a late autumn afternoon when I saw something so simple it not only changed my day and brought a smile to my face, but it even turned my whole week around.

I felt buried by responsibilities. It was one of those times when work was full of stress and the duties of domestic life seemed far more numerous than the rewards. I'd taken the dog out for a walk.

As we approached the village green, the dog was stopping to sniff every tree and bench we passed by. Because we rarely walked this far on our daily outings, he had many new smells to discover. I stopped paying attention to him after a while and was looking off into the distance. It was a beautiful day; the sun was shining. Across the street, I saw a man emerging from the courthouse. He wore a suit and tie and a nicely pressed white shirt. His shoes looked polished. And he walked out the back door of the courthouse, yanked at his tie as if to breathe deeply for the first time in a long while, knelt on the grass and kissed the earth.

I watched him for a full minute and realized he wasn't just kissing the grass. He was shaking slightly with sobs of joy. I began to feel I was eavesdropping, so the dog and I moved on, but I think the man had just been delivered from something that was hanging over his head in that courtroom, and now he was free. The feeling overwhelmed him. He was forgiven.

I'm overwhelmed, Lord, because I, too, am forgiven.
—JON SWEENEY

Sat 17

Quicken us, and we will call upon thy name. —PSALM 80:18

Our son Timothy calls his grandparents Grammie and Grampie, and that's how he introduces them to his friends. That's just who they are.

One fall weekend Tim was in a production of *Richard II* at his college. He didn't have a big part, just a few lines to say and a great gold cape to wear along with a beard. We couldn't go out to California to see the show, but Mom and Dad live only thirty-five minutes away from the school, and good grandparents that they are, they decided to go to the Saturday matinee. "I wouldn't miss it for the world," said my mom.

They showed up at the theater on campus in plenty of time. Tim had assured them he'd leave tickets at the box office with their name. "We've come to pick up our tickets," Mom said. "They'd be under *H* for Hamlin."

The girl at the box office looked through her stack of envelopes. "I'm sorry; I don't have anything under Hamlin."

"That's funny," Mom said. "He promised." And a promise to a pair of grandparents was a *promise*. She turned to Dad, pausing. Had Tim forgotten? And if he didn't reserve tickets in their name, would there still be a place for them in the small theater? Then she had an idea.

"Try *G*," she said confidently. "Under Grammie and Grampie."

The girl looked through her stack of envelopes. "Yes," she said. "Here they are. Grammie and Grampie."

It's often been pointed out that Jesus called God "Abba," which is like saying "Papa" or "Dad." Our loved ones know what we call them and answer to their names.

Jesus, Lord, You hear me when I call Your name.
—Rick Hamlin

Sun 18

Like newborn babies, crave pure spiritual milk, so that by it you may grow up in your salvation.
—I Peter 2:2 (niv)

When I opened up my Bible to share a favorite passage with my friend Ann, she stopped me. "Wait a minute!" she exclaimed. "Look how marked up your Bible is! You have notes scribbled in the margins!"

"Sure do," I replied. I thumbed through the brightly colored pages. "I've even highlighted my favorite passages in bright yellow."

"Wow," Ann said, "I've never written in my Bible."

"I hadn't, either," I told her, "until my ninth-grade Sunday school teacher taught me otherwise. She taught home economics in high school, and one day she brought her favorite cookbook to our Sunday school class. The margins were crammed with handwritten notes, and the corners of her favorite pages were folded down. Colorful tabs marked some often-used recipes.

"'Why did you write all over your cookbook?' we asked.

"'Because that's the best way for me to use what's inside of it,' she replied.

"Then she showed us her Bible. Her favorite Scriptures were underlined in green ink, and she had notes written in the margins, while stars and asterisks pointed to favorite passages.

"'Your Bible is just like a good cookbook,' she explained. 'It, too, nourishes you, sustains you and allows you to grow. And just like my favorite cookbook, the Bible is meant to be used.' She held up some brightly colored pens and said, 'So let's dig in!'

"And for the next year of Sundays we studied the Bible, marking our favorite passages in red, blue and purple ink, and jotting down key words in the margins."

Thank You for Your Words, Lord,
which nourish my soul.
—MELODY BONNETTE

Mon 19

I thank God, whom I serve, as my forefathers did, with a clear conscience, as night and day I constantly remember you in my prayers. —II TIMOTHY 1:3 (NIV)

I recently recorded some videos for the OurPrayer.org Web site. One of the questions I was asked was "Who's had the most influence on your prayer life?" This was an easy one for me. Without a doubt, it's my parents. Each of them has taught me something special about the power of prayer. They believe no problem or issue is too big or small for God.

When I was a boy, if I'd get up at night to get a drink of water, I'd find my dad in the living room of our small apartment on his knees, praying out loud in Spanish in the dark: *"Dios, te doy las gracias por todas las bendiciones recibidas....* God, thank You for all the blessings we have received. Thank You for the home we have...." He would pray for each member of his family by name and need: "God, please bless my sister Antonia with strength to care for her family." At other times he was lifting up us children in prayer. "O God, watch and protect Pablo, Sandy and Orlando."

Mom had her very own unique and practical ways of "praying without ceasing" as Scripture teaches. I often would find her at the kitchen sink while she was doing the dishes or preparing dinner, singing and praying. A woman of few words, Mom prayed in silence. Many times I've seen her with tears streaming down her cheeks, pouring her heart out to God.

Today, in their golden years, they're still praying people, still showing me the power of prayer.

Thank You, Lord, for the many ways my parents have shown me Your way.
—PABLO DIAZ

EDITOR'S NOTE: *Join us today for our annual Thanksgiving Day of Prayer. Visit us online at OurPrayer.org, where you can request prayer, volunteer to pray for others or help support our prayer ministry.*

Tue 20

I sought the Lord, and he answered me; he delivered me from all my fears. —PSALM 34:4 (NIV)

I was out walking on one of those cold, gray, forlorn days that come with late autumn, when the trees are bare and winter is dead ahead. A light, raw drizzle dampened me to the bone, and the wind tore at my jacket. I turned up my collar and hunched my shoulders against it. A fog of fear enveloped me: fear of the future, fear for our retirement, fear that in the years ahead our money would be gone. With the economic downturn, the possibility was real.

By the time I crossed the railroad tracks I was one anxious woman, convinced that the winds of time would blow me away like the leaves gusting in the gutter and pushing me down the street. This wicked wind turned over a garbage can, flapped open a barn door and dragged a heavy tarp across a lawn. But it hadn't dislodged a fist-sized puff in a young tree ahead of me.

The empty bird's nest was wedged at my eye level. I stood there amazed at this perfectly shaped bowl woven from twigs and grasses, this seemingly fragile abode that should have sailed away or fallen to bits and pieces in the first gale. But here it was—strong, built to last. A tiny architectural wonder woven by a lowly sparrow, whose pattern came from the hand of the Creator Who cares for her.

As I turned around and headed back into the stiff wind, the words of our Lord enveloped me: "Look at the birds of the air. . . . Are you not much more valuable than they?" (Matthew 6:26, NIV)

> *Our Father in heaven, thank You that the true*
> *underpinnings of our lives are woven and*
> *held by Your almighty hand.*
> —SHARI SMYTH

Wed 21

Do not withhold good from those to whom it is due, When it is in your power to do it.
—PROVERBS 3:27 (NAS)

At eighty-eight, my mother is living on her own. She has a great group of friends in her small town who look out for her. Ken and Donna Neale give her rides to the airport and accompany her to medical appointments. They keep her stocked up with food and sundries when they warehouse-shop, and Mom borrows freezer space from them. Ken helps with her home repairs. She is a mentor to Donna and an adopted grandmother to the couple's four children.

The most touching thing Ken and Donna do happens at Thanksgiving. Each year mom is a guest at their holiday table. And she goes home with an uncommon leftover: the turkey carcass, so she can make her favorite turkey vegetable soup. Every year she tells me, "And Ken really left a lot of meat on the bones."

The Neales' kindness reminds me of the Old Testament story of Ruth. A poor young widow recently arrived in Bethlehem with her mother-in-law, also widowed, Ruth went into the fields to glean grain. The owner of one field—knowing Ruth's circumstances—told his servants to "purposely pull out for her some grain from the bundles and leave it that she may glean, and do not rebuke her" (Ruth 2:16, NAS).

There are many ways to give, whether it's a helping hand or some meaty turkey bones. And did I mention that my mother's name is Ruth?

Great and giving God, show me how I can
give simply and meaningfully.
—CAROL KNAPP

November

Thu 22

You have granted him his heart's desire and have not withheld the request of his lips.
—PSALM 21:2 (NIV)

I stared at the landscape outside my window. Everything was a shade of gray or brown; not a single bright blossom broke the gloom. Frost had claimed the last of even my hearty mums. It was the day before Thanksgiving, but I wasn't feeling very grateful. *Oh, God*, I whined. *Must everything be so drab?*

I'd already begun to feel desperate for color. How could I go months (and months) with nothing but this bleakness to look at?

Then this morning I awoke earlier than usual. I slipped out of bed and into my warm robe and house shoes. I was mentally going over the menu for Thanksgiving dinner (*Should I double the corn casserole or triple it?*) as I pulled open the drapes. And there, on the eastern horizon, was the color I'd been craving: periwinkle and pale lemon and streaks of magenta. I grabbed my camera and clicked. I adjusted the settings and aimed again. Everything was different. Now a startling palette of peach and orange and mauve filled the sky. *How could it change so quickly?*

I do, truly, have many things to be grateful for this Thanksgiving. A loving (and growing!)

family, friends far and near, a church where I feel welcome and nourished. But especially I'm grateful for fall and winter sunrises. They remind me that even though my world is fraught with change, it's also rich in unexpected surprises and answered prayers.

And color, if I have the tenacity to look for it.

Giver of all that is good, how grateful I am for Your abundant kindness—even when I whine.
—MARY LOU CARNEY

Fri 23   *I planted, Apollos watered, but God was causing the growth.*
—I CORINTHIANS 3:6 (NAS)

Recently we bought a new house, and the front porch is lined with flower boxes. So although I've never been a gardener, I decided I'd learn to grow flowers.

My mother, who has a natural green thumb, spent Thanksgiving with us this year. "Mom," I asked, "winter is coming. What kind of flowers can I plant that will thrive in cold weather?"

"Plant pansies," she answered. "They're beautiful, colorful and easy to grow."

So I planted pansies. Mother was right: They thrived. All I had to do was plant them and enjoy them. The soil provided nutrients, God gave the rain and they flourished in the first frost of winter.

Yesterday as I climbed our front porch steps, I noticed the pansies drooping. I stuck my finger into the soil and noted that it was bone dry. Then I remembered that it hadn't rained in two weeks. God had been doing the watering for me; I hadn't remembered that God needed me to do a little watering too.

Yesterday I drenched the pansies and today they look magnificent. Feeling good about my ability to fill a watering can and sprinkle flowers, I stopped at my favorite coffee shop on the way to work. As I parked and walked toward the door, a man sidled up to me and said, "Hey, mister, I'm hungry. Can you help me out?"

I backed up a step and quietly checked for blood-shot eyes and whiskey breath. Then God clobbered me; it was as if I could hear His voice: *All right, Walker, if I need help to water flowers, then I need help with people too. It doesn't matter if the man's half drunk and floundering; he's hungry. Give him a cup of coffee and one of those two donuts you always buy. I need you to help Me water this flower.*

> *Lord, help me remember that when it doesn't rain,*
> *I should help You water Your flowers.*
> —SCOTT WALKER

Sat 24

For I know the thoughts that I think toward you, saith the Lord, thoughts of peace, and not of evil, to give you an unexpected end. —JEREMIAH 29:11

After we returned from that second trip to Africa, Corinne's and my wedding day came around quickly. There were all the usual preparations, a few parties, and then there we were, standing at the altar in front of my minister-father.

"You didn't get here by accident," he was saying, "and you stand to have an extraordinary marriage if you'll remember how God has brought you together."

I thought back to that first lonely trip to Africa...

"Your journeys haven't been easy," he continued. "You both have been through the 'refiner's fire.' And, of course, you couldn't have had a clue what God was doing."

I looked at Corinne and smiled. God's finger had drawn the map that had brought us to this very place. He even went to the trouble to send us to the other side of the world, not once but twice, to weave together His perfect plan for us.

"But why the long wait?" Dad was saying. "Why draw you through that dry emotional desert?

"Well, because the most precious gifts are fully appreciated only by those who've gone through the fire—a fire that burns away the *me* to open room for *Thee*."

It was all making perfect sense. I certainly had my share of rough edges and for sure I had experienced plenty of disappointments. But God had never forgotten me, just as He had never forgotten Corinne in her own difficulties. In a way, I suppose He was biding His time, getting us ready and burning away the *me*'s that blocked the way to a new life together.

I looked at my bride and she looked at me. We didn't need to say a single word—except, of course, "I do."

Father, You have given us far more than we could ever expect. Your peace completes us. Thank You.
—BROCK KIDD

Sun 25

From the place of His dwelling He looks on all the inhabitants of the earth. —PSALM 33:14 (NKJV)

Each year on the weekend that follows Thanksgiving, I journey to the attic to haul down the boxes that contain our Christmas decorations. My husband Bill goes to the local tree farmer and strolls for hours through the tall evergreens looking for just the right tree. Before I take even a single trinket out of the box, I put on a CD of Christmas music that lifts my heart with joyful anticipation.

With the tree finally settled into its corner, I pour a fresh cup of coffee and begin slowly unpacking, relishing the memories each of the ornaments brings. As I gently lift up the top of a flat box, I see the green plastic pieces of the gumdrop tree and recall visits to my grandmother's home on the north shore of Long Island.

The ceilings in her dining room were fifteen feet high, and there in the center of her large mahogany table sat—glimmering and colorful—a solid crystal gumdrop tree. I was too small to reach it, but I'd stand there and gaze in amazement at the beauty of its clear glass arms stretched out to hold more gumdrops than I could count. I loved the tree's grandeur and magic.

I pick up the plastic pieces of my own humble gumdrop tree, thankful for the joy of remembering it brings me each year. By reminding me of those long-ago Christmas visits, it shimmers with a magic of its own.

*Lord, thank You for the memories that bring back
my past and give me a foretaste of my
future in heaven with You.*
—Patricia Pusey

Mon 26

In his heart a man plans his course, but the Lord determines his steps. —PROVERBS 16:9 (NIV)

I was tempted to reply to the e-mail and tell them it was just flat-out impossible.

The e-mail was from my publisher. My book, *Just Don't Fall*, was coming out in six months and it was time to get blurbs, the endorsement quotes found on book jackets. I was expected to find five published authors who would write blurbs for my book. And not just published authors—best-selling authors.

A few minutes later I was on the phone with my father. "But Dad, I don't even know any best-selling authors," I said. "It's impossible."

"Joshua, the important thing is to take the first step. At least give it a shot. Don't quit before you even try."

I sighed. "All right," I said. "I'll try."

I spent the next several weeks compiling a list of best-selling authors who might like the book, searching for their addresses and writing them letters. And then I waited. And waited. Then the blurbs started coming back. I ended up with not just the five I was aiming for, but eleven!

A few months later I was seated at a conference table at my publisher's office in New York. "What's your secret for getting blurbs?" someone asked. "We are amazed at your success."

I laughed. "No secret," I said, "other than taking the first step."

Lord, in which areas of my life is it time
for me to take the first step?
—JOSHUA SUNDQUIST

Tue 27

For they deal falsely, the thief breaks in, and the bandits raid without.
—HOSEA 7:1 (RSV)

My husband Larry and I were recently scammed. We have since learned we had fallen for the number-one scam in America for older people. It's called "Help Me, Grandma."

The scam is complicated and well-organized, involving several thieves who gather information about a young woman and her family. Then an actress, crying so hysterically that her voice is disguised, calls the young woman's grandmother and convinces her that she is her granddaughter, in serious trouble and needing a large sum of money at once.

Larry and I are usually skeptical about things like that, and yet we believed the story and sent the money to our "granddaughter."

We didn't lose a devastating amount of money (some people have lost thousands), but we lost enough so that Christmas for our family this year will be slimmer than usual.

I think often of those scammers, and I wonder if they feel any guilt over what they do. It's taken me a while to forgive them, but I think I'm getting there. Meanwhile, I keep them in my prayers, asking God to touch their hearts and their souls.

Heavenly Father, many people in this world don't know You or Your Word, including Your commandment "Thou Shall Not Steal." Please help me be a messenger for You.
—MADGE HARRAH

Wed 28

*Fear not, neither be thou dismayed.... —*JOSHUA 8:1

The pounding of my heart woke me up. Something was in bed with me! And I'd gone to bed alone! In my prayer, I'd specifically asked God to protect me in these unfamiliar surroundings, my friend Mabel's cottage. I kept my eyes shut, but then I sniffed. *What is that odd smell?* It smelled like . . . tuna fish?

That brought me back to reality. I opened one eye and looked at Mabel's cat Thundercloud, who was inches from my face and looking at me as if I had no right to be in her owner's bed. "Good morning, tuna breath," I said, suddenly wondering why nobody marketed a peppermint mouthwash for cats.

I was wide awake now, and my thoughts returned from the ridiculous to the serious. After thanking God that my intruder was nothing more dangerous than the long-haired gray animal who was purring, I thought of other middle-of-the-night fears I'd had over the past two decades. Two years ago, when I stopped substitute-teaching, I would wake up at 3:00 AM, fearing I'd never work again. Now I was teaching two workshops, one on overcoming clutter, and I was enjoying them more than I'd ever enjoyed subbing. And what about when I was single? I'd lie in bed alone, wondering if I'd ever fall in love. Now my husband Paul and I have been married seventeen happy years.

"Middle of the night madness," Thundercloud's owner had called it when I'd confessed it to her several months back. "Do two things," Mabel had instructed me. "Turn over and turn it over. Change your position in bed—or even get up—and share your problem with the Lord."

God, when I'm in the midst of "middle of the night madness," let me come to You for comfort.
—LINDA NEUKRUG

Thu 29

My peace I give unto you. . . .
—JOHN 14:27

Near the door to the garage at the apartment complex where we now live stands a rust-pitted old bicycle. It's covered with dust, its tires are flat, its handlebar askew. And on it some wit has hung a sign: RUST IN PEACE.

I didn't think the joke was funny. All right, this is a retirement community, nobody here younger than sixty-two, but that didn't mean we'd come here to rust. I was twenty-five years older than that minimum age and going strong—still working, still traveling.

Then I had quadruple-bypass surgery and was put on a strict regimen. No driving, no lifting anything over ten pounds, no raising my arms above my head—all kinds of irksome restrictions. It would be six months or longer before I'd be back to normal. Well, I, for one, was not going to start "rusting." I'd astonish everyone! I'd be walking a mile a day by the end of the month! I'd try lifting twelve pounds, fifteen, twenty . . .

And, of course, I pushed myself too hard. My chest ached, my breath was hard to catch. Instead of speeding my healing up, I'd set it back.

That was when a different word in the sign on the old bike began to speak to me. I'd bristled at *rust,* but *peace*...Maybe that was something I needed to pay heed to. Some amount of rust, I was beginning to concede, was inevitable as bodies age: Bones get brittle, arteries harden. What wasn't inevitable was the attitude I took toward these inescapable changes.

What if instead of chafing at them, I acknowledged them with grace and humor? What if peace, instead of battle, was my response to the gift of years?

Give me that peace, Father,
that passes understanding.
—JOHN SHERRILL

Fri 30   *Jesus said, "Let the little children come to me, and do not hinder them, for the kingdom of heaven belongs to such as these."* —MATTHEW 19:14 (NIV)

I was at an airport during one of those seemingly interminable waits between planes when restless passengers choose between looking at wristwatches or something to read. A young mother flopped onto a nearby bench, parking her baby in his stroller alongside.

The baby boy, probably about nine months old, jiggled up and down and back and forth, clenching and opening dimpled fingers while eyeing a paper sack his mother took from her purse. The sack contained a small jar of applesauce from which the mother began to feed her baby. The child's mouth mechanically opened each time she spooned in applesauce, but it was the sack itself that kept his attention.

It's just a sack, *for goodness sakes,* I told myself. *What's so special about that?*

To the little fellow, it wasn't "just a sack"; it was a toy. And it made noise! Two flying hands pounding the sack brought crackling, crunching sounds while the boy alternated between rapt awe and excited squeals.

It was hard to tell who found more pleasure: the boy or we amused, formerly bored passengers now watching his antics.

I also noticed something else: My fellow travelers were no longer looking at their watches or for something to read. Maybe they, too, were thinking of the verse above or of the painted depictions of Jesus surrounded by clusters of kids.

Father, too many years have passed since I've looked at the world through the eyes of a child. Please open my understanding, so I can see Your wonders in the ordinary.
—Isabel Wolseley

MY PATHWAY TO PEACE

1 _____

2 _____

3 _____

4 _____

5 _____

6 _____

7 _____

8 _____

9 _____

10 _____

11 _____

12 _____

13 _____

14 _____

15 _____

November

16 _____

17 _____

18 _____

19 _____

20 _____

21 _____

22 _____

23 _____

24 _____

25 _____

26 _____

27 _____

28 _____

29 _____

30 _____

December

Glory to God in the highest, and on earth peace, good will toward men.

—LUKE 2:14

❧ THIS I KNOW

Sat 1

And she . . . laid him in a manger. . . .
—LUKE 2:7

SMELLING THE HAY

I am standing face-to-face with the *Adoration of the Magi* by the Dutch painter Hieronymus Bosch. But instead of feeling exhilaration, I'm feeling fairly flat.

My husband David and I are visiting the Prado Museum in Madrid, and after viewing a good number of the thousands of paintings, from Rubens to Velazquez to Goya, I'm far from inspired. In fact, I'm confused.

From Raphael's *Holy Family* to El Greco's *Adoration of the Shepherds*, I'm just not smelling the hay. It seems that artists from the Renaissance forward were intent on gilding the Nativity and all that followed.

I, for one, have little need of a gold-leafed Jesus. I need an on-the-ground example to follow, someone who tells me how to get by in this world with all its greed and sharp edges. Mother Mary in a lavishly embroidered robe and Joseph with an ornate staff aren't helping. I need to remember the donkey and the rough-hewn stable.

David explains to me that the great artists painted the way their patrons paid them to paint. The thought makes me more uncomfortable than ever. Just as surely as those artists turned the hay to gold in their paintings, sometimes I have a tendency to bend Jesus' teachings to fit my comfort zone. Feeding the hungry and caring for the homeless are great ideas—just don't raise my taxes to make it happen!

Outside the museum, the day is bright. The art was beautiful, but for me, it was the personal message that was truly profound. This I know: A gilded Jesus doesn't work. I need to go back to the Book and study His teachings. I need to do what He says.

Already, I'm beginning to smell the hay.

Father, take me back to the manger.
Show me Your way. —PAM KIDD

LIVING CHRISTMAS

Sun 2   *And now you have become living building-stones for God's use in building his house....*
—I PETER 2:5 (TLB)

FIRST SUNDAY IN ADVENT:
JUMPING FOR JOY

At the pool on a warm Florida November day, my friend Paula and I were talking about

Advent. Paula recalled that as a kid in Vermont, she spent Advent preparing for the annual Christmas pageant. The grade school children memorized lines, polished their acting skills and worked on costumes so they could delight the community.

Paula remembers one year when the students were supposed to do various things to entertain the baby Jesus. Some delivered special gifts, one sang a song, a few danced. One little girl was asked to jump rope. Unfortunately, as the little girl jumped up and down, her bloomers fell down around her ankles. Paula says the little girl just kicked them away and kept on jumping for joy.

Paula's story reminded me of the problems that seem to crop up during the four weeks before Christmas. The season is supposed to be about preparing our hearts to welcome Jesus into our lives, but often it becomes a time of too much to do, too little time and too much stress.

Sometimes extra gifts must be purchased and wrapped when unexpected guests announce their impending arrival. Or maybe a new holiday cookie recipe falls flat. Or there's a mess of broken ornaments when a little one (like my little sister years ago) knocks over the Christmas tree.

The very nature of Advent means it's a time to settle down, take a deep breath and concentrate on what's important. And when things don't go perfectly as planned, I need to plant that smile on my face, sweep up the mess and keep on jumping for joy.

Lord, as the Advent season sweeps over me, keep me calm and enjoying the anticipation of an event so amazing it changed the world.
—PATRICIA LORENZ

Mon 3   *But even the very hairs of your head are all numbered....* —LUKE 12:7

What's your favorite place to pray? I'd been asking that question of some of our *Guideposts* readers and people who use the OurPrayer Web site. We'd received a slew of answers, such as "in my car" or "the old sofa in the living room" or "at the kitchen table."

I was thinking about just what my answer would be when I walked by the barber's. I popped my head in. "Jacob," I asked. "Do you have time to cut my hair?"

"Sh." He put a finger to his lips and gestured, "Come in, come in." He slapped the barber chair with his towel, pinned a smock around my neck and took out his comb and clippers. "I'm so glad you could fit me in," I said. Again he put a finger to his lips and this time he pointed to a chair in the back where a man was sitting with his head swathed in warm towels, his feet up and his hands over his chest.

"The guy fell asleep," Jacob whispered. "I didn't want to wake him. And then you walked by." He started combing and clipping. Inspired by the sleeping customer and Jacob's silence, I closed my eyes, breathed deeply, listened to the traffic outside and closed out the world. I thought of several people who needed a measure of peace in their lives, including me. *Lord, have mercy* . . . I prayed.

Fifteen minutes later Jacob whisked off the smock and held up a mirror so I could admire his handiwork. "Great," I said. "Thanks." I gave him a good tip because he'd given me one: A barber chair is a great place to pray—as long as you can trust your barber with your hair while you're practicing trusting God.

I put my trust in You, Lord, for You know me
better than I know myself.
—RICK HAMLIN

Tue 4   *"Blessed are the pure in heart. . . . "*
—MATTHEW 5:8 (NAS)

I'd been having atrial fibrillation episodes for three months. My heart would gallop in my chest like a racehorse pounding down the track. Eventually I had an echocardiogram—an ultrasound of the heart—and then met with a cardiologist to discuss the findings.

In his soothing Greek-accented voice, Dr. Iskos explained to me that the heart is like an orchestra, and the nest of cells called the sinus node is the conductor. It directs the other cells as if they were musicians playing a symphony. But over in this chamber, the atrium, are players who decide not to follow the conductor, going off on their own tangent—hence my atrial fibrillation.

After prescribing some medicine that would help me maintain a regular heart rhythm, Dr. Iskos told me the results of my echocardiogram: "Your heart," he said, "looks pristine."

In Dr. Iskos's analogy I recognized the movement of God's grace in my life. When I fail to follow my Maestro and go off in my own direction, my heart gallops farther away from its Lord. But Jesus lived and died to forgive and cleanse all our hearts. Because of this, I have the immense privilege of knowing that when God looks at my heart, He sees it as pristine.

Jesus, You are the Keeper of my heart,
making it pure and perfect.
*—*Carol Knapp

Wed 5

I am the good shepherd, and know my sheep.... —JOHN 10:14

I'd hit a snag in my daily devotional time. "It's no big deal," I told myself. "I can handle this."

For about ten years I'd been using a daily Bible reading plan. The problem developed when I started going out in the early morning dark to get the newspaper. I'd put it on the sofa until I finished my quiet time in my prayer chair. Occasionally I'd read it first, before the Bible. Of course, there's nothing inherently wrong with that. But it began to trouble me. I couldn't concentrate on God's Word after man's words. I tried to reason with myself: "This is silly. It's legalism to have to read the Bible before the newspaper."

During my inner struggle, I refused to ask for God's help. I wanted to do it myself. Then the day arrived when I began routinely reading the paper first. For four months, I didn't have a quiet time. "I could simply stop taking the paper," I told my stubborn, defeated self. I didn't. I lost the battle and my quiet time, and what's more, I didn't enjoy reading the newspaper.

Then one day a letter arrived from the newspaper company: For financial reasons, delivery to our home would no longer be possible; we were thirteen miles outside the new delivery zone. A check was enclosed for the balance of our subscription.

I had my quiet time back.

I'm overjoyed, Father. I know the paper would probably have stopped coming if I'd never struggled. But I also know You cared about my dilemma.
—MARION BOND WEST

Thu 6

"And he will go on before the Lord . . . to turn the hearts of the fathers to their children and the disobedient to the wisdom of the righteous—to make ready a people prepared for the Lord."
—LUKE 1:17 (NIV)

When I was a kid, my favorite video game was a pretty geeky one, "The Oregon Trail." By today's standards, it had remarkably lame graphics with a pretty basic premise: You had to get your wagon and your family from the East to Oregon during the pioneer days.

You might think from its name that the game is won or lost on the trail—your party can be unexpectedly hit by snakebite or dysentery, you can lose supplies or even a life while trying to ford a river, hot weather can take a toll on the health of your party. But one of the pivotal decisions in the game takes place before you even depart: How will you equip your wagon for the long, arduous trek? How many spare axles do you need? How about food?

The game came to mind one day recently while I was thinking about the spiritual development of my two young nephews. A child's early years are much like that initial part of the game. It's the responsibility of the parent to equip a child well and give his or her faith its best chance to blossom when the reality of life, with all its joys and difficulties, hits.

I think my nephews are lucky: My sister and brother-in-law are devoted, wise and wonderful parents who know that, in the end, their children's spiritual foundation matters a lot more than how many Legos they have accumulated. I'd say those boys will grow up with the spare axles they need for their journey.

Lord, let me be ready to help the next generation acquire a full set of spiritual tools.
—JEFF CHU

Fri 7   *"Now what I am commanding you today is not too difficult for you or beyond your reach."* —DEUTERONOMY 30:11 (NIV)

It was a frigid December morning, and I was deep in prayer over my worries about my job directing a new prayer ministry. Turning the corner toward home, I saw a torn plastic garbage bag, its load of kitchen waste strewn down the middle of the road.

What a mess! I thought as I walked around it. Then I remembered meeting a woman named Valerie Beeson-Lyles, who actually looks for trash on her prayer walks! As she picks up each piece, she uses it as a subject for her prayers. Valerie always carries plastic grocery bags in her pockets, just in case she finds trash to pray over.

I shook my head. *I can't possibly do anything about this mess. It's way too big, I can barely pick up anything in these mittens, and I don't have a bag.* Then a strange thought came into my mind: *At least try.*

I bent down and discovered a small bag under some of the garbage. I awkwardly filled it and set it on the sidewalk. Then I kicked at a mound of wet beige plastic; lo and behold, it was a lump of plastic grocery bags! I found three with decent handles and went to work stuffing in the rest of the trash.

As I carried the trash home, I realized I'd thought that dealing with the mess was well beyond my resources and abilities. Once I decided to try, the mess itself had yielded up the things I needed to handle it. The resources had all been right there, but I hadn't discovered them until I was tackling the heap.

I smiled, the message loud and clear in my mind: *Get started on your leadership task, and when you do, you'll find some unexpected help.*

> *Dear Lord, I have a job that looks too big for me to tackle. Help me to trust that You'll provide the resources I need to get the job done.*
> —KAREN BARBER

Sat 8

> *I have strayed like a lost sheep. Seek your servant, for I have not forgotten your commands.* —PSALM 119:176 (NIV)

Snow was beginning to fall. We shivered as branches snapped beneath our feet. Brambles grabbed at our sweaters. It had been dark for hours, and we started to worry that our flashlight's batteries would fail.

My four best friends and I were lost in the woods. We had set up our tent in the fading light of sunset and then decided to go out in search of a beautiful quarry I'd seen behind the forest years ago.

Now that looked like a mistake. It was getting later, getting colder, and my friend Ted had just pointed out a bush we'd seen twenty minutes ago—we were walking in circles, unable to find either the quarry or our campsite. What's more, it wasn't warm enough to sleep without blankets, so I feared we'd have to keep walking aimlessly until the sun came up to stave off the cold.

Then Brian said, "Look at this!" He was pointing at the string of old telephone poles we knew led back to camp. If we could just follow it in the right direction . . . except no one knew which direction we should take.

We decided to go right, and after half an hour of scrambling over a path choked with thorns, I saw the leaf-covered hill I knew led to the quarry. We'd gone the wrong way, but we'd found what we'd been searching for.

When we climbed to the top of the hill, we all stood in awe of the abyss before us, surrounded by sheer rock, illuminated in moonlight. We sat down on the ridge, arms around each other's shoulders, watching the dark water slosh at the quarry's floor, in awe of the majesty of God's creation.

Thank You, Lord, for when I am lost,
You lead me to where I need to be.
—SAM ADRIANCE

🔳 LIVING CHRISTMAS

Sun 9

The voice of one crying in the wilderness, Prepare ye the way of the Lord, make his paths straight.
—MATTHEW 3:3

SECOND SUNDAY IN ADVENT: MAKING TIME

Almost like clockwork, on the second Sunday of Advent I'd start making excuses about why I didn't have time to write letters or personal notes inside my Christmas cards. I know Advent is the time we reach out to all our loved ones, but by this time of year I'm often complaining that I don't even have time to buy, sign, seal and send the cards themselves, never mind writing a personal note in each one.

Then a friend suggested, "Tell yourself that you only have to write three personal notes a day and start writing the cards in September if you have to."

That year I wrote over three dozen letters. I did it by finding lots of little twenty-minute chunks of time: waiting for the roast to finish cooking or the clothes to finish drying; sitting in the doctor's or dentist's office; during the commercials of my favorite TV show; while enjoying my morning cup of tea.

I used to look at that pile of Christmas cards and shudder. Now I divide the task into small, manageable bites of two or three letters a day. Before I know it, I'm heading to the post office, job completed.

This year I'm sending twenty-four Christmas letters to friends and family around the country. I'm writing three letters a day. In eight days I'll be finished. And this year my letters are going to include reasons the person I'm writing to is so special to me.

Isn't that what Advent is all about? Building up others so their hearts expand enough to also welcome the Christ Child into their lives on a daily, permanent basis?

Heavenly Father, as I write personal notes to my loved ones this Advent, help me to help them see how You are a very real presence in our lives.
—PATRICIA LORENZ

Mon 10

The hail will sweep away the refuge of lies. . . .
—ISAIAH 28:17 (NKJV)

When I was in kindergarten, my older sister moved to New York City. On a visit back home, she brought me a gift-souvenir: a miniature Empire State Building. My parsonage family didn't travel much; my world was small. Proud of this connection to the big, bold city, I took the memento to school for show-and-tell. My metallic replica of the tallest building in the world impressed my classmates—even Sammy, the only boy whose opinion mattered to me.

In first grade, my teacher announced another show-and-tell. I couldn't think of anything better to bring than my little Empire State. All I really remember of the day is the shame I felt after Sammy said: "You brought the same thing last year." Old story, as boring as a rerun.

I haven't seen Sammy in forty years, and yet the implications of his remark have lingered all this time. Then last week I traveled to New York City. Heading for the bus to return home, I stopped short at the sight of a window display featuring Empire State Building replicas about four inches high. Were they from the same mold as my sister's golden gift? That's what I imagine now, but then I grappled with a first-grader's emotion. Right there on Seventh Avenue, I confronted the voice: *You're unimaginative and ill-equipped.* I asked an elementary question: *True or false?* My very presence in New York—to see a creative colleague, to enjoy the sites—belied the claim.

With a burst of confidence—to quiet Sammy forever—I bought the kitschy keepsake. It sits now on my windowsill, silently beckoning me back to New York.

> *Lord, in your grace, show me ways to silence
> the old lies I've believed for too long.*
> —EVELYN BENCE

Tue 11 And my God will supply every need of yours. . . .
—PHILIPPIANS 4:19 (RSV)

I pulled it from a cracked patent-leather pocket-book in a bottom drawer—a piece of paper with a message in my husband John's handwriting: *1 hour total care for Scotty.*

The words sent my thoughts back nearly fifty years. Short of cash, instead of gifts one Christmas, John pinned "promissory notes" to the tree. *Breakfast in bed. House vacuumed. A week doing the dishes alone.*

For me the best gift was this one, a dozen or so of them: sixty minutes when I could entrust the care of an active toddler to someone else! To know that when John got home from work I could produce one of these notes and turn all supervision of Scotty over to his father! Here in a forgotten pocketbook was one I'd apparently hoarded, unspent. It had been peace of mind simply to have in my possession the means of providing all Scotty might need at a certain moment—food, comfort, safety—from a source outside myself.

Scott has been a father himself now for many years. His moment-by-moment needs today in far-off Nashville are unknown to me. But I carry that long-ago Christmas gift in my wallet today to remind me of the promise of his heavenly Father: *total care for Scotty.* Not for an hour, not for a dozen hours, but every hour, every day . . . protection, guidance, peace, all that he needs.

As a new year nears, Father, remind me of Your promise: total care for those I love, now and forever.
—ELIZABETH SHERRILL

Wed 12   *If we confess our sins, he is faithful and just to forgive us our sins, and to cleanse us from all unrighteousness.* —I JOHN 1:9

At a store that carries everything imaginable for the bedroom, bathroom and beyond, my husband, daughter and I were on a mission to find a feather comforter. I opened the plastic covers and laid out each one for so long that my family finally went in search of something more interesting.

As I zipped one open, I felt a prick on my finger. It wasn't bad enough to interrupt my search, but a few minutes later I noticed a red smear there. *Oh dear, it's probably on the comforter too*, I thought. I went back to the last one I'd looked at and, sure enough, there it was: a small spot on the white comforter that I didn't want to buy. So what did I do? I found my family, left the store and tried to put it out of my mind.

But for the next two hours I could think of nothing else. I couldn't concentrate on the book I was trying to read or focus on the TV show my husband was watching. Instead, a movie of me on a security camera played repeatedly in my head.

Finally, I spilled everything to my husband. "I want to go buy it," I said.

He thought for a second and then offered wisely, "Why don't you call the manager?"

I got the manager on the phone and related the whole story. But instead of asking for my credit card number, he kindly said, "It's no problem, ma'am. I'll take care of it." I hung up the phone, feeling a great deal of gratitude and a little weepy with the joy of an unburdened heart.

Thank You, Holy Spirit, for convincing
me to do the right thing.
—LUCILE ALLEN

Thu 13

We do not know what we ought to pray for, but the Spirit himself intercedes for us with groans that words cannot express.
—ROMANS 8: 26 (NIV)

The sounds of morning drifted into my dream, waking me before the alarm. I lay in bed, my mind drifting over the busy day ahead, and remembered that my husband Andrew had said our son John needed extra prayers today. And so, with my first conscious, collected thoughts, I willed my mind toward God. *Good morning, Jesus, and thank You for bringing me to this day. I ask you to comfort my son John . . .*

A few moments later my thoughts were on what I was going to bake for breakfast. I began again. *Jesus, I bring before you John, who needs help dealing with some difficult residents in his new home . . .*

This time I ended up dickering with myself over the best words for my prayer. I tried beginning a third time, and a fourth. I tried praying for the other boys in John's residential program. I tried praying for the staff. The results were the same: distraction. How odd that it was so hard to connect with God this morning, and yet I'd pretty much been awakened so I could pray! *No, that's not odd at all. That means someone doesn't want me to pray.*

I sat up in bed, wide awake with the knowledge that it was utterly essential to pray. I went into the living room, where I wouldn't disturb Andrew's sleep. "Father and Creator," I prayed out loud, struggling to form each word. "You are my Lord and God," I said, and then slowly, slowly prayed, my mind a scramble of half-formed thoughts.

When I'd prayed what I could, I turned over the rest of what was in my heart to the Holy Spirit. And then I went to the kitchen and made coconut almond muffins for breakfast, wishing my boy were at home to enjoy them.

Search my heart, Holy Spirit, and speak the words
my heart is unable to utter.
—JULIA ATTAWAY

Fri 14

I long for your salvation, O Lord, and your law is my delight.
—PSALM 119:174 (NKJV)

When I was a boy, the best part of Christmas was the anticipation. I just knew I was going to get a genuine Lionel train, with a diesel engine, a two hundred-watt transformer, and all the accessories. What I really got, because we were poor, was akin to soda cans with wheels, but still, it was fun to dream.

Philosopher Bertrand Russell said, "To be without some of the things you want is an indispensable part of happiness." When we stop dreaming, we stop living.

I told my children's literature class that the works of Hans Christian Andersen are popular because his characters have the same longings we have: the Little Mermaid, who longed to be human; Thumbelina, who longed to be big; the Steadfast Tin Soldier, who longed to be faithful, even though he had just one leg.

Andersen himself had many cravings. The saddest was for the hand of opera singer Jenny Lind, but he didn't have a chance with her. He was an ugly duckling, with a big nose and ears and thick lips. Yet from this failed romance came his beloved story "The Nightingale," a tribute to her.

The Hans Christian Andersen Award is the most coveted children's literature award in the world, but without Andersen's yearnings, we might never have heard of him. His beautiful tales came from a lonely heart.

Christmas is the perfect time to look at our wish lists. Like the Little Match Girl, we light some matches and catch a glimpse of heaven.

Lord, only You know my deepest longings,
the ones that can only be fulfilled in heaven.
Until then, be Thou my portion.
—DANIEL SCHANTZ

A GRACE-FILLED JOURNEY

Sat 15

[He] hath made of one blood all nations. . . . —ACTS 17:25

HOLY WISDOM

Today we are in Istanbul, Turkey, our last stop before sailing back to Athens for our flight home.

Istanbul is a city of ancient buildings, rich treasures and an unexpected blending of religions. Hagia Sophia is a gorgeous cathedral built for Christian worship by the Byzantine emperor Justinian in the sixth century. Its name means "holy wisdom." Nearly a thousand years later it became a mosque, where Muslims worshipped. Now it is a museum. I am deeply moved by a mysterious light that quietly infuses the sacred halls of this magnificent house of worship. Our last stop today is the Blue Mosque, with mosaics composed of over twenty thousand brilliantly colored tiles. Our Turkish guide tells us that Istanbul is a secular city, but this is not what I observed. In both of the city's most elaborate religious buildings, I am touched by a spirit of the sacred. Could this city someday be a place where people of all religions will worship together in peace?

This grace-filled voyage has opened my eyes, my heart and my soul. And it all began with a rainbow promise.

Thank You, Holy One, for fulfilling Your rainbow covenant! And may there be peace on earth.
—MARILYN MORGAN KING

LIVING CHRISTMAS

Sun 16

Gray hair is a crown of glory; it is gained by living a godly life.
—PROVERBS 16:31 (NLT)

THIRD SUNDAY IN ADVENT: ADOPTING WILMA

During the summer of 2010 three bad things happened to me: I ended up without a car; my friend Jack ended our relationship; and my eyes got so bad I couldn't drive, read, bike or watch TV.

By the time Advent rolled around, medical treatments had fixed my eyes. And I even had a few interesting dates that fall.

But Wilma, the eighty-five-year-old mother-in-law of one of my friends, was truly the best thing that happened to me during those awful months. When Wilma moved from California that summer she had her 1992 Thunderbird shipped to Florida. But sadly, shortly after she arrived, Wilma discovered she couldn't pass the eye test for driving and had to sell her baby.

I bought Wilma's car and at the same time fell in love with the spunky oldster. That Advent I decided instead of spreading myself thin doing a little bit for a number of church groups or charities, I'd concentrate on Wilma. That Advent she and I enjoyed a few restaurant breakfasts, a holiday shopping excursion, chocolate milk shakes afterward and a long gab fest on my lanai. She listened and offered motherly advice as I spilled my heartaches about my ended relationship.

Adopting Wilma during Advent helped erase all the sad things that happened to me the previous summer. I not only made a new friend, but I also found that when I step out of my own miseries and into the waiting arms of someone who needs a new friend and neighbor, the Christmas season begins to sparkle in ways I'd only imagined. Giving time to others is the secret.

Jesus, thank You for answering my prayers, and thank You especially for Wilma, who brightened my Advent, my Christmas and my whole year.
—Patricia Lorenz

Mon 17

If you seek him, he will be found by you. . . .
—I CHRONICLES 28:9 (NIV)

I lost Jesus!

I couldn't believe it, but I couldn't find the baby in the manger that I'd taken to church as a visual aid for a devotional about giving and receiving. Somewhere between church and home, I'd lost this most precious piece of our Nativity scene.

I searched and researched the canvas bag I'd used to carry my Bible, notes and props. I dug around in my car. I went back to the church and scoured the room where I'd been. I e-mailed Glenda in the church office. "I've lost Jesus," I moaned in my message. I think she thought my message sounded a bit loony, but she kindly dug through everything in the lost and found closet. My Jesus wasn't there.

I put the other figures on a table, and every time I walked by, I grieved the absence of Jesus.

On Christmas Eve morning, I sat at my desk and once again saw the bag I'd carried to church that day a couple of weeks earlier. "Oh, please, Lord, let Jesus be somewhere in that bag. . . . Let me find Him."

I picked up the bag with a hopeless feeling because I'd already thoroughly checked it. I squished it next to me, feeling the fabric in every part. And lo and behold, I felt something small and hard! I unzipped the pocket leading to that spot and there—way down deep inside—was Jesus in the manger!

I just smiled and smiled and marched back to the Nativity on the table, as if I was part of some divinely planned procession, and put Jesus right where He belongs on Christmas Eve: in front of Mary and Joseph.

Lord, loss and absence sometimes magnify
the importance of what we long for, and
I'm so thankful for the reminder that Jesus can
be found everywhere. Even in the deep
dark pockets of a canvas bag.
—CAROL KUYKENDALL

Tue 18

The true light, which enlightens everyone, was coming into the world. —JOHN 1:9 (ESV)

It is a week before Christmas, and we're decorating our new house for this special season. It's a two-story wooden house, full of character and beauty, sitting on a tree-covered ridge that descends to the Ocmulgee River in Macon, Georgia. Tonight

I wonder where the various families who lived in the house since it was built in 1854 placed their Christmas trees and what their holiday traditions were.

In the midst of my reverie I began to look for the packing box that contains our most treasured Christmas-tree ornaments. After three hours of searching, I still hadn't found them. I looked through every box we had not yet unpacked, as well as in the basement, the attic and every closet.

I wistfully pictured each ornament in my mind: the wooden toy soldiers Beth and I purchased for our first Christmas together, the wooden ornaments carved from the trunk of our first Christmas tree, the older ornaments saved from each of our childhoods, the gifts given by special friends throughout the years.

Anxious and discouraged, I sat down on the living-room couch and reached up to turn on a reading lamp. The bulb didn't light, and I looked behind the couch to see if the lamp was unplugged. Suddenly the box of decorations came into view, tucked beneath the couch. I sheepishly remembered that months ago while unpacking, I had placed the box behind the couch for temporary safekeeping.

It's easy to lose the memories we've tucked away through the years and hidden in our hearts. Christmas is a time to rekindle our memories as we hang each ornament, read each Christmas card and recall every Christmas we've experienced through the years. But the most precious memory we can rediscover is the memory of God's gift to us through Jesus Christ.

> *Father, may I find again the Christmas box that shelters faith, hope and love.*
> —SCOTT WALKER

READER'S ROOM

When I was twenty, I lost my mother. I blamed God and walked away from Him for quite some time. What a difference the years have made! Each day for the past fourteen years, all of you at Guideposts have walked my life's journey with me, encouraging me to continue moving forward, trusting in our Lord and His promises.

—*Nancy Morrison, Marshfield, Massachusetts*

Wed 19 *You refined us like silver.*
—PSALM 66:10 (NIV)

I almost suggested we skip our porch party the week of our wedding anniversary in December. As we settled into our rocking chairs and covered up with blankets, I felt a complaint rising: *It's too cold. This is crazy.* But according to our porch party rules, we can't say anything negative.

I glanced at my husband Rick. We're in our fifties now; he has high blood pressure, and I've developed a couple of autoimmune illnesses. As I sat there, still and quiet, my mind skipped back to the days when we were dating. Sweet memories surfaced.

Pulling the red fleece blanket around me, I remembered riding to school with Rick when we were teenagers. His 1965 GTO didn't have a heater, but he kept a blanket handy for me.

On Christmas Eve 1975, he filled a stocking for me. He still does. And every November, he strings white lights around our porch and decorates the trees near the front door. He'd turned on the front porch Christmas lights that morning. The bright glow slipped into my heart.

Just then, a buck and a doe wandered across our driveway. A cardinal darted to the birdfeeder.

When it was almost time to go inside the house, I spoke. "What are you thinking?"

"Not many things are all that important, are they?"

"Just what I was thinking."

After thirty-one years of marriage, our love is stronger. Deeper. We've grown a little quieter, maybe a little more content. He doesn't always have to be right, and I don't have to say everything I'm thinking.

Lord, thank You for thirty-one years with Rick, and
for all those quiet moments on our porch.
—JULIE GARMON

Thu 20 *Now the birth of Jesus Christ was on this wise.... —*MATTHEW 1:18

It's that time of year again when all the nitpicking killjoys try to ruin the Christmas season for me.

I'm talking about those folks who take delight in exposing the inaccuracies of many of our most cherished Christmas images.

First off, the date is wrong, they point out. No right-minded emperor would call for a census in the middle of winter when travel was nearly impossible. More likely Joseph and Mary journeyed to Bethlehem much earlier in the year when it was still quite warm. In fact, not only did we get the season wrong, we got the year wrong. Most historians agree Jesus was born in about 6 BC, which makes absolutely no sense to say.

Then there are the three wise men. Wrong again. No evidence exists that there were any specific number of wise men, apart from the fact that three distinct offerings are mentioned in Matthew. Nor is there any reason to think they were kings, and they most certainly weren't there at the birth of

Christ. In fact, scholars speculate they may have arrived several years later.

And, of course, we have all the pagan underpinnings of the holiday to worry about: The tree harks back to pantheism; December 25 was chosen by the early church to coincide with and thereby replace the ancient festivals celebrating the Roman sun god and the Persian god Mithras; and mistletoe in pre-Christian Europe was a symbol of fertility.

Fine, fine. I'm happy to know the facts about Christmas. I don't want to be ignorant. But for me Christmas is a swelling of the soul, filled with light and hope and love and the promise of eternal life and all that fills your heart. The facts are the facts. But Christmas will always be Christmas.

Lord, Your birth redeems the world from darkness.
You enter our lives in infinite and unexpected
ways, even as a Child in a manger, and
Your presence is beyond dispute.
—EDWARD GRINNAN

Fri 21   *Remember, and forget not....*
—DEUTERONOMY 9:7

I grew up skating on the frozen ponds in suburban Philadelphia. My best friend Nell and I used to take our skates, bundle warmly and get one of our mothers to drive us to the nearest body of water. When it had been cold enough for long enough, we even skated on the reservoir, which gave us miles of smooth surface on which to glide.

After college, I moved to Los Angeles and missed skating as much as I missed winter. Southern California never froze, but there were rinks. I found one where some Olympic team members practiced in the early mornings. I signed up for a class there.

Excited, I showed up for my first class, which was divided into beginning, intermediate and advanced.

The teacher didn't ask anything about my skills, just waved me to the beginners group. I thought I was better than that, but I didn't say anything. We began with some exercises and then some straight free skating; the teacher divided her attention among the three groups. I thought that by the end of the first class, she'd see I didn't really belong in the beginners group. I carefully did the movements I knew I did well, to show her how good a skater I was. But when the lesson ended, all she said was, "See you next week."

For three weeks, it was the same. Then the fourth week, I tried a jump during the free skating and fell with a great splat onto the ice.

Embarrassed, I climbed to my feet. The teacher came over to me. "I wondered if you'd ever get out of your comfort zone," she said. "Go join the intermediate class."

December

Thank You, God, for sending people to remind me that winter, too, is a time for growth and learning.
—RHODA BLECKER

Sat 22

Blessed are those who mourn, for they shall be comforted.
—MATTHEW 5:4 (NKJV)

Christmas Eve is one of the busiest days of the year. There's the last-minute gift shopping, food to be purchased and prepared and, of course, the evening church service to attend. But this Christmas Eve I had another concern. It was about my doctor.

My doctor is always helpful. He continues to make house calls, and he visits the sick in nursing homes. He loves medicine and his patients. And in addition to being my doctor, he's my friend.

Just before Christmas, the doctor's young wife died. Her funeral was to be held on Christmas Eve. I was afraid that because of the day, only a scattering of people would be able to attend.

I was wrong: The church was overflowing. The doctor's mentor, a monk as well as a medical doctor, was in the sanctuary, robed to take part in the service. I felt sad, but my heart was warmed because the community and the doctor's patients were there to support and to comfort him.

During the service, I wondered what I could do to help. There seemed no answer. But as I was leaving the church, I heard a lady whisper, "I feel so sad saying good-bye to this young lady whose life was cut so short. There's nothing we can do for her. But we can do everything for the doctor and his four children."

I had my answer. When the doctor and his family felt alone, I would be there for them.

Understanding Lord, reaching out to comfort is
the gift You gave us two thousand years ago.
—OSCAR GREENE

LIVING CHRISTMAS

Sun 23   *There are many ways in which God works in our lives, but it is the same God who does the work in and through all of us who are his.*
—I CORINTHIANS 12:6 (TLB)

FOURTH SUNDAY IN ADVENT:
A LEGACY OF LOVE

Today as I watched a fellow parishioner light the last candle on the Advent wreath at church, I thought about what it means to prepare for Christmas. For most of us, it is finding ways to give to others. It also means keeping the traditions alive that have been in our families for generations.

My friend Paula is Polish. During Advent her mother and grandmother made their favorite holiday treat: *pierogi*, a ravioli-like dumpling filled with farmer's cheese, sauerkraut and mushrooms, mashed potatoes, meats or plums.

My stepmother Bev is Norwegian. Bev remembers her mother preparing warm fruit soup and *Jule Kaga*, a rich moist bread with fruits and citron. Most of all she remembers her father playing the accordion and her sister Marge playing the piano while they both sang Christmas songs in Norwegian. Food and music blended to create holiday magic.

When I was a child, we always had oyster stew for dinner on Christmas Eve, which was a German custom. My Dad is German, and even though mother was Scottish, Irish and English, she made oyster stew every Christmas Eve. I grew to love it, and I still serve it in my home the night before Christmas.

Today as we prepare for the birth of the Christ Child, I'll say a prayer of thanks for this tiny baby, known round a world filled with many traditions, tastes and customs that make us so diverse and yet so united in our love for Him.

Lord, open my heart to all those around me who are different in background, looks, customs and traditions, and help me to love each the way You do.
—PATRICIA LORENZ

LIVING CHRISTMAS

Mon 24

Yes Lord, let your constant love surround us, for our hopes are in you alone. —PSALM 33:22 (TLB)

CHRISTMAS EVE: A JOYFUL NOISE

On Christmas Eve in medieval England, Scotland and Ireland, the village church bells tolled mournfully and slowly for an hour before midnight. It was the annual celebration of the devil's funeral. Then, just at the stroke of midnight, the bells rang out loudly, jubilantly, because it was believed that the devil died when Jesus was born.

Tonight, before the joyous bells ring, let's pray for the lonely, sad, frightened people who aren't having as grand a Christmas as we are. Let's resolve to find at least one person who needs a good friend and help that person find a joy and peace in the coming year. Perhaps we can find a way to help them bury their struggles, just as the devil was buried in medieval times.

Tonight as church bells and carillons call us to church to rejoice that the Savior is born, let's shout more than just "Merry Christmas!" Tonight and every day this next year, let's shout joyfully,

> "God bless you!"
> "May I help?"
> "Thank you!"
> "How are you?"
> "Welcome home!"
> "I need you."
> "I forgive you."
> "I love you."

Father, help me sing out these beautiful words
of Christmas every day in many ways
to everyone I meet.
—Patricia Lorenz

LIVING CHRISTMAS

Tue 25   *For even darkness cannot hide from God; to you the night shines as bright as day....* —Psalm 139:12 (TLB)

CHRISTMAS: AN OPEN HEART

Last Christmas Day dawned sunny and warm here in Florida, but for me, without the excitement of Christmases past. Because my dad and stepmom Bev had been staying in the building next door and were going back to Illinois on December 27, I'd made arrangements to fly to Ohio that same day to visit my son Michael and his family. My daughter Julia and her children would join us there from Wisconsin. But waking up on Christmas morning without anyone in my home but me felt strange.

The night before, Dad and Bev and I had gone to the service at Bev's Lutheran church. And early Christmas morning the three of us went to my church. Then I served a holiday brunch for my folks, my sister, her husband and their daughter. But by noon they'd all gone home, and I was alone for the second time that day.

I talked to my four children on the phone and then started packing for my trip. Later that day, since none of us wanted to cook, we gathered eighty-year-old Dick, who lives alone in my building, and Rob, a young man with no family in Florida, and went out to a Chinese buffet.

Later, alone for the third time that day, the melancholy started welling up. I listened to Christmas carols, wrote some thank-you notes, made a few phone calls and ate some Christmas candy and cookies. Before long, I felt that although it wasn't a traditional sort of Christmas, my day was blessed, punctuated with family, friends and a sense of peace.

And when I finally hugged my children and grandchildren two days later, I learned that the joy the Christ Child brings can flow into the days and weeks that follow, if I just open my heart.

Jesus, today You bring me the gift of Yourself.
Help me pass on that gift to others.
—PATRICIA LORENZ

Wed 26 *"Write down the revelation and make it plain on tablets. . . . "*
—HABAKKUK 2:2 (NIV)

All of us have experienced situations where something we said or wrote was misunderstood by the person hearing or reading our words. Sometimes misunderstandings can be comical, like one I ran into in Africa recently.

My new job in Texas involves working with people who translate the Scriptures into "easy-to-read" versions in the most common languages used around the world. The main purpose is as old as the Lord's command to the ancient prophet Habakkuk to "make it plain." In Bible translation a tension often arises between being literal and preserving meaning. "Whiter than snow" has no meaning in the Sudanese desert. So last year I was in Tanzania working with our team to do a new translation of Swahili. Because this was my first visit with them, I asked why a new effort was needed. Typically I heard that "the old one requires me to read the English version to figure out what the Swahili says" or "the old version is very hard on young ears" until one of the group was asked to explain with a story.

"In Swahili," he said with a big smile, "there is only one letter different between the word for 'wise men' and the word for 'lizard.' So even I myself, after attending seminary and earning high marks, preached my first Christmas sermon proclaiming, "The birth of the Savior Jesus was of such importance that even the lowly lizards crawled from the east to worship at the manger!"

When the laughter in the room died down, we agreed that providing a translation whose meaning could be clearly and simply understood was important. I mean, do you want to go out and buy a rubber lizard to add to your Nativity scene?

Lord, help me to take care in the words I say and write
so that understanding will grow and
misunderstanding will fade away in my work,
my family and my faith.
—ERIC FELLMAN

December

Thu 27

Christ Jesus came into the world to save sinners....
—I TIMOTHY 1:15

My friend Victoria was in charge of the live nativity our church was staging on the courthouse lawn. She found plenty of folks to play Mary, Joseph, the wise men and the shepherds. Local farmers brought in animals; our choir transformed into singing angels. The only thing missing? Baby Jesus. Turns out Victoria couldn't get enough babies signed up for the fifteen-minute intervals she'd planned.

The solution? "Draft" babies from the crowd. "Excuse me, could I borrow your baby?" Victoria said again and again.

I was delightfully surprised when I arrived on the scene to see my fifteen-month-old grandson Knox in the manger. He sat there in his knit hat and gold-tinsel halo, patiently surveying the scene.

Eventually, of course, the straw started to itch and he was cold and wanted his mama. Stacy bundled Knox into her arms—and suddenly all the pretense fell away. I saw the young mother Mary, enveloping her Son in a protective hug. I saw a helpless babe nestling into the only human flesh He had ever known: God the creator, come in all lowliness and love, to dwell among us.

I took a backward glance at the manger. It was empty, but I knew it wouldn't be for long—because Jesus always comes where He is welcome... whether it's a bed of hay or a human heart.

Make my heart Your home, sweet Baby Jesus.
—MARY LOU CARNEY

Fri 28   *And David and all Israel played before God with all their might, and with singing, and with harps, and with psalteries, and with timbrels, and with cymbals, and with trumpets.*
—I CHRONICLES 13:8

A few years ago, I joined the twenty-first century and bought an MP3 player—those tiny, palm-size music players that carry a couple of hundred hand-picked songs. Every time I plug it in, I'm amazed.

At the risk of speaking heresy, I think we live in the golden age of music. So many songs are at our fingertips, covering every genre, every era, every continent. My playlist makes me feel... cosmopolitan. South Africa's Ladysmith Black Mambazo followed by Bach followed by blues singer Susan Tedeschi. It's as if I've invited an international concert to perform in my head.

Then I borrow my wife's player or my daughters' players, and it's like I've never heard music before: Robert Johnson; Cellofourte; Cowboy Junkies; Kiri Te Kanawa singing "O mio babbino caro"; Matisyahu, an Orthodox Jewish rapper (!), singing "One good thing about music—it makes you feel okay"; Nusrat Fateh Ali Khan's plaintive voice in Jonathan Elias' *Prayer Cycle*. All this interspersed with Led Zeppelin, The Neville Brothers' "By the Rivers of Babylon," Bruce Springsteen and Joe Grusecky bemoaning the tortured life of early twentieth-century coal miners. Listening to Smashing Pumpkins smash against "Foggy Mountain Breakdown" causes acoustic whiplash. It also causes unbridled joy.

When I was in grade school, Sister Mary Celine said that grace was an undeserved gift from God. When I plug in my miraculously small player and hear the Christmas chorus sing how all flesh—every genre, every era, every continent—shall see Him together, I think I know what she means.

It's a wide world You made, Lord. Thank You for the joyful sounds that rise from every corner of it.
—MARK COLLINS

Sat 29

David strengthened himself in the Lord his God.
—I SAMUEL 30:6 (RSV)

Last week the phone rang, and a good friend told me that my husband Bill's and my names had come up. A local troupe was looking for a couple to dance the waltz in a musical this weekend at our local center for the performing arts.

My heart soared because I love, love, love to dance and, wow, to be onstage—what a thrill! There would be one rehearsal and then three nights of performance. Plus, they would provide the costumes.

I told my friend I would talk to Bill and get back to her with our decision. As I hung up, I prayed, "Thank You, Lord, for it all. For makeup, smiles and twirling around the stage."

Suddenly, though, a blip appeared on my inner radar. *You can't do it. What if it snows and Bill has to plow? Who would we find to stay with our daughter Brittany and mind the bed-and-breakfast while we are away late at night?*

For a split second, before I realized that we had responsibilities that prevented us from being in the show, the thought of being a "celebrity" was magical. But it was okay. I loved being asked, and I know there will be other opportunities to "dance with the stars."

> *When I keep my heart and my eyes on You, Lord,*
> *You will lead me where I need to be.*
> —Patricia Pusey

Sun 30

Restore us to You, O Lord, that we may be restored; Renew, our days as of old. —Lamentations 5:21 (nas)

It began when we got home from church. While the "little kids," Maggie and Stephen, worked on a craft kit they'd been given for Christmas and Mary pored over her new French cookbook, Elizabeth and John headed for the sofa. They'd seen each other briefly at Thanksgiving, but now, with Elizabeth home from college for her winter break and John making weekend and holiday visits from his group home, they were making up for four months of being apart.

They'd created their own role-playing game, and they went at it with an almost desperate enthusiasm. Attuned to each other and to their places in their imaginary world, they played happily—and loudly.

As I sat on the other sofa pretending to read a book, I looked at them and savored their happiness. And I thought back to other Christmases, when baby John would delight in knocking over his big sister's toy animals; when toddler John helped Elizabeth show off her new magic set (he was her official "distracter," charged with misdirecting the audience); when the Attaway Family Circus featured Elizamath, the mistress of numbers, and the Amazing John, strongman extraordinaire; when, as dinosaurs, they pranced across the room or acted out earthquakes and volcanic explosions. They were close, constant companions, each other's best friend.

Then, when John reached school age, things changed. Urged on by his anxiety, John's behavior swung out of control. In the face of his unpredictability, their friendship cooled, adding more weight to the resentment John carried and breaking his sister's heart. But for today, at least, they had reached back behind those years to the days when being together was a joy. And when it was time for Julia to take John back to the group home, Elizabeth insisted on coming along to enjoy their closeness just a little longer.

Lord, King of all hearts, heal the wounds in our hearts and give us strength, peace and joy in the coming year.
—ANDREW ATTAWAY

Mon 31

Therefore, if anyone is in Christ, he is a new creation; the old has gone, the new has come!
—II CORINTHIANS 5:17 (NIV)

I love to decorate my home for the holidays. I hang twinkling white lights and fresh garlands around the front door. The Christmas tree, all ten feet of it, is filled with ornaments old and new, and under it is a hand-carved crèche, made for small hands to rearrange the stable animals who await the arrival of Baby Jesus. Crystal, ceramic and wooden angels of all shapes and sizes fill the fireplace mantel.

Then, as quickly as it all began, Christmas is over and the time comes to take down the decorations and look toward the new year.

When all of the boxes are back in the attic, I sit down on the sofa and open up my journal, ready to write down my resolutions. I've thought about my goals and how I'll achieve them; it's all clear and organized in my head. I pause for a moment and look around the living room, which looks bare now that it is free of its holiday trappings. I, too, must get back to the basics. So I begin from my heart and start with a prayer:

Lord, a brand new year is before me. I offer myself to You and ask You to guide me during this year ahead. Work through me, Lord; guide my steps, lead my way and inspire my words so others see You through me. And, Lord, no matter what lies ahead for me this year, I want to pray without ceasing, love my fellow men and honor You with my heart and my soul. Amen.

My most important resolution, Lord, is to walk hand in hand with You each day of the year.
—MELODY BONNETTE

MY PATHWAY TO PEACE

1 _____

2 _____

3 _____

4 _____

5 _____

6 _____

7 _____

8 _____

9 _____

10 _____

11 _____

12 _____

13 _____

14 _____

15 _____

December

16 _____

17 _____

18 _____

19 _____

20 _____

21 _____

22 _____

23 _____

24 _____

25 _____

26 _____

27 _____

28 _____

29 _____

30 _____

31 _____

ANNE ADRIANCE of Oldwick, New Jersey, writes: "A wise friend recently pointed out to me that nothing in nature ever stays the same—everything is either growing or dying. I opt to be of the growing sort, and my sense of peace has come from working to accept the fact that change *is* a fact. This year, I've gotten my sea legs in the role of mom to college-age sons just in time to ready myself for more changes as Sam will graduate in the spring and Ned will be away on an internship in Washington. At Guideposts I have had the great good fortune to help create and nurture a whole new brand, Hope Springs, that will bring a fresh and optimistic spirit to all kinds of products for everyday living. I hope it will help many people across America 'fill their lives with Hope.'"

"This year has been challenging in many ways," says SAM ADRIANCE of Oldwick, New Jersey. "After four great years at St. John's College in Santa Fe, New Mexico, my school career is coming to an end. As graduation approaches, I'm facing new fears and uncertainties, having to throw myself into the job market for the first time. Even so, this year has been a time of peace: I once again got to spend a relaxing few weeks in Maine with my mom, dad and brother Ned. Even with very little idea of what the future holds in store, I've found peace in knowing that the people I care about most will always be there with me, cheering me on."

The past year has been one in which MARCI ALBORGHETTI of New London, Connecticut, and her husband Charlie Duffy have been yearning for peace, for the world and for themselves. Changes in their work and a move to a new address have kept them busy and turning to God for guidance and enlightenment. One good change: Marci's latest book, *A Willing Heart*, was published by Ave Maria Press. Marci and Charlie continue to enjoy living in New England, while spending the winter in the San Francisco Bay Area. Their latest trip to California saw them moving to the East Bay, where they attend St. Columba, a wonderful African American church in Oakland. They approach the future praying for personal and global peace and putting their trust in God.

LUCILE ALLEN of Montrose, Colorado, writes: "My favorite illustration of peace is a mama bird, her nest tucked securely in the branches of a bush, watching serenely over her babies while a violent storm rages around her. Plenty of storms raged around our 'nest' this year: a major move out of full-time ministry into a job search for my husband Curtis and within the month back into full-time ministry; my mother's newly discovered serious heart health issues; my sister's breast cancer; our graduating only child Deanna who is ready to be free from her mama watching over her (serenely or not) and preparing to attend Seattle Pacific University in the fall. A tumultuous year, yes, but with peace in the midst of it."

 FAY ANGUS of Sierra Madre, California, writes: "With this edition, I'm celebrating twenty years as a part of the *Daily Guideposts* family of writers and readers, the most blessed and inspirational years of my life! Month by month, the messages of encouragement and love, all under the promise of the Holy Scriptures, have fortified my faith and shown me the grace of God. For me, the greatest miracle of that grace is that our Lord has chosen to make the human heart His home. He is as close as our unspoken thoughts, our hidden tears, our silent dreams, and our whispered prayers. I continue to depend on the power of His Presence to be my strength: strength to do, strength to love and strength to live."

"It's been a year of transitions," says outgoing *Daily Guideposts* editor ANDREW ATTAWAY of New York City, "for the children—especially John, 14, in a residential program, and Elizabeth, 16, off to college—and for Julia and me. And though change can be stressful, we've found peace in the knowledge that God is in charge and in the support of our Guideposts family. As for what's ahead? Check this space next year!"

"Peace is more difficult some years than others," writes JULIA ATTAWAY of New York City. Mere weeks after Elizabeth, 16, headed off for her freshman year at MIT, John, 14, moved into a residential facility. The one-two punch of absence took its toll on the whole family. And yet the relative quiet has also allowed time for everyone to re-find their footing after a tumultuous summer. "What I'm learning about peace is that even if it's like a river, there are still rocky spots and rapids that don't exactly feel calm. It helps to remember that Christ is the Living Water and that His love supports us through even the hardest times."

KAREN BARBER of Alpharetta, Georgia, reports that it's been another busy year fitting in family time with her husband Gordon, their sons and daughter-in-law and their granddaughter Kendall, who's 2. Karen says, "As the founding director of a new nonprofit called Prayer Igniters, I've been challenged to do things that seem impossibly beyond my resources, talents and abilities. Sometimes I get really worried! Thankfully, I was given the opportunity to write fifty-two Scripture lessons on prayer for the Guideposts book *Daily Talks with God.* I mentally immersed myself in the daily world of Jesus and imagined how I might react when seeing His ministry go through so many twists and turns. After finishing my life-altering journey with Jesus in prayer I had an unshakable sense of peace that comes from knowing that when Jesus leads you, you're always going in the right direction."

"Last fall, a painful case of shingles with prolonged aftereffects meant I had to keep my body rested and my mind preoccupied over most of the winter," writes ALMA BARKMAN of Winnipeg, Manitoba, Canada. "So with my husband Leo assuming more of the cooking, cleaning and gardening, I managed to complete a book of devotionals titled *Everyday Moments with God.* We survived our respective ordeals with a better appreciation for the health we'd perhaps come to take for granted. Another evidence of Romans 8:28 ('All things work together for good to them that love God') is that a humorous piece I wrote about my experiences in hospital emergency rooms led to a regular column in our city's newspaper."

EVELYN BENCE of Arlington, Virginia, writes, "After church on Sunday a woman asked me what was new. While I analyzed my life and tried to formulate a response, she kept talking: 'Same old, same old?' The easy answer was 'Yes, you got it.' But that's not the whole picture. I'm energized by daily front-stoop encounters with a neighborhood girl: doing puzzles, sorting and counting old buttons, reading books—helping her learn to read. I still smile at the memory of an October outing in Pennsylvania, stomping sauerkraut with cousins, and a festive December getaway to colonial Williamsburg. I delight in the mercies of God, anticipating something new every morning."

"We have had a year that was thankfully dominated by serenity," says RHODA BLECKER of Bellingham, Washington, "and yet there were a few exciting moments.

My novel, *A Song of Awakening*, was published after almost ten years of rewriting, and I'm very proud of it. Tests showed that Keith remains cancer-free, which is cause for much celebration. The animals—our greyhound Anjin and the two cats, Chi and L.E.—are doing well. The cats are almost on speaking terms with one another, which means the atmosphere at home is much quieter than before. Our community of friends keeps growing, and I am serving on eight committees at the synagogue, which Keith refers to as 'utter madness.' Luckily, two of them are inactive right now! In addition, I find great fulfillment in weekly group study of the Torah and in doing individual study with our rabbi."

 "Even though finishing up my PhD at the University of Southern Mississippi while working full time keeps me busy, I still find time to do the things that make for peace," writes MELODY BONNETTE of Mandeville, Louisiana. "Just today I went to church and then lunched with my family. I spent the afternoon planting flowers: caladiums around the oak tree, hot-pink knockout roses in front of the dining-room windows and pink-and-white impatiens under the cherry blossom tree. My day ended with a visit from my son Christopher and his family, which includes 2-week-old Macie Ann, my ninth grandchild! We sat in the backyard and shared tall

glasses of raspberry iced tea while I held this precious bundle of God's love. My heart was filled with gratitude for pink flowers, sweet babies and the glorious gift of God's perfect peace."

"What a fun, clamorous year it's been!" says MARY LOU CARNEY of Chesterton, Indiana. "Last summer we welcomed a new grandchild—another boy—making it an even half dozen." The family bought an old cottage near a small lake, a place where they all get together for food and board games, for karaoke and boating. Mary Lou's husband Gary had emergency surgery at Mayo Clinic when doctors found he had an abdominal aortic aneurysm. "It was a miracle it hadn't burst. Even the surgeon said so." Mary Lou collaborated on another children's book with her friend and *Daily Guideposts* contributor Debbie Macomber. Look for *The Yippy Yappy Yorkie in a Green Doggie Sweater* in bookstores this year. "Every day I feel God's peace and grace, embracing and sustaining me. Life continues to be an adventure!" You can read about Mary Lou's adventures on her blog at OurPrayer.org.

JEFF CHU is still an articles editor at the business magazine *Fast Company*, despite the publishing world's tumult. Now at work on his first, faith-related book, Jeff has been traveling around

America, meeting with believers of various denominations and none. This experience of collecting stories—many of them about truly heartbreaking events in people's lives—has compelled him to consider how we rely on God for the "peace that passes understanding" or, more often, struggle to do so. He recently moved to a quiet Brooklyn apartment, an oasis from New York City's bustle—except when the thundering herd downstairs (aka his neighbors' two young children) decide to do laps around their home, yelling, shaking the place to its foundations and reminding Jeff what peace is by highlighting its absence.

 "I can't believe my youngest son Henry enters kindergarten this fall," writes SABRA CIANCANELLI of Tivoli, New York. "I have to admit I'm dreading the first day of school, though it will be comforting to see Henry board the bus with his big brother Solomon. I'm not sure how I'll feel that September morning with both my boys in school and the house to myself. Relieved, I suppose, with moments of longing and then the wonderful reassurance that will come from seeing them dash off the school bus with smiles and stories from their day. I'll have more writing time, I hope, and dare I say, the energy to organize the attic." Sabra is a freelance writer and editor for OurPrayer.org.

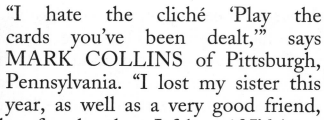

"I hate the cliché 'Play the cards you've been dealt,'" says MARK COLLINS of Pittsburgh, Pennsylvania. "I lost my sister this year, as well as a very good friend, within months of each other. I felt as if I'd been dealt jokers or was forced to play pinochle with a poker deck. Then I'm reminded of a line from the *Book of Common Prayer*, 'Deliver me from the presumption of coming to this Table for solace only, and not for strength.' Maybe I'll just sit out this hand, maybe take a break and come back again ready to play." Among the players around Mark's table are seminary instructor and wife Sandee; college sophomore Faith, 20; college freshman Hope, 19; and high school newbie Grace, 15. "There are times when it looks like the chips are down," Mark says, "but I'm reminded that some chips are beyond counting, and in those chips I'm rich beyond belief."

"This past summer we drove down from New York City to Virginia Beach for a family vacation," says PABLO DIAZ of Carmel, New York. "Early into our drive, we discovered some things never change. Paul and Christine slept most of the ride or poked fun at each other, and selecting a restaurant that appeased everyone's preference had its unique twist and turns.

Yet for several days we laughed, prayed, played and were together. Elba and I could not have been happier. Once we returned home, the children got back to their individual activities and, as for us, we were grateful to God for the peaceful time with our kids."

"What gives me peace?" writes BRIAN DOYLE of Portland, Oregon. "In order? Okay: all children, a small and lovely and mysterious spouse, excellent basketball teams, the dog remembering to close the door after himself for a change, honest spiritual talk, politicians who do not lie, no wet towels left on the bathroom floor, spiderwebs woven overnight, sudden herons, decent coffee, the way America is still such a riveting verb and possibility despite our yen for violence, sudden small checks in the mail, the mail, the mailman's airy wave, Bruce Springsteen's masterpiece *The Rising*, the fact that this soil hatched Mark Twain and Flannery O'Connor and Abraham Lincoln, the whistle of osprey, the crash of surf, sudden parking spots opening just as you are despairing utterly, cotton shirts, all berries, and the way women flip their hair back unconsciously with one hand—I love that. Also, the laugh that always rises in me when I say the wild words *my new novel*. Finally wrote one. *Mink River*. Impossible to explain."

"Three things help me find peace in the digital age," says ERIC FELLMAN of Keller, Texas. "First, years ago, Ruth Stafford Peale found me working late one night and gently chided me: 'Eric, don't forget your in-box will be full the day you die. Someone else will come along and take care of it.' Spiritually, as life seems to speed up, Jesus' promise to give us His peace rings more clearly in my thoughts and heart. I have developed the habit of simply whispering His name, 'Jesus,' to remember His presence. Personally, having my granddaughter Ella Grace sit on my lap and tell me the latest about her day is incredibly peaceful, if not restful. Her unconditional love, expectant expression and excitement over the pending arrival of her baby brother are precious, and holding what's precious in my lap gives peace."

SHARON FOSTER of Durham, North Carolina, writes: "What a pleasure to share stories of Bible Witness Camp. Though my 'roomie' has gone home to be with the Lord, I have found peace in her resting place and being able to share the stories with her before her passing. I continue to find joy and peace in my family: Chase will sing in Tel Aviv this summer and then it's on to Chicago to sing in *Showboat*

at the Lyric Opera. Lanea continues to shine as she serves running Durham's homeless program. After five years, my next book, *The Resurrection of Nat Turner*, will release in two parts in August 2011 (Part 1) and February 2012 (Part 2). Please keep us in your prayers. It's a joy to talk to my dad, friends and family. But my greatest peace comes from knowing the love, strength and faithfulness of the Lord."

JULIE GARMON of Monroe, Georgia, writes: "This year I'm focusing on a new way of thinking: I'm choosing to seek God's peace every single day. Absolutely nothing is worth losing it—no events in my past, no bitterness in the present, no fear about the future. No one has the power to take my peace from me; I have to choose to give it away. After all, no one can change my thoughts but me. Peace follows surrender. Each morning now I whisper, 'Thank You, Lord, for a cup of coffee, another day and someone to love.'"

"Others," writes OSCAR GREENE of West Medford, Massachusetts, "helped to bring the things that make for peace. In April, my cataract surgery was so successful I sometimes neglect to don my glasses. After six-and-a-half years, our beloved pastor accepted an out-of-state parish. Our interim priest suggested a person our parish had never seen. He arrived, served as priest-in-charge and is now our eighteenth rector. Once again our home is a gathering place for others to visit and to share their deepest concerns. We feel so blessed."

"Last year, I finished writing a book called *The Promise of Hope: How True Stories of Hope and Inspiration Saved My Life and How They Can Transform Yours*," says EDWARD GRINNAN, editor-in-chief of *Guideposts* magazine. "This year it has been all about promoting the book, which means I have spent a lot of time on the road, going to signings and giving readings. The travel can be grueling and monotonous, but I love meeting *Guideposts* readers. It always puts me in a great mood." How has the book been received? "Since a portion of the book is my untold personal story of struggle and redemption, I was worried about how my family and friends might respond. But everyone has been extremely supportive." Edward lives in Manhattan with his wife Julee and their golden retriever Millie. You can order *The Promise of Hope* at Guideposts.org, EdwardGrinnan.com or your favorite bookstore.

This past year has been a poignant one for RICK HAMLIN of New York City. In February, he lost his father after a long decline. "I flew out to California to be with him and with the rest of the family and was glad to be there for his last days. Then we mobilized our familial forces for a memorial service. Since he had always worn bow ties, we wore his bow ties—even the women, who tied them on their wrists. And because he had been in the submarine corps in World War II and loved Richard Rodgers' score to *Victory at Sea*, I sang a song from *Victory at Sea*. He'd lived a good long life full of faith and in our final farewell we did as he would have wished; using one of his favorite words, we *rejoiced*."

"I've been thinking a lot lately about peace, or lack of peace," writes MADGE HARRAH of Albuquerque, New Mexico. "America has been in six wars during my lifetime. And many people these days don't seem to be as kind and well-behaved as when I was younger. What can I do about this? Maybe not much, but as a first step I can continue to follow Jesus' greatest commandment: 'Thou shalt love the Lord thy God with all thy heart, and with all thy soul, and with all thy strength, and with all thy mind; and thy neighbor as thyself" (Luke 10:27). My parents taught me to live that commandment, and Larry and I have tried to teach our children and grandchildren to do so too."

HAROLD HOSTETLER of Poughkeepsie, New York, writes: "The highlight of this past year was joining our daughter Laurel and granddaughter Kaila on a trip to Hawaii for Kaila's thirteenth birthday, which falls on June 11, King Kamehameha Day. Her wish was to attend a luau, which we did at the Polynesian Cultural Center, and we followed that with the usual sightseeing around Oahu and swimming at Kailua Beach. But the trip had an additional special meaning for us. For Laurel, it was a return to the place where she and her sister Kristal were born. For Carol and me, it was a return to one of our favorite places on Earth, the island where we'd lived and I had worked as a newspaper reporter for ten years. But most important, it was a return to our spiritual birthplace and the church where we'd had the single most transforming experience of our lives, coming to real faith in Christ. We've been to Hawaii only twice in the thirty-five years since we moved back to the mainland, but in more ways than one it still feels like home."

"I never thought I'd find myself in Florida," says ASHLEY KAPPEL, "but it's a wonderful place to be!" A happy resident of the Sunshine State's Jacksonville, Ashley has enjoyed a year heaped full of blessings. She welcomed two nephews, making her an aunt nine times over, and enjoyed a year of travel, work and fun with Brian, her husband. The sworn Lifelong Honeymooners will celebrate their second anniversary this year. When not freelancing, Ashley works at her dream job as a baker in a local bakery and revels in the fact that it's awfully hard to be grumpy when ordering a birthday cake. Life is good and, thankfully, heaped with blessings along the way.

"Following a truly storybook romance," writes BROCK KIDD of Nashville, Tennessee, "Corinne and I were engaged. As my son Harrison, 10, said, 'Dad, Corinne was worth the wait for us! Six months later my family ventured on a mission trip to an orphanage in Zimbabwe. When we arrived at Home of Hope, Harrison and Corinne were welcomed by our African brothers and sisters as long-lost family members. Through the traditional welcome songs, God brought me a peace that I had never felt before. Corinne and I were married less than one month later. As my father conducted the ceremony and Harrison stood beside me, it was hard to imagine that things could be more miraculous in my life. Little did we know then that the next spring would bring news of a most wonderful anniversary present: Harrison will have a little sister in October!"

Life is mighty good in PAM KIDD's family of Nashville, Tennessee. "For my husband David, *freedom* is another word for retirement, and it's fun to see him doing the things he never had time to do. From 'accidentally' buying a Harley Davidson, teaching New Testament at a local university and joining me in my community passions, he keeps me laughing more and worrying less. My daughter Keri and I still do real estate, a necessity to keep our work in Zimbabwe going. See what we're up to at childrenofzimbabwe.com. My son Brock and Corinne were married *last* October and are expecting a little girl to join their family *this* October! Harrison is very excited about his sister-in-waiting! My good news spreads out to my mother who is recovering from a health scare, under the watchful eye of Herb. And we just found out that Herb can cook!"

MARILYN MORGAN KING of Green Mountain Falls, Colorado, says, "I'd like to share with you three of the many lessons my eight decades have taught me. One: Wrapped up in every difficult passage in life is a gift from the Spirit. In times of trouble, I've learned to ask myself, 'How does this serve?' and 'What is its gift?' Two: What happens to me does not really matter; how I respond is what counts. If I can keep releasing everything to Spirit, peace of mind comes. Three: Inner peace happens when I intentionally feed my sense of wonder by immersing myself in the beauty of God's creation and by breathing in music, art and poetry, while trusting God to take care of the rest."

CAROL KNAPP of Lakeville, Minnesota, writes: "Unbelievable! Grandcuties numbers fourteen and fifteen are on their way, while the oldest grandchild turns 13. Our Alaskan son married a Texas girl here in Minnesota. I loved best serving a wedding breakfast under the apple tree, and all of us singing, 'This Is My Father's World.' I've awakened a passion for creating a *real-but-not* world through an advanced fiction-writing course at St. Olaf College. I kept up with my twenty-something classmates by eating peanut M&Ms during breaks! Just now the phone rang—my daughter Brenda is undergoing emergency surgery for a ruptured appendix. I am terribly worried. I turn to Jesus, my Prince of Peace—and to my Bible, the gospel of peace—and in this seeking and pursuing, I find repose for heart, mind and soul."

"I have a peacemaker implanted within me," writes CAROL KUYKENDALL of Boulder, Colorado, "and it's called deep breathing. Slow, focused, lung-filling breathing, made more rhythmic by repeating a simple prayer such as 'Come, Lord Jesus' or 'Father, I am Yours.' Inhale on the first word; exhale on the rest. The words and oxygen fill not only my lungs but also my soul with life-giving, calming reminders of God's indwelling presence and peace. They have helped me reach the five-year anniversary of my diagnosis of stage 4 ovarian cancer. My husband Lynn is also a survivor, currently in remission with his brain tumor. So we are refilling our bucket lists with plans for some new adventures. Our favorite weekend activity is spontaneous family dinners with our children and grandchildren. Never peaceful but always wonderful."

"As I contemplate God's comforting presence with me in the valley of cancer treatment," says HELEN GRACE LESCHEID of Sumas, Washington, "I have incredible peace. God knows the outcome of all of this, and it will be good. Comfort also comes from my children's presence. They have come from many parts of the world to support me at this time—Esther and Cathy from Ontario, Jonathan and Cheryl from

Vancouver, British Columbia, and Elizabeth from Australia. The prayers of many dear friends also add to my peace of mind." For more news about Helen and information on her new book *Prayer: When Answers Aren't Enough*, visit her Web site at helenlescheid.com.

 PATRICIA LORENZ of Largo, Florida, is trying hard to stay happy, healthy and peaceful by following a simple rule: eat less, eat better, exercise more. "I've learned that as I age (yes, I'm finally on Medicare and Social Security!), taking care of the body and mind God entrusted to me is even more important. For the past couple of years I've been biking on the wonderful Pinellas County Bike Trail and in the many parks around my home. Riding around a gorgeous lake is the perfect time to say my morning prayers. Working at being healthy (still doing water aerobics every day) gives me energy to travel to speaking opportunities and to visit my four children and eight grandchildren scattered around the country. It's a fun, peaceful life and never dull, that's for sure!"

 "People often ask what keeps me sane," reports DEBBIE MACOMBER of Port Orchard, Washington. "The answer is easy. Whether I'm traveling or at home, I

begin each day at 4:00 AM by reading the Bible and a daily devotional, writing in my gratitude journal, and swimming a half mile in the local high-school pool. Starting the day with God centers me and gives me peace. As for the evening, I leave business at the office and head home to cook dinner and spend quality time with my husband Wayne. My day ends with another endeavor that enables me to relax and think over the many blessings God has bestowed on me: knitting. I always have a project for one of our nine grandchildren on my needles!"

 When ROBERTA MESSNER was hospitalized this past year for pneumonia, she found a tremendous source of strength and peace in the old hymns of the church. "Alone in my hospital room and in isolation for possible tuberculosis, the words of those precious songs flooded my mind," she says. "It's wonderful to know they never, ever leave us. It was as if I were on the third row, piano side, at Seventh Avenue Baptist Church, singing them with that beloved congregation of my youth." Roberta's favorite peace-filled hymn? "It Is Well with My Soul." Roberta has fully recovered from her bout of pneumonia and continues to work as an infection control practitioner in Huntington, West Virginia.

LINDA NEUKRUG lives in Walnut Creek, California. She enjoys her job in a bookstore, and she has two cats, Prince and Junior (who, she discovered, was raised in Alaska with sled dogs before he chose the warmer weather here). This year, Linda visited an old school friend who lives in Florida. They both agreed they are remarkably unchanged. Linda has been reading a biography a week this past year, which she hopes will inspire her, and has also rediscovered the timeless and uplifting book *The Little Locksmith*. As she continues her attempts to simplify her life, Linda still subscribes to flylady.net. She has planted a blackberry bush on her patio—no fruit yet, but hoping—and is trying to practice gratitude daily for good health, good relationships and good memories.

"It doesn't *seem* like I'm traveling all the time," says MARY ANN O'ROARK of New York City, "but my friends sweetly point out that I'm never home!" In the spring Mary Ann went wandering through emerald-green Ireland, delighted by the Dingle Peninsula and Ring of Kerry, and in the winter she was off to London, where the bustling city glistened in a snowstorm. But best of all were the in-between months when she visited family and friends in

Ohio, Pennsylvania, Michigan, Arizona and Georgia. Then, when back at home in her Manhattan apartment, she settled in for purr therapy with her rambunctious cats, The Jersey Boys. Mary Ann still leads journaling workshops around the country and is working on a book of short stories called *Things with Wings.*

 PATRICIA PUSEY of Halifax, Vermont, writes: "One of the greatest compensations for aging is seeing the reflections of my children in the faces of their children. This past year I have seen my oldest grandchild Liam graduate from Army boot camp and shared the excitement of my youngest, Chloe, speaking in full sentences. The seven grandchildren in between have also been shining stars, each in his or her own way. My husband Billy reminds me that 'Life is good when we can still dance every time the music comes on.' Sometimes I dance, sometimes I just stand and marvel, sometimes I struggle to know how to help those I love, but always I know that God is in my heart and in my life—and that makes for peace."

 DANIEL SCHANTZ and wife Sharon of Moberly, Missouri, find great peace in traveling together. Almost every day they take a country drive to relax and talk. In April

they went through the Little House on the Prairie Museum at Mansfield, Missouri, where Dan got some books for his children's literature class, and then stopped at the famous Baker Seed Company to get some exotic heirloom seeds. In May, they spent some time in Paducah, Kentucky, where Sharon shopped for quilts while Dan rode his bike along the Ohio River. And in July, they visited Dan's mother in South Bend, Indiana, and took in the many Amish shops around Elkhart. Dan bought some Amish-grown popping corn, his favorite food.

 GAIL THORELL SCHILLING of Concord, New Hampshire, experienced an extraordinary year when her son Tom sent her to France for a month, a trip deferred for more than forty years. "God gives me peace no matter where I am, so traveling alone felt perfectly comfortable to me. I found wonderful people to converse with at bed-and-breakfasts, at hostels and on the trains. Mostly we spoke French with many hand gestures. The deep quiet of churches hundreds of years old—Chartres Cathedral and Mont St. Michel, for example—offered stunningly beautiful oases of peace. Even Notre Dame and St. Germain des Près soothed my spirit despite Parisian street life throbbing just outside their doors." En route by bus to Mont St. Michel, Gail met a very helpful woman who negotiated with

the non-English–speaking driver. Her companion's name? Angel, of course!

"Years ago I received a card that read, 'Peace is not a season, it is a way of life,'" writes PENNEY SCHWAB of Copeland, Kansas. "I've come to realize the profound truth of that statement. Starting each day with devotions and prayer reminds me that inner peace is possible throughout even the busiest and most anxious times." Penney is retired but still does some grant writing and freelance work. While she wouldn't describe their six grandchildren as a source of peace, Penney and Don get great enjoyment from attending their sports, choir and band events. Ryan has recovered from facial surgery and is graduating from Texas Tech this year. David is a sophomore at Oklahoma State, and cousins Mark and Caleb are high school sophomores. Olivia is in eighth grade, and second-grader Caden went to Inventor's Camp during the summer.

The longest day of ELIZABETH SHERRILL's life was in October when her husband John underwent quadruple bypass heart surgery. Doctors at the Shapiro Cardiac Center in Boston had warned that, at 87, John might not survive. "John was sedated," Elizabeth says, "so he doesn't remember me kissing him good-bye in the little curtained alcove next to the operating room." The surgery lasted seven hours—seven hours when she didn't know if John would live. "There was a special waiting room for relatives. When I saw the sign on the door, Family Waiting Room, I had the most incredible sense of peace. I wasn't alone! All the people in that room had a wife, a father, a child undergoing heart surgery right at that moment. In times of shared stress, I realized, we're all of us family." The only time Elizabeth cried all day, she says, was when the surgeon came to tell her John had done well.

For years, JOHN SHERRILL of Hingham, Massachusetts, lived by "Plan your work, and work your plan." So he wasn't sure he liked a new assignment from *Guideposts*: He and his wife Elizabeth were to travel back-roads America, with no destination in mind, searching for glimpses of God at work. Their second night on the trip they stopped at a restaurant whose marquee proclaimed: All Food Grown Locally! "That must take a lot of planning," John commented to the owner-manager. "No, I don't do a lot of planning," the man said. "I listen. When I spend my time listening for guidance instead of planning, I'm more relaxed, have more fun, and in the end achieve more than I could otherwise." John's trying to put the man's wisdom to work as the trip continues. "I'm discovering that excessive planning can be the enemy of peace. When I listen for what God may have in store, my whole outlook is more relaxed."

 SHARI SMYTH of Nashville, Tennessee, writes: "God's peace surrounds us. Whitney and I continue to experience God's provision in these economic hard times. A highlight of the year was a monthlong visit from our daughter Wendy, who lives in Hawaii. We welcomed Elijah, a German shepherd, to our household—a real joy after the devastating loss of our dog Isaiah. I go to the YMCA to keep the old bones fit. Our wonderful grandson Frank, who just turned 6, lives down the road with our daughter Sanna and son-in-law Glen. A few weeks before Easter, I overheard Frank practicing the Peace, which we exchange every Sunday in church. 'Peace be with you,' he said. Then he answered, 'And also with you.' After a pause, he added, 'Because Jesus is risen.' All the bells of Easter rang in my head. Frank gets it!"

 JOSHUA SUNDQUIST of Arlington, Virginia, reports, "This year I've spent a lot of time making videos for the Web site YouTube. I've had a lot of fun and have built up something of a following; my videos have been viewed more than

eight million times. And while I've enjoyed it, it has not given me much—shall we say—peace. In fact, quite the opposite. Producing videos is often stressful and tiring. And that stress has forced me to take a step back and reconnect with the things that do give me peace: going on walks, reading books about spiritual matters, journaling, spending time with family and friends. In short, I've been trying to become more of a human *being* instead of a human *doing.*"

 JON SWEENEY of Woodstock, Vermont, is anticipating having a bit more trouble finding peace in the coming year, given that his wife is about to give birth to a baby—and they already have two teenagers (including one who just started college) in the house. "What a blessing this child will be in our lives!" Jon says. "You know, peace and quiet don't have to go together." An author, editor and speaker, Jon has written many books, including *The Road to Assisi: The Essential Biography of St. Francis, The St. Francis Prayer Book,* and *Verily, Verily: The King James Bible—400 Years of Influence and Beauty,* which was featured on PBS's *Religion and Ethics Newsweekly* last spring. Does Jon have a secret recipe for outer and inner peace? "Not at all, but I do thank God every day for His many blessings!"

"My wife and I are now settled in Macon, Georgia," says SCOTT WALKER, "and are engaged in life and work at Mercer University. Beth works with study abroad programs and service learning opportunities. I am directing the Institute of Life Purpose, teaching three classes and have started Service First, a new program that connects graduating seniors with opportunities to do yearlong international service projects in China, Thailand, the Philippines, Hungary, the Czech Republic, Liberia and South Korea. I'm also writing a biography, speaking frequently concerning my newest book, *The Edge of Terror*, enjoying long bike rides, rediscovering many beautiful regions of Georgia, and Beth and I are leading a Bible study for students in our home each Sunday night. Our three children are now grown and pursuing careers in South Carolina, Washington, DC, and Georgia. As a result, our three golden retrievers receive more attention and care than ever before!"

DOLPHUS WEARY of Richland, Mississippi, writes, "Our daughter Danita continues to practice medicine as a pediatrician in Natchez. Our son Ryan is working, using his marketing and communication skills, but really wants to become a sound engineer. Our grandson Lil' Reggie is almost 8 and continues to be the centerpiece of our lives." Dolphus and his wife Rosie are focused on REAL Christian Foundation, which connects resources and provides mentoring and training for rural ministry leaders. Rosie has finished her book *Stepping Out from the Shadows*, proceeds from which go to support REAL. Dolphus' second book, *I Can't (Never) Leave*, came out in May 2011.

"As you will know from reading my devotionals this year, I have retired," says BRIGITTE WEEKS of New York City. "It's a big step for me, and searching for peace without my daily work routine to keep everything neatly in place has not been easy. But I am getting there. Sometimes peace comes in the noisiest, most demanding and fun shapes: such as five small children gathered around, who suddenly become intently quiet and fix their eyes on me as I read from *The Cat in the Hat*. So I visit with my grandchildren—the very young—and the hospice patients where I volunteer—many of them very old—and I marvel at the breadth and depth of God's creation."

MARION BOND WEST of Watkinsville, Georgia, writes: "Things I reasoned would make for peace this year didn't: trying hard, practically never missing church, helping loved ones out of jams, keeping a short to-do list. I've been here before; I'm a slow learner, so I had to relearn: God helps those who can't help themselves; church is anywhere, anytime one of His own is willing to be used by Him. I'm trying to practice being still and quiet and letting God be God."

 "A full-time job has not been forthcoming," writes BRENDA WILBEE, "but a more than satis-factory arrangement sees me writing at home in Birch Bay, Washington, during the winter and acting as a driver guide in Skagway, Alaska, during the summer. It's a lovely balance, and I invite anyone inter-ested in my adventures to tune into my blogs: Winter, BrendaWilbee.blogspot.com; Summer, SkagwayEtc.blogspot.com. In addition, I'm now a grandmother of seven, the seventh still on the way from Haiti: a little girl orphaned by the earthquake. Alice, my sixth grandchild, came to us from China in July 2010; a joyful little girl suffering brittle bone disease. We are all so grateful she belongs to us and delight in the happiness of this little child God saw and sees. My son Blake? Oh yes, he's in Skagway, driving motor coaches with me!"

"This is my tenth year of telling you what I accomplished during the past year and what I would accomplish the next," says TIM WILLIAMS of Durango, Colorado. "Each year I've been wrong about what I was going to do. Whenever Jesus said 'Follow Me' in the past, I ignored him and kept fishing. I was in control, and the fishing would only get better—or so I thought. After a decade of unplanned melanoma, broken bones, early retirement, a tighter budget, and still no grandchildren, I give up. I find no peace in making my own plans. So please forgive me for not being specific this year. I only know I'm ready to follow Jesus, and his path for me will be more peaceful than my own."

"In 1979 I began writing for *Daily Guideposts*," says ISABEL WOLSELEY, "and six years before that, I became part of the Guideposts family. As I look back on what's transpired during these subsequent thirty-nine years, I am grateful for so much: I've been in all fifty states and on all seven continents; both my sons returned safely from their tours in Vietnam, and their wives have become the daughters I never gave birth to; my six grandchildren and two great-grands are my delight. It's been said that each of us needs two things: someone to love and someone to be loved by. In addition—as I Timothy 6:8 puts it, 'If we have food and clothing, we will be content with that.' (UPDATED NIV) I have all these, plus much more. I am content." Isabel and her husband Lawrence Torrey live in King City, Oregon.

SCRIPTURE REFERENCE INDEX

Scripture Reference Index

AUTHORS, TITLES AND SUBJECTS INDEX

Authors, Titles and Subjects Index

Authors, Titles and Subjects Index

Authors, Titles and Subjects Index

A NOTE FROM THE EDITORS

Daily Guideposts is created each year by the Books and Inspirational Media Division of Guideposts, a nonprofit organization that touches millions of lives every day through products and services that inspire, encourage and uplift. Our magazines, books, prayer network (OurPrayer.org) and outreach programs help people connect their faith-filled values to daily life.

Your purchase of *Daily Guideposts* makes a difference. When you buy Guideposts products, you're helping fund our many outreach programs to military personnel, prisons, hospitals, nursing homes and educational institutions.

To learn more about our outreach ministry, visit GuidepostsFoundation.org. For more information about *Daily Guideposts*, visit DailyGuideposts.org. To find out about our other publications, such as *Guideposts Daily Planner*, visit Guideposts.org or write Guideposts, PO Box 5815, Harlan, Iowa 51593.